The following guides by Dawn Apgar are available from Springer Publishing to assist social workers with studying for and passing the ASWB® examinations necessary for licensure.

Bachelors *(forthcoming)*

The Social Work ASWB® Bachelors Exam Guide: A Comprehensive Guide for Success

Test focuses on knowledge acquired while obtaining a Baccalaureate degree in Social Work (BSW). A small number of jurisdictions license social workers at an Associate level and require the ASWB Associate examination. The Associate examination is identical to the ASWB Bachelors examination, but the Associate examination requires a lower score in order to pass.

Masters

The Social Work ASWB® Masters Exam Guide: A Comprehensive Guide for Success

Test focuses on knowledge acquired while obtaining a Master's degree in Social Work (MSW). There is no postgraduate supervision needed.

Clinical

The Social Work ASWB® Clinical Exam Guide: A Comprehensive Guide for Success

Test focuses on knowledge acquired while obtaining a Master's degree in Social Work (MSW). It is usually taken by those with postgraduate supervised experience.

Dawn Apgar, PhD, LSW, ACSW, has helped thousands of social workers across the country pass the ASWB® examinations associated with all levels of licensure. In recent years, she has consulted in numerous states to assist with establishing licensure test preparation programs, including training the instructors.

Dr. Apgar has done research on licensure funded by the American Foundation for Research and Consumer Education in Social Work Regulation and is currently chairperson of her state's social work licensing board. She is a past President of the New Jersey Chapter of NASW and has been on its National Board of Directors. In 2014, the Chapter presented her with a Lifetime Achievement Award. Dr. Apgar has taught in both undergraduate and graduate social work programs and has extensive direct practice, policy, and management experience in the social work field.

Social Work ASWB® Masters Exam Guide

A Comprehensive Study Guide for Success

Dawn Apgar, PhD, LSW, ACSW

SPRINGER PUBLISHING COMPANY
NEW YORK

Springer Publishing Company, LLC
11 West 42nd Street
New York, NY 10036
www.springerpub.com

Acquisitions Editor: Stephanie Drew
Production Editor: Michael O'Connor
Composition: DiacriTech

ISBN: 978-0-8261-7203-7
e-book ISBN: 978-0-8261-7204-4

15 16 17 18 19 / 5 4 3

Publisher's Acknowledgment

Springer Publishing Company recognizes that the ASWB® is a registered service mark of the Association of Social Work Boards and has applied this service mark to the first mention of the association in each of the chapters in the book and its cover. The Association of Social Work Boards neither sponsors or endorses this product.

The author and the publisher of this Work have made every effort to use sources believed to be reliable to provide information that is accurate and compatible with the standards generally accepted at the time of publication. The author and publisher shall not be liable for any special, consequential, or exemplary damages resulting, in whole or in part, from the readers' use of, or reliance on, the information contained in this book. The publisher has no responsibility for the persistence or accuracy of URLs for external or third-party Internet websites referred to in this publication and does not guarantee that any content on such websites is, or will remain, accurate or appropriate.

Library of Congress Cataloging-in-Publication Data

CIP data is available from the Library of Congress.

Special discounts on bulk quantities of our books are available to corporations, professional associations, pharmaceutical companies, health care organizations, and other qualifying groups. If you are interested in a custom book, including chapters from more than one of our titles, we can provide that service as well.

For details, please contact:
Special Sales Department, Springer Publishing Company, LLC
11 West 42nd Street, 15th Floor, New York, NY 10036-8002
Phone: 877-687-7476 or 212-431-4370; Fax: 212-941-7842
E-mail: sales@springerpub.com

Printed in the United States of America by McNaughton & Gunn.

Contents

Preface

Congratulations on getting to this point in your social work career. The decision to become licensed is significant, and passing the licensing examination demonstrates that you have the basic knowledge necessary to safely practice. Social workers are employed in all kinds of settings including hospitals, correctional facilities, mental health and addictions agencies, government offices, and private practices. It is essential that those served have some assurance that these practitioners are competent to provide the services that they are charged with delivering.

Regulation through certification and licensure helps to assure that social workers will interact in an ethical and safe manner, and there is oversight to address actions that are not consistent with this standard.

Passing the licensing exam is only one step in becoming certified or licensed, but it is usually the most difficult challenge faced after graduating with your degree.

This guide aims to assist helping you through this process in several important ways. It will:

1. Increase your knowledge of the Association of Social Work Boards (ASWB®) examination, including testing conditions and scoring

2. Provide valuable test-taking strategies that will assist in developing a good study plan and in analyzing question wording in order to select the correct answer

3. Summarize content areas that may be included on the examination as per the Knowledge, Skills, and Abilities (KSA) statements published by ASWB, which are used by test developers to formulate actual questions

4. Supply sample questions that can be used to simulate an actual examination experience

Although there are other test preparation materials produced, this guide provides all these essential elements in a single, manageable, easy-to-use guide.

Individuals who are studying for the social work licensing examination have a primary concern and request. They are worried that they do not know important information about the tests that will prove to be a barrier to passing, and they want a "place" to go that will have all the necessary materials in a single location. They want to focus their efforts on studying for the exam—not hunting around for what needs to be studied!

This guide was created based on this important information, and it has been gathered from thousands of social workers just like you. Although it is not produced by or affiliated with ASWB in any way, and does not guarantee a passing score on the examinations, the test-taking techniques have been developed and used successfully by others who were faced with the same challenge that you are—others who are now certified and licensed social workers! They found this information so helpful in passing because the skills that it takes to be a good social worker in practice can be very different than the skills that it takes to pass the examination.

Best wishes as you study for the examination. And remember that there is never only one way to achieve a goal, so use this guide in a way that works for you as you prepare. In choosing this guide as your roadmap, you have taken an important first step on the journey of passing the examination for certification and licensure.

Acknowledgments

Although I have taught this material for nearly 20 years and have helped tens of thousands of social workers pass the examinations, writing this guide proved to be a challenging undertaking. Many people assisted in getting the guide written and produced in an aggressive time frame. In some instances, they provided direct support in ensuring that the guide was comprehensive and easy to use, whereas others gave me strength throughout the process.

I want to thank:

- The National Association of Social Workers (NASW), who granted permission for me to reprint a section of the Code of Ethics, which was essential material for Unit IV, Professional Relationships, Values, and Ethics:

  National Association of Social Workers. (1999). *Code of ethics of the National Association of Social Workers.* Washington, DC: NASW Press.

- Trainers with whom I have worked to help countless social workers prepare for the examinations
- Social workers in my examination preparation classes who were the best educators about what works and what doesn't in preparing for and passing the examinations
- Stephanie Drew, my editor at Springer Publishing Company, who first approached me about writing this guide, and who was persistent even when I was procrastinating
- Bill, Ryan, and Alex, who are my support system and always inspire me to be a better person

Social Work ASWB® Masters
Exam Guide

Introduction

About the Examination

Generally, when social workers are getting ready to take the ASWB® tests, they are anxious not only about knowing the content, but also about the examinations themselves. They have many questions about the number of questions that will be asked and the number of correct answers required to pass. Becoming familiar with the examination basics will assist in making you more comfortable with the examination conditions and structure, thereby reducing your anxiety about the unknown.

10 THINGS THAT YOU SHOULD KNOW ABOUT THE ASWB EXAMINATIONS

1. All of the ASWB examinations have the same format, meaning that each has the same number of questions that each test-taker is given the same amount of time to complete. There are **170 multiple-choice questions** and you will have **4 hours** from the time that you start answering the questions. You can take a brief restroom break or stand to stretch, but the clock does not stop and these activities will be included in your 4-hour limit, so you want to be judicious with your time.

2. Although you will be answering a total of 170 questions, **20 of these questions are non-scored items** that are being piloted for possible inclusion as scored questions on future ASWB examinations. Thus, only 150 questions will determine whether you pass or not. However, you will never know which 20 are pilot items because they are mixed in with scored items, so you will need to try to select the right answers on all 170 questions.

3. You **do not want to leave any questions blank**; answer all 170 questions in the 4 hours.

4. The examination is **computerized**, but requires no specialized computer knowledge. There is a brief computer tutorial that will assist you when you first sit down and look at the screen, and spending time getting to feel comfortable with the device at that time is a good idea, since it will not count toward your 4-hour time limit.

5. You will be taking your examination at a **testing center with others who are being tested in different disciplines** and may be taking shorter or longer examinations, so do not be concerned if they finish before or after you.

6. Testing center activities are **closely monitored**, and you will need to leave all of your belongings, including your watch, in a provided locker. You can ask for earplugs, scrap paper, or a pencil, but will not be able to bring anything into the room with you. The room may be hot or cold, so you should dress in comfortable layers. All testing accommodations related to documented disabilities must be approved by your state licensing board and arranged in advance with ASWB. *Some* states allow for extra time or foreign language dictionaries as accommodations for those who do not have English as a first language.

7. You will leave the testing center with an unofficial copy of your examination results. It will tell you how many questions you were asked and how many you got correct in each of the four areas or domains. You will never know which specific answers were correct and incorrect. You will also not find out the correct answers for those that you answered incorrrectly. **The exam is pass/fail**, and a passing score can be used for certification or licensure in any state.

8. Although the KSAs are in four content areas and you may structure your studying to learn all the related material in a given domain before moving on to the next, **the questions on the examination are in random order** and skip across topics. There is not a separate section of questions labeled Human Development, Diversity, and Behavior in the Environment, or so on. You may have a human behavior question followed by one on ethics, so you really need to clear your head between questions and avoid trying to relate them to one another in any way. Each question stands alone as a way to assess knowledge related to a distinct KSA.

9. Social workers always want to know how many questions of the 150 scored items they will need to answer correctly to pass the exam. Although this sounds like an easy question, it is not! Not all questions on the ASWB examinations are the same level of difficulty as determined by the pilot process, so individuals who are asked to answer harder questions that have been randomly selected from the

test bank will need to answer fewer questions correctly than those who were lucky enough to have easier questions randomly assigned. This method ensures that the examination is fair for all those who are taking it, regardless of which questions were chosen. **The number of questions that you have to get correct** *generally* **varies from 93 to 106 of the 150 scored items.** You will find out how many needed to be answered correctly only after you are finished with your examination and it is immediately scored electronically. When you examine your unofficial test results, which are provided in a printout prior to leaving the testing center, you will be able to gauge the difficulty of your examination. If you needed to get closer to 93 correct, you had a harder combination of questions, and if you needed to get 106 or above correct, you had an easier combination.

10. **If you do not pass the examination, you will not have the same questions repeated on any of your examinations in the future.** Other questions in the four areas will be selected from the test bank. As the four domains are so broad, you may find that the topics of the questions may be quite different than those on a previous examination. To be adequately prepared, it is best to go back and study all the KSAs listed for a content area and not just those that may have caused you problems. If you do not pass, you will have to wait 90 days before taking the examination again.

If you have questions about the examination or scoring, such as the process for sending your passing exam score to another state in which you want to be licensed, visit the ASWB website at www.aswb.org for additional information and necessary forms. The *ASWB Examination Candidate Handbook*, which is free and located on this website, provides additional information about registering for the examination that may be useful.

Test-Taking Strategies

Social workers studying for the ASWB® examinations always want to know techniques that will assist them in studying wisely and answering questions correctly. Remember that there are no replacements for good old-fashioned work, and test-taking strategies are not enough on their own to eliminate all of the incorrect answers. Usually, applying test-taking strategies can help you dismiss two of four possible multiple-choice responses and it is your knowledge of the content area that will be needed to select the correct answer from the two that are remaining. Thus, you will need to make sure that you are well versed in the examination content in order to pass the examination.

However, there are two types of strategies that may assist. The first concerns things to remember when developing your study plan. These are important pieces of information that may help when you are trying to decide what to learn and how to learn it. The second includes those strategies that can assist you when actually answering the questions. These "tips" are important to remember after you have learned all the needed content and are tasked with applying it in the proper way to select the correct answer.

As both of these strategy types are keys to success on the examinations, they are outlined here.

10 ESSENTIAL STRATEGIES FOR STUDY SUCCESS

Tip 1

This is an examination to assess knowledge of social work content, so you will need to make sure that you can describe an overview of the key concepts and terms related to each of the KSAs. You will know if you are ready to take the examinations when you are able to briefly explain these areas to someone who does not have any prior knowledge of them. The difference between passing and not passing the examinations almost always is a result of gaps in knowledge, not application of test-taking strategies, so you need to make sure that the bulk of your studying is aimed at filling in knowledge gaps or refreshing information already learned.

Tip 2

You will never be "ready" to take the ASWB examination. Not unlike other standardized examinations, such as the Scholastic Aptitude Test (SAT) or Graduate Record Examination (GRE), you cannot judge readiness as knowing everything about the content areas. The ASWB® examinations are not designed for test takers to "know it all" in order to pass. Often, picking a test date is the hardest task; as with the SAT or GRE, a deadline for admission to college or graduate school forces individuals to select a date even when they do not feel ready. For the ASWB examination, you will need to select a date in the next few weeks or months, perhaps dictated by job opportunities or promotions predicated on being licensed. You will walk into the examination without feeling totally ready, but this is typical of others who have passed.

Tip 3

You need to limit your study materials to this guide or other key resources that summarize material. This is *not* the time to go back and read your textbooks! There are so many topics that you are asked to know about under each KSA that you cannot and are not expected to know everything related to the topic. This guide is geared to provide important information on these areas "under one roof." It will be hard enough to read through all this material. You should only use outside materials if something in this guide is unclear or you feel that you need more than the information included, perhaps because you never learned this area in the first place. In these instances, you can use free resources on the Internet or any other documents that have no more than a paragraph summarizing key points. Remember, you do not need to read a book on Freud to understand his work and its importance in explaining human development.

Tip 4

Although individuals like to study from sample questions, this is *not* advisable. There are many reasons why using this technique will hurt you on the examinations, but here are just a few:

1. Although it makes individuals feel better when they get an answer correct on a sample test, getting an answer correct is not a valid indicator of really knowing the content in the KSA for which the question was developed. Studying from the KSAs and the topics within them will ensure that you are able to answer any question, not just the one that is in a sample test.

2. Your answers to sample questions inappropriately influence your decisions on the actual examinations when asked about similar topics. For example, you may see an answer that is similar to one that was correct or incorrect in a practice test and you will be more apt or less apt to select it based upon this prior experience. However, the question in the "real" examination will not be exactly the same as the one on the practice test, and you must evaluate all four answers independently without any undue bias that may be caused by your practice question experience.

3. The sample questions that you study are not going to be on your examination and probably are not even written by those who developed items for your test. Thus, the idea that many social workers have of wanting to "get into the head" of the individuals writing the exam or understand their logic is not valid—though it might make them good clinicians in real life!

Tip 5

If you have access to sample questions, such as those in the last section of this guide, you should use them to create a "mock" examination. Most people have trouble resisting the urge to look at the answer key to see if they were correct immediately after selecting a response. However, a far better way to use these questions is to pretend that they are an actual examination.

1. *After* you are done studying the content and think you are ready to take the ASWB examination, select a 4-hour period where you can create a quiet environment without interruptions.

2. Answer the questions as you would on the actual examination—using the strategies and having to pick *one* answer—even if you are not completely sure that it is correct.

3. If you do not take unnecessary breaks, you will see that you can easily get through 170 questions in the 4 hours allotted. This experience should relieve some of your anxiety about the timed nature of the examination.

4. See which answers that you got correct and incorrect. The "mock" examination is not to be used to determine whether you are ready to take the actual test—even if getting 93 to 106 puts you in the range of having the knowledge to pass the actual examination. Instead, it gives you some idea of the length of the examination and how long you will need to focus, while giving you the confidence that you can get most of the answers correct within the time period allotted.

Tip 6

It probably has been a long time since you had to sit for a 4-hour examination—if ever! Our lives are hectic, and we rarely get a chance to really focus on a single task or have the luxury of thinking about a single topic in a way that allows us to really understand it. Thus, many people find it helpful to study in 4-hour blocks of time rather than for a few minutes here and there. This may be difficult, but it will be beneficial because it will get you prepared to not lose your concentration or focus during such a long period. Remember, runners do not start with marathons, they need to build their strength and endurance over time before they can tackle 26.2 miles. Your preparation is similar: You do not want the first time that you have to sit and engage in critical thinking to be your actual examination.

Tip 7

There is always a time lag between the generation of new social work content and when it appears on the ASWB examinations. It takes time to write and pretest questions on new material. For example, when the Health Insurance Portability and Accountability Act (HIPAA) of 1996 was passed, there were several years before questions related to this law were asked. Although the *DSM-5* was published in 2013, ASWB announced that it would not be included on examinations until July 2015. This lag is good and bad. The good news is that you do not have to know the "latest and greatest" in all content areas. It is hard to keep completely up to date in a profession that is changing so rapidly. Now for the bad news! For many, especially if they are working in a particular specialty area, some of the content or answers may appear to be dated. This is often the case in the area of psychopharmacology, because new medications are being approved and used rapidly. Remember the time lapse in your studying, and do not rely on breaking news or even practices in your own agency as information sources.

Tip 8

As you think about what is important to learn or remember when you are reviewing this guide, you should recognize that social workers who have attended social work programs at different schools, as well as courses within a program taught by various instructors, have passed the examinations. Thus, although there is always information to add to a KSA related to experience or depth of knowledge, there are "core" elements included in any overview or lecture on the topic, regardless of school or professor. These elements are the ones that have to be learned and remembered because they are the basis of the knowledge being tested. In addition, there are also "core" or essential areas that contain information that is seen as critical to competent practice. Can you imagine a social worker leaving an undergraduate or graduate program without reviewing the signs of child abuse and neglect and his or her duty as a mandatory reporter? Of course not! This is a "core" topic that often is the basis of examination questions. The list of these areas is not fixed, but includes confidentiality, assessment of danger to self and others, cultural competence, and so on. You should ask yourself when studying, "Is this something that every social worker needs to know, regardless of setting or specialization?" If so, it may be essential to include it in your review of a topic because it is likely to be included on the examination.

Tip 9

When studying, it is not necessary to memorize the content because you will not have to recall a term or definition from memory. The ASWB examinations are not tests geared to test your memory. Instead, they require you to be able to pick the one of several answers that most directly relates to the topic or is the best based on your knowledge of the content area. Thus, it is much more important that you understand each of the KSAs and are not focused on memorizing fancy terms or facts. If you stumble when asked a question about something that you are saying about a KSA, or cannot go off script when discussing these areas, you may be just memorizing the material instead of really understanding it.

Tip 10

Often, social workers are focused on using the clinical and other jargon that they learned in their MSW programs; however, they may be unable to explain what these concepts mean in plain and understandable terms. For example, when asked what should happen when meeting with a client for the first time, social workers often use phrases such as "You need to build rapport," "It is essential that you start where a client is," or "Social workers should show empathy as to what a client is going through." Though all true, these statements give little insight into any real actions that a social worker should take in this first meeting. What should a social worker do to "build rapport"? How would a client know if a social worker was being "empathetic"? What would a social worker be doing or saying? Having to explain the KSAs to someone who knows little about social work practice and will ask you *lots* of questions about the content area can be a far better strategy than studying with a social work colleague who will not challenge you when you use jargon or technical terms without having to explain the basics.

20 TIPS YOU NEED TO USE TO ANSWER QUESTIONS CORRECTLY

Tip 1

This is an examination of your knowledge of social work content. Often, what we learn in the classroom and how we might act in practice based upon practice wisdom and clinical judgments are different. **When selecting an answer, you should base it upon the content that you studied from this guide and what you learned in the classroom.** Each question is written to make sure that you know requisite information about the KSAs. Thus, ask yourself—"What did I study in the guide that relates to this question?" or "Which KSA is being tested and what do I know about this content area?" If you are inappropriately asking, "What would I do in this case vignette?" or "How should I handle this situation?" you will be drawing upon your practice experience rather than the existing knowledge in a domain that is the basis for selecting the correct answer.

Remember, there is only one correct answer for each question. Since everyone has different practice experience, basing your answers on what you see or do in the field may lead you to a different response than someone else taking the examination. However, the textbook or existing body of knowledge on the KSAs is universal, regardless of setting or practice experience. Basing your responses on the information that is taught in the classroom and in social work textbooks, as outlined in this guide, will ensure that you get to the same correct response as others.

Tip 2

You may have a negative opinion about the need to take a standardized 4-hour examination after having successfully graduated from your social work program and even gotten the requisite clinical experience. However, it is a requirement for licensure and seen as a way of determining whether social workers possess the knowledge needed to practice safely. Just as the SAT and GRE are viewed as ways of determining the ability to perform in college or graduate school, the ASWB examinations are seen as indicators of proper social work preparation to successfully practice at various levels. You probably know individuals who have done well on the SAT and GRE and did not do well in postsecondary education and vice versa.

The use of standardized tests in social work and other life areas "is what it is" and **it will hurt your performance if you "fight" the use of such examinations**—in other words, *do not* approach the test with negative attitudes and resentment about having to take it.

It is important to approach the examination with a positive attitude and realize that your performance on this examination will not define your social work career. Passing it should not be viewed as an end in itself, but rather a step in the licensure process—just as the SAT is a step in the college acceptance process. Being resentful about the use of standardized testing as an indicator of competence or future performance will only get in your way.

Tip 3

Although there may be some questions that require you to simply "recall" content in a content area, many of them will be focused on you "applying" information to a particular situation or scenario. These questions come in the form of case vignettes and are often the ones in which social workers make mistakes. In practice, social workers often alter their actions based on many contextual variables. However, remember that the questions on the examination are about the application of social work knowledge within the KSAs, and this knowledge does not change regardless of the setting in the vignette. **You should not get "lost" in the scenario.** For example, the core components of a discharge plan are the same if it is prepared for a client leaving the hospital, a drug treatment facility, or an inpatient psychiatric treatment setting. The content within the components (i.e., history/assessment, treatment provided, follow-up needed) may be different, but each discharge plan has to contain information in these critical areas.

Thus, you need to stay focused on the content being tested and remember that it is not necessary to have worked in all the settings mentioned in the vignettes (schools, hospitals, drug treatment centers, nursing homes, etc.)

to pass the examination; the KSAs or core social work content being tested is universal, regardless of venue.

Tip 4

The ASWB examination that you are taking is used for licensure in virtually every state. The correct answer to a question is the same for all social workers taking the examination. However, the systems of care and laws in each state differ; thus, responses to situations may be varied in real-life, everyday work. This is not the case on the examination, as **there is only one correct answer to each question**. Thus, if you are thinking about "rules" or laws that apply in your state, or resources that may be available, you are likely to get yourself in trouble on the examination because these vary between states and cannot influence your answer selection.

A simple way to avoid unconsciously using state-specific information when answering questions is to think of a state that you envision is very different than your own and ask yourself, "What answer would a social worker living in [insert name of state here] pick as the correct answer?" If your response is, "I don't know because I am not sure how things are done there," you are mistakenly drawing upon practice systems and rules that may differ between states and should *not* be considered. However, if your response is, "It would be the same as mine," you have considered the core social work content that applies to practice in all states.

Tip 5

Standardized examinations are often difficult and test-takers often find themselves struggling to identify the correct answer from several listed. In these instances, social workers can make a common mistake such as selecting the answer that has catchy social work phrases, such as "from a client's perspective" or "focus on a client's strengths and skills." Although these are important social work concepts, you need to make sure that these answers fit the scenario or question asked. **The "best" answer is not always the correct answer.** If you are judging answers solely based on the inclusion of important social work terms—independent of what the question is really asking—you will often be drawn to the "best" answers (judged to be so solely based on the inclusion of important social work terms or concepts), but they may not be correct. Remember, you always want to ask yourself, "What is the right answer to this question on the examination?"

Tip 6

If you are asked to select between four listed terms, diagnoses, or theories, and you do not know with certainty what all the terms listed mean or the criteria for all of the named diagnoses, you should only choose between those that you know. When they are uncertain about the answer to a question, social workers often mistakenly think that it must be the term, diagnosis, or theory listed that they do not know and will gravitate toward selecting this answer. It seems to make logical sense in their minds—"I am uncertain of the answer to the question and I am uncertain as to what this answer means, so they must go together." Although common, this logic is problematic.

Instead, you should concentrate on choosing between the answers that you know. **Only in instances in which you are able to eliminate with 100% certainty the three choices that you know—which is almost never the case— should you choose the "mystery" term, diagnosis, or theory.**

Tip 7

You will have plenty of time to answer the questions. Although the examination is timed, most people finish with a half-hour or more left in the 4 hours. However, you may be nervous about the time and feel rushed due to your anxiety. Use your time wisely, reading carefully and applying the tips described. You should answer the questions in the order in which they are listed. Skipping around will waste time. The most time that you will spend on a question is determining what the question is asking, so not answering a question after you have done this analysis serves no purpose because you will not have an epiphany or any more information that will be helpful to you later in the examination than you do at that moment. You need to select an answer and move on. You also will need to commit to an answer after having read the question no more than two to three times and applying the strategies. Individuals who run out of time are "stuck" because they are waiting for the feeling of certainty in their answers that does not come in these types of standardized examinations.

Tip 8

Look for qualifying words in examination questions. These words are often capitalized, but not always. Examples of qualifying words are "best," "next," "least," "most," "first," and "not." Whenever you see a qualifying word, it is the key to selecting the correct answer from the others and is directly related to the answer. Thus, when you read each of the response choices or answers, you should put the qualifying word in front of it to ensure that you are focusing on what, in this question, is important. You will repeat the qualifying word before reading each answer. By repeating the word before each response choice, you are making sure that you are focusing on what is important when selecting between the answers.

Tip 9

The examinations require you to have basic knowledge about many theories, practice models, and perspectives related to social work practice. A theory is a set of interrelated concepts that are organized in a way that explain aspects of everyday life. A practice model is a way in which a theory is operationalized. And a perspective is a point of view that is usually broader and at a higher level of abstraction (i.e., strengths perspective). Having a basic understanding of various theories, practice models, and perspectives, as well as the terms that are rooted in them, is necessary. Sometimes there are recall questions about theories, practice models, or perspectives, but knowledge in these areas is often tested through questions related to case vignettes. For example, the last sentence before the response choices or answers may state, "*Using a systems approach,* a social worker can expect this recent medical diagnosis to...." Examining the response choices or answers through the "lens" of systems theory is essential to selecting the correct answer. Systems theory states that individuals are in continual interaction with their environment and that parts within a system are interrelated. Thus, when one subsystem is affected, they are all affected. In this example, you would need to have this knowledge in order to select the correct answer, and you would be looking for the response choice that reflects the medical diagnosis affecting others in the family or other aspects of a client's life beyond health.

You do not have to be an expert in all theories, practice models, or perspectives. Instead, your knowledge base needs to be "an inch deep, but a mile wide." You do not need to know the material in great depth, but you do need to have basic knowledge about a lot of paradigms.

Remember to always make sure that you are determining whether a question asks you to use a particular theory, practice model, or perspective when selecting the correct answer. If so, it is not about what might be best to address the problem; instead, identify which answer most closely relates to the paradigm identified.

When studying the theories, practice models, and perspectives, make sure to also focus on their related terms. Sometimes questions do not specify paradigms, but use related terms that you would only know if you studied them.

Tip 10

Perhaps the biggest mistake that social workers make when taking the examinations is adding material to the questions. This is done unconsciously when social workers mistakenly think of a client or situation in their own lives that is similar to what is described in a question. Unfortunately, when this occurs, information related to this real-life client or situation is added to the information that you are considering when selecting the correct response choice or answer, even when it is not actually included in the question. For example, if a man is described as psychotic, you may inappropriately think that he is a danger to himself or others because you recently worked with someone who was psychotic and was exhibiting harm to self or others. However, being psychotic does not necessarily mean that you are posing any danger. This added information may cause you to choose the incorrect information.

In order to determine whether you are adding material to a question, ask yourself what a non–social worker might answer. If the non–social worker's answer would be different from your answer, you may be adding material based on practice experience, not what is stated in the question. Remember, the question has all the information needed to select the correct answer. **You should stay with the material in the question and not add information based upon practice experience.**

Tip 11

Look for quotation marks throughout the question or clues in the last sentence before the response choices, because both are often the keys to selecting the correct answers. For example, a case vignette may describe a client who walks into the first therapy session and states, "I don't have to tell you anything and I don't want to be here," followed by a question for a social worker's best actions. Although this question does not explicitly state that it is asking how to best address resistance, it is implied by the client's verbal statement as described in the quoted statement. These words are there for a reason and are usually important clues to the KSA being tested or the critical information needed to select between correct and incorrect answers.

In addition, a case vignette may ask you to use a particular practice modality or theoretical approach to select the correct response choice. The "lens" that you should use is often mentioned in the last sentence before the answers are listed. For example, a case vignette that ends with "*using a task-centered treatment approach*, a social worker should. . ." requires you to look at the response choices to see which relates to an intervention that is brief, highly structured, and focused on quick results in which a client can take a very active role. The correct answer would be very different if a social worker, responding to the same case vignette, was asked to use a "psychodynamic model."

Tip 12

Many of the response choices to questions on the examination often begin with verbs. **If you are debating between multiple answers, the verb choices can often provide some clues.** For example, some answers describe a social worker doing something for a client that he or she should be doing or for which he or she should be taking responsibility. These response choices often begin with the word "provide" when the question asks what a social worker should do in a particular situation.

SW over'doing

In addition, some verbs may denote less of an empowerment approach, which may help rule them out. "Explore" and "engage" are active verbs that usually indicate that a social worker is relying on a client to come up with the answer or be responsible for the treatment process. "Ignore" or "wait" may indicate that a social worker is not taking critical information into account or acting when needed.

Although examining the verb used in the response choices is only one piece of information that should be used when selecting the correct response choice, and may not be as critical in some instances as other selection criteria, it is a vital tool to consider when two response choices appear equally viable.

Tip 13

Often, questions on the examinations require social workers to identify what they would do "first" or "next" or to pick out the issue or problem that is "most" important in a case scenario. In practice, such decisions are often somewhat subjective and driven by practice wisdom that takes into account many clinical and contextual factors. However, for the examination, all social workers must select the same correct answer. **A useful framework for prioritizing client needs and addressing them sequentially is Maslow's hierarchy of needs.**

Although it is unlikely that Maslow's hierarchy of needs would ever be explicitly asked about on the examination, it is a tool that will be used repeatedly in questions that want the social worker to prioritize problems or order actions based on client need.

A social worker should always address health and safety issues before moving on to issues that relate to self-esteem and relationships. Thus, when the question includes the qualifying word "first," the answers should be considered in light of the health and safety needs of a client. Social workers should also provide concrete services to meet basic needs, such as housing, employment, and transportation, before moving up the hierarchy. Maslow's framework indicates that without health, safety, and basic needs being met first, a client cannot meet his or her higher level needs.

Tip 14

eapiet

Another critical tool available to select the correct answer is the problem-solving process (i.e., engagement, assessment, planning, intervention, evaluation, and termination). Understanding the goal of each phase and the tasks to be completed therein is critical because many questions on the examination focus on making sure that things are happening in the correct order. For example, if the question is about the first session or meeting with a client, the activities of a social worker should be focused on engagement. Engagement includes finding out why a client is there and why he or she is seeking services now, explaining the role of a social worker and what to expect in treatment, listening to a client as he or she explains his or her situation, and explaining the limits of confidentiality. Including a reference to a specific session in the question is a clue for a social worker in determining what stage of the problem-solving process a social worker and client are in and what activities are appropriate for this stage.

When a question asks what actions a social worker should take when interacting with a client, attention should be paid to what part of the problem-solving process a social worker and client are theoretically engaged in. A social worker's response may be quite different if it is the beginning of the process versus the end. Although questions will rarely explicitly state the phase, it can be identified by what has occurred, such as "when gathering information on the problem" to indicate assessment or "when developing the contract" to indicate planning. Also, it may be useful to classify response choices into these stages in order to select what comes "first" or "next."

Tip 15

If the age of a client or others is included in a case vignette, it is usually relevant to selecting the correct response choice. For example, having an imaginary friend at age 4 is very different than having one at age 34. Imaginary friends in childhood are an extension of pretend play and part of Piaget's preoperational stage. However, having one in later life might be an indicator of psychosis resulting from a hallucination or delusion. Thus, in the former instance, a social worker would view this behavior as typical, which would require no special intervention, whereas in the latter, a social worker may need to do a mental status examination or refer for a psychiatric evaluation.

When studying, a social worker does not need to memorize the exact age at which an individual leaves one stage of development or reaches a milestone. However, when mentioned in a question, the age can be a useful hint as to where a client is in the life course and what may be expected.

Tip 16

Often, questions on the examinations aim to assess whether a social worker is appropriately placing a client as the priority and respecting his or her right to self-determination. Questions may focus on conflicts between meeting a client's needs versus adhering to practices or policies created by an agency. When there is a barrier to meeting a client's needs, a social worker should always take responsibility for trying to remove the barrier.

Answers indicating that a social worker should provide advice to a client because he or she has better solutions to a client's problems are never correct.

In practice, a social worker may often encounter practices or policies that limit a client's alternatives or rights to self-determination, and fighting to change these "rules" may seem unrealistic and futile. However, whether or not a social worker will be successful does not change the mandate to challenge them. Do not dismiss an answer just because it seems difficult to achieve.

A client is the expert on his or her situation and should be regarded as such. The supervisor in case vignettes is there to ensure that a client receives the most effective and efficient services possible—not to make things easier for a social worker or enforce agency mandates.

Always look at the answers through the lens of what is best for a client. The self-determination of a client is only limited in situations that would cause harm to a client or others. The correct response choice is always the one that puts a client first.

Tip 17

It is essential that the question is thoroughly understood before looking at the answers. The most difficult part of selecting the correct answer is understanding the knowledge area or concept that is being tested. In order to ensure that proper attention is given to understanding the question, a multistep process should be undertaken.

1. Read the question exactly as it is written, paying attention to qualifying words and those in quotes. Do not look at the response choices yet!

2. Ask "What is this question about?" to determine which of the KSAs is being tested.

3. Think about the important concepts related to the KSA; they will be essential in selecting the correct answers from the incorrect ones.

4. Examine the question again to confirm that your assumption about which KSA is being tested is correct and to determine how the important concepts related to the KSA are relevant to the question.

5. Now look at the response choices for the first time! Read each carefully.

6. Eliminate any that do not appear to be correct. If more than one response choice appears to be viable, go back and read the question again—looking only at the remaining viable responses. It is difficult to eliminate three of four possible answers immediately, so this process may involve multiple iterations. Each time a response choice is eliminated, read the question and the answers that are left. Going back to the question each time you are unable to dismiss all but one response choice will assist in selecting the correct answer for that particular question.

Tip 18

It is critical not to be influenced to select a response choice simply because it has social work "buzz words" such as "rapport," "empathy," "support system," "joining with a client," "strengths perspective," "from a client's perspective," and so on. Often, social workers have a hard time eliminating response choices that contain terms that are important to effective service delivery. These are key concepts that are the cornerstone of competent social work services. However, a word or catch phrase does not make a response choice correct. An answer may not be correct because the other parts of it are inadequate, false, or simply do not address what the question is asking. When you see these social work "buzz words" in a response choice, it is essential to read the rest of the answer critically. You might want to ask yourself whether the answer would still be as appealing if a synonym was used in place of the "buzz word." The entire answer has to stand on its merits as correct, even when the actual term that is making it so appealing is omitted.

Tip 19

Often, social workers view the examinations as a vehicle by which to demonstrate their clinical knowledge and skills. They view all client behaviors through a psychotherapeutic lens and are inappropriately quick to attribute actions to symptomology of disorders or dysfunction. Social workers also are more apt on the ASWB examinations to wrongly view clinical attributes as the focus of treatment or intervention.

For example, if a client has just experienced unsuccessful infertility treatments, she may be likely to feel depressed, frustrated, and hopeless. These are typical reactions to her inability to get pregnant as a result of this medical intervention. The presence of these feelings does not mean that they must be the focus of social work treatment or clinically analyzed and diagnosed. Perhaps the client simply needs support for pursuing alternative methods for becoming a mother, such as through adoption or surrogacy.

You should not be quick to diagnose a client with a disorder on the examinations unless ALL the required clinical criteria are present. You should also not make all client feelings or behaviors clinical issues to be addressed as part of an intervention or treatment.

The ASWB examinations, including the Clinical Examination, are taken by social workers employed in all types of settings and roles. Clinical work does not always imply the need for psychotherapy. Unless the setting or type of intervention to be employed is explicitly stated in a case vignette, you should use a more generalist approach to selecting the correct answer.

Tip 20

Most questions do not ask a social worker to "solve the problem" or even take action that will directly lead to resolving the issue or situation. For example, a question may ask what a social worker should do FIRST when having an issue with his or her supervisor or not getting a verbal response from a colleague. Although speaking directly to a supervisor or putting the request to a colleague in writing may likely not result in an acceptable outcome, such as getting a client a service, they are required steps in ensuring adherence to chain of command or appropriate documentation procedures. It is also important to remember that it is possible to speak to your supervisor first, even if it won't achieve the desired outcome, and then go to an agency directly immediately after—perhaps even the same day—in order to follow the proper chain of command.

Social workers like to get results, and this desire can cause them to choose answers that will make a difference even when questions are not asking for resolution.

There are not long waiting lists, scarce resources, or delays in referrals in examination case vignettes unless they are explicitly stated. In actual practice, social workers encounter these realities daily and often base their decisions and actions to ensure results despite these constraints. These factors should not influence selecting a response choice unless they are explicitly stated in the question.

Assessing Examination Difficulties

If you are having difficulty answering practice questions or even passing the examinations, it is useful to try to diagnose what is causing your problem. You should re-examine the tips outlined in this guide to see what strategies may be helpful in preparing for the examinations and/or answering questions. You also might want to relook at the self-assessment to determine which content areas require more studying.

Although strategies are important, failing the examinations is almost always a result of gaps in knowledge of social work content.

The ASWB examinations are very reliable. Thus, if you study using the same strategy or methods, you are likely to get the same results.

Just like in social work practice, a thorough assessment is critical to ensuring a strategy or intervention is created to address the targeted problem(s). A social worker should spend time analyzing what is causing the difficulties before taking an examination again. For example, difficulties with anxiety will not be addressed by "hitting the books." In addition, knowledge gaps cannot be filled by simply reviewing the test-taking strategies.

Although social workers who have failed the examinations may be anxious to start studying so that they can take the tests again in 90 days, it is worth spending time *critically* reflecting on the strategies used to study and answer questions so that corrections can be made before trying again.

Dealing With Test Anxiety

Perhaps one of the biggest issues that social workers have to address when preparing for and actually taking the examinations is anxiety. Although not designed to be an exhaustive resource on how to address test anxiety, this guide would be incomplete if it did not provide some guidance to social workers to assist with anxiety during this stressful time in their professional development.

It is important to acknowledge that anxiety can be useful during this process because it helps you prioritize studying and preparing above other demands placed upon you in everyday life. There are no magic ways to instill the necessary knowledge in your brain besides good old-fashioned studying. Anxiety can be a motivator to keep going over the material even when there are more interesting things you could be doing!

Remember, everyone who is studying for the examinations is feeling the same way. This stress is typical, and you are not alone in feeling anxious.

However, it is essential to manage this anxiety, and there are several strategies that can help.

1. *Make a Study Plan and Work the Plan*
   A great way to instill confidence is being able to walk into the testing center having prepared the way that you set out to do. A study plan will help you break the material into smaller manageable segments and avoid last minute cramming.

2. *Don't Forget the Basics*
   You need to make sure that you don't neglect your biological, emotional, and social needs leading up to and on the day of the examination. Get plenty of rest, build in relaxation time to your study plan, and eat well to give you energy during this exhausting process.

3. *Familiarize Yourself With the Test Environment*
Before the day of the examination, drive to the testing center so you know how to get there. Arrive early so you are not rushed. Take your time reviewing the tutorial on the computer before you start the examination.

4. *Use Relaxation Techniques*
Breathe and give yourself permission to relax during the examination. You may need to shut your eyes and stretch your neck or stand up several times during the 4-hour exam to help you to refocus.

5. *Put the Examination Into Perspective*
Rarely do people get the score that they want the first time taking any standardized test. Taking the SATs or GREs more than once is the rule rather than the exception. Social workers often attach too much meaning to whether or not they pass the examination the first or second time. They walk into the testing center feeling their entire career rests on the results. This is not true. There are many outstanding social workers who have had to take the test multiple times. Remember that you will be able to retake the examination if you do not pass—this is not your only chance. Not passing is not in any way reflective of your ability to practice social work. You *will* eventually pass, whether it is this time or another, so don't let the test define you. Avoid thinking in "all or nothing" terms.

6. *Expect Setbacks*
The road to licensure is not different than other journeys in life and not usually without unexpected delays or even disappointments. It is important to see these as typical parts of the process and not ends in themselves. Try to figure out why these setbacks in studying or passing are occurring and how you can use this information as feedback for making improvements. You did not get a social work degree without some disappointments and challenges. Studying for and passing the examination will also not be easy, but you will be successful if you keep focused and learn from challenges encountered.

7. *Reward Yourself*
You don't have to wait until you pass in order to celebrate. Build some enjoyment into the test-taking experience by creating little incentives or rewards along the way. Go out to dinner after having studied for 4 hours on a Saturday afternoon. Get up early and study before work so you can enjoy a movie when you get home. Improving your attitude about the test-taking experience can actually help you study more and improve your performance on the examination.

8. *Acknowledge and Address the Anxiety*
Ignoring the anxiety that accompanies this process will not help. It is impossible to completely eliminate it through any of the techniques mentioned. However, you do need to assess whether it is

manageable and can be addressed by some of these suggestions or if it is interfering so significantly with the learning process that you are "blanking out" or having problems in other areas of your life because of its presence. If this is the case, you may need more intensive anxiety reduction interventions. Repeatedly studying the content over and over will not reduce your anxiety. Although most people can develop their own strategies for anxiety management, others need outside help. Usually, individuals who need the assistance of others are those who have experienced debilitating anxiety in other areas of life prior to taking the examinations. No matter what the severity—anxiety management is a critical part of every study plan!

Examination Content

Although it is impossible to identify the information that will be tested in your examination, ASWB® provides a listing of all content areas that are used as the basis for all question construction. These areas are identified by social workers in the field via a practice analysis conducted by ASWB. Through this process, a listing of topics that describe the Knowledge, Skills, and Abilities (KSAs) that are important to the job of a social worker are used to make sure that questions focus on the areas of critical importance to social workers.

Although there is a separate set of KSAs for each of the four ASWB examinations (Bachelors, Masters, Advanced Generalist, and Clinical), there is tremendous overlap across these tests. Sometimes a KSA is not listed in the same content area or is described slightly differently (for example, "theories of human development" versus "developmental theories"). However, upon review, you will see a tremendous overlap across the examinations.

This is good news, because doing well on one ASWB examination often means that you will do well on another. It is always easier to refresh your memory about a topic area than to learn it for the first time!

You do not have to be an expert in each of the KSAs, but you will need to recall critical content, as well as key concepts and terms that may be related to the area. Many people question whether they know enough or are ready to take the examination. With regard to content, it is challenging because individuals often define readiness by being an expert or highly skilled in each area.

For the examinations, you can use the following as a guide to assessing your readiness in having the requisite knowledge.

1. Would you be able to summarize the most relevant points related to the content area in a 5-minute "lecture" on the topic?

2. Do you understand the relevancy to social work practice and how social workers use this information to make decisions when interacting with clients?

3. Do you know how this content area relates to the assessment and treatment of clients? Does it in any way impact problems or issues that they may be experiencing?

In order to get the right answers, your exam questions may require you to broadly apply the overall key theme related to a theory or area (e.g., the understanding that what happens to a client early in life can influence later functioning) or specific terms associated with the area, even if the construct is not mentioned (e.g., picking a response that best represents "family homeostasis"). In order to help you to determine the areas in which you need to concentrate in your preparation for the examination, you should review KSAs, listed in the Self-Assessment in this guide. They are the basis for individual test questions.

If you feel that you have the requisite knowledge, you may only need to quickly review by reading through the content outlined in the subsequent pages of this guide. If you have gaps in content, you should mark the sections in this guide that relate to the topic and go over them in detail so you can get to the point that you have enough knowledge to recall the key concepts and terms. If you have never heard of the concept or recall little about its relevance to social work practice, do not worry—everyone has gaps in knowledge, but this just means that you will have to spend some extra time learning about the topic.

There are different learning styles and you will need to determine which one best fits you because researchers have shown that individuals perform better on examinations if they use study techniques that are consistent with their styles of learning.

The following are some suggested techniques for each learning style that can help fill in content gaps that may exist.

VISUAL LEARNERS

Visual learners learn best through what they see. Although lectures can be boring for visual learners, they benefit from the use of diagrams, PowerPoint slides, and charts.

- Use colored highlighters in this guide to draw attention to key terms.
- Develop outlines or take notes on the concepts in the guide.
- Write talking points for each of the KSAs on separate white index cards.
- Create a coding schema of symbols and write them in this guide next to material and terms that require further study.
- Study in an environment that is away from visual distractions such as television, people moving around, or clutter.

AUDITORY LEARNERS

Auditory learners learn best through what they hear. They may have difficulty remembering material that they read in this guide, but can easily recall it if it is read to them.

- Tape record yourself summarizing the material as you are studying it—listen to your notes as a way to reinforce what you read.
- Have a study partner explain the relevant concepts and terms related to the KSAs.
- Read the text from this guide aloud if you are having trouble remembering it.
- Find free podcasts or YouTube videos on the Internet on the content areas that are short and easy to understand to assist with learning.
- Talk to yourself about the content as you study—emphasizing what is important to remember related to each KSA.

KINESTHETIC OR HANDS-ON LEARNERS

Kinesthetic learners learn through tactile approaches aimed at experiencing or doing. They need activities and physical activities as a foundation for instruction.

- Make flashcards on material because writing it down will assist with remembering the content.
- Use as many different senses as possible when studying—read material when you are on your treadmill, use highlighters, talk aloud about content, and/or listen to a study partner.
- Develop mnemonic devices to aid in information retention (for example—EAPIET or *EAt PIE* Today is a great way to remember the social work problem-solving process (Engaging, Assessing, Planning, Intervening, Evaluating, and Terminating).
- Write notes and important terms in your guide margins.
- Ask a study partner to quiz you on material—turn it into a game and see how many KSAs you can discuss or how long you can talk about a content area before running out of material.

One important thing to remember is that success on the examination does not require a lot of memorization of material, but rather the ability to recall terms when you see them and to draw upon your knowledge of multiple concepts to select the correct course of action in hypothetical vignettes or scenarios. Thus, spend your time really understanding the KSAs and not just being able to recite definitions.

Self-Assessment

In order to help you determine the areas in which you need to concentrate in your preparation for the examination, please review the Knowledge, Skills, and Abilities (KSAs) below that describe the discrete knowledge components that may be tested as part of the examination and are the basis for individual test questions.

If you are not able to recall basic content and/or key terms, indicate the need to study this area thoroughly by circling "1." If you have some basic information about the content and/or key terms, indicate the need to fill in knowledge gaps by circling "2." If you are able to summarize the key concepts and terms, as well as answer questions about its applicability to social work practice and impacts on client functioning, you may be well prepared and can circle "3." Adequate preparation should not be indicated until you can synthesize material from multiple content areas and can discuss all aspects of the KSAs easily and fluidly.

Association of Social Work Boards' Content Outline for *Masters* Examination

	3	2	1
	Well Prepared	Somewhat Prepared	Not Prepared

I. Human Development, Diversity, and Behavior in the Environment (28%)

Theories and Models

Developmental theories	3	2	1
Systems theories	3	2	1
Family theories	3	2	1
Group theories	3	2	1

(continued)

Psychodynamic theories	3	2	1
Behavioral, cognitive, and learning theories	3	2	1
Community development theories	3	2	1
Person-in-environment	3	2	1
Addiction theories and concepts	3	2	1
Communication theories	3	2	1
Defense mechanisms	3	2	1
Normal and abnormal behavior	3	2	1
Indicators of normal physical growth and development	3	2	1
Adult development	3	2	1
Effects of life crises	3	2	1
Impact of stress, trauma, and violence	3	2	1
Emotional development	3	2	1
Sexual development	3	2	1
Aging processes	3	2	1
Family life cycle	3	2	1
Family dynamics and functioning	3	2	1
Cognitive development	3	2	1
Social development	3	2	1
Child development	3	2	1
Basic human needs	3	2	1
Adolescent development	3	2	1
Human genetics	3	2	1
Gender roles	3	2	1
Impact of environment on individuals	3	2	1
Impact of physical, mental, and cognitive disabilities on human development	3	2	1
Interplay of biological, psychological, and social factors	3	2	1
Effects of family dynamics on individuals	3	2	1
Dynamics of grief and loss	3	2	1
Impact of economic changes on client systems	3	2	1
Effects of body image on self and relationships	3	2	1
Cultural, racial, and ethnic identity development	3	2	1
Strengths perspective	3	2	1

Abuse and Neglect

Abuse and neglect concepts	3	2	1
Indicators and dynamics of sexual abuse	3	2	1
Indicators and dynamics of psychological abuse and neglect	3	2	1
Indicators and dynamics of physical abuse and neglect	3	2	1
Characteristics of abuse perpetrators	3	2	1

Indicators and dynamics of exploitation   3 2 1

Diversity, Social/Economic Justice, and Oppression

Influences of culture, race, and/or ethnicity on behaviors and
    attitudes   3 2 1

Influence of sexual orientation and/or gender identity on
    behavior and attitudes   3 2 1

Influence of disability on behavior and attitudes   3 2 1

Effects of differences in values   3 2 1

Impact of cultural heritage on self-image   3 2 1

Impact of spirituality and/or religious beliefs on behaviors
    and attitudes   3 2 1

Effects of discrimination   3 2 1

Systematic (institutionalized) discrimination   3 2 1

Professional commitment to promoting justice   3 2 1

Impact of social institutions on society   3 2 1

Impact of diversity in styles of communicating   3 2 1

Influence of age on behaviors and attitudes   3 2 1

II.   Assessment and Intervention Planning (24%)

Biopsychosocial History and Collateral Data

Psychopharmacology   3 2 1

Components of a biopsychosocial history   3 2 1

Components of a sexual history   3 2 1

Common prescription medications   3 2 1

Components of a family history   3 2 1

Basic medical terminology   3 2 1

Symptoms of neurologic and organic processes   3 2 1

Indicators of sexual dysfunction   3 2 1

Indicators of psychosocial stress   3 2 1

Indicators of traumatic stress and violence   3 2 1

Indicators of substance abuse and other addictions   3 2 1

Use of Assessment Methods and Techniques

Use of collateral sources to obtain relevant information   3 2 1

Methods to evaluate collateral information   3 2 1

Process used in problem identification   3 2 1

Methods of involving client's communication skills   3 2 1

Use of observation   3 2 1

Methods of involving clients in identifying problems   3 2 1

(continued)

Indicators of client's strengths and challenges	3	2	1
Use of assessment/diagnostic instruments in practice	3	2	1
Methods used to organize information	3	2	1
Current *DSM* diagnostic framework and criteria	3	2	1
Components and function of the mental status examination	3	2	1
Process of social work assessment/diagnosis	3	2	1
Methods used in assessing ego strengths	3	2	1
Methods used to assess community strengths and challenges	3	2	1
Methods used in risk assessment	3	2	1
Indicators of client danger to self and others	3	2	1
Indicators of motivation and resistance	3	2	1
Methods used to identify service needs of clients	3	2	1
Use of interviewing techniques	3	2	1
Process of assessing the client's needed level of care	3	2	1

Intervention Planning

Factors used in determining the client's readiness/ability to participate in services	3	2	1
Criteria used in selecting intervention modalities	3	2	1
Components of an intervention or service plan	3	2	1
Human development considerations in the creation of an intervention plan	3	2	1
Methods used to develop an intervention plan	3	2	1
Techniques used to establish measurable intervention or service plans	3	2	1
Methods used to involve clients in intervention planning	3	2	1
Methods for planning interventions with groups	3	2	1
Methods for planning interventions with organizations and communities	3	2	1
Cultural considerations in the creation of an intervention plan	3	2	1

III. Direct and Indirect Practice (21%)

Direct (Micro)

Client advocacy	3	2	1
Empowerment process	3	2	1
Methods used in working with involuntary clients	3	2	1
Psychosocial approach	3	2	1
Components of the problem-solving process	3	2	1
Crisis intervention approach	3	2	1
Task-centered practice	3	2	1

Short-term interventions	3 2 1
Methods used to provide educational services to clients	3 2 1
Methods of conflict resolution	3 2 1
Use of case management	3 2 1
Techniques used to evaluate a client's progress	3 2 1
Use of contracting and goal-setting with client systems	3 2 1
Use of timing in intervention	3 2 1
Phases of intervention	3 2 1
Indicators of client readiness for termination	3 2 1
Techniques used for follow-up in social work practice	3 2 1
Use of active listening skills	3 2 1
Techniques used to motivate clients	3 2 1
Techniques used to teach skills to clients	3 2 1
Use and effects of out-of-home placement	3 2 1
Methods used to develop behavioral objectives	3 2 1
Client self-motivating techniques	3 2 1
Techniques of role play	3 2 1
Assertiveness training	3 2 1
Role-modeling techniques	3 2 1
Limit setting	3 2 1
Methods used to develop learning objectives with clients	3 2 1
Models of intervention with families	3 2 1
Couples intervention/treatment approaches	3 2 1
Interventions with groups	3 2 1
Techniques for working with individuals within the group context	3 2 1
Use of expertise from other disciplines	3 2 1
Approaches used in consultation	3 2 1
Processes of interdisciplinary collaboration	3 2 1
Methods used to coordinate services among service providers	3 2 1
Multidisciplinary team approach	3 2 1
Case recording and record-keeping	3 2 1
Methods used to facilitate communication	3 2 1
Verbal and nonverbal communication techniques	3 2 1
Techniques that explore underlying meaning of communication	3 2 1
Methods used to obtain/provide feedback	3 2 1
Methods used to interpret and communicate policies and procedures	3 2 1
Methods used to clarify the benefits and limitations of resources with clients	3 2 1

(continued)

Use of case recording for practice evaluation or supervision	3 2 1
Use of single-subject design in practice	3 2 1
Evaluation of practice	3 2 1
Interpreting and applying research findings to practice	3 2 1
Process used to refer clients for services	3 2 1
Use of cognitive behavioral techniques	3 2 1
Culturally competent social work practice	3 2 1

Indirect (Macro)

Applying concepts of organizational theories	3 2 1
Impact of social welfare legislation on social work practice	3 2 1
Methods used to establish service networks or community resources	3 2 1
Techniques for mobilizing community participation	3 2 1
Techniques of social planning methods	3 2 1
Techniques of social policy analysis	3 2 1
Techniques to influence social policy	3 2 1
Techniques of working with large groups	3 2 1
Use of networking	3 2 1
Approaches to culturally competent practice with organizations and communities	3 2 1
Advocacy with communities and organizations	3 2 1
Impact of agency policy and function on service delivery	3 2 1

IV Professional Relationships, Values, and Ethics (27%)

Professional Values and Ethical Issues

Professional values and ethics	3 2 1
Client self-determination	3 2 1
Intrinsic worth and value of the individual	3 2 1
Client's right to refuse service	3 2 1
Ethical issues regarding termination	3 2 1
Bioethical issues	3 2 1
Identification and resolution of ethical dilemmas	3 2 1
Applying ethics to practice issues	3 2 1
Responsibility to seek supervision	3 2 1
Use of professional development to improve practice	3 2 1
Professional boundaries	3 2 1

Confidentiality

Legal and ethical issues regarding confidentiality, including electronic communication	3 2 1

Use of client records	3	2	1
Ethical and legal issues regarding mandatory reporting	3	2	1
Obtaining informed consent	3	2	1

Social Worker Roles and Responsibilities

Social worker–client relationship patterns	3	2	1
Concepts of empathy	3	2	1
Process of engagement in social work practice	3	2	1
Concept of a helping relationship	3	2	1
Principles of relationship building	3	2	1
Professional objectivity in the social worker–client relationship	3	2	1
Concepts of transference and countertransference	3	2	1
Use of social worker–client relationship as an intervention tool	3	2	1
Social worker–client relationships in work with communities and organizations	3	2	1
Social worker–client relationships in work with small groups	3	2	1
Methods used to clarify roles of the social worker	3	2	1
Social worker's roles in the problem-solving process	3	2	1
Client's roles in the problem-solving process	3	2	1
Influence of the social worker's values on the social worker–client relationship	3	2	1
Dual relationships	3	2	1
Influence of cultural diversity on the social worker–client relationship	3	2	1

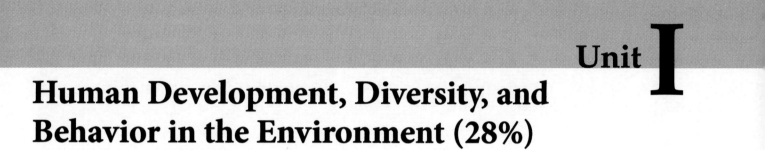

Human Development, Diversity, and Behavior in the Environment (28%)

Theories and Models

1

DEVELOPMENTAL THEORIES

Social work theories are general explanations that are supported by evidence obtained through the scientific method. A theory may explain human behavior by describing how humans interact with each other or react to certain stimuli. Because human behavior is so complex, numerous theories are utilized to guide practice. You need to understand these systems and use them as conceptual tools.

Often, the name of the theory will not be used in a question, but understanding it will be essential to selecting the correct answer.

Study the theories *broadly* to understand their general theme or focus, and *deeply* enough to know the meaning of terms originating from them that may be mentioned in exam questions.

SYSTEMS THEORY

A system is a whole comprising component parts that work together. Applied to social work, systems theory views human behavior through larger contexts, such as members of families, communities, and broader society.

Important to this theory is the concept that when one thing changes within a system, the whole system is affected.

Systems tend toward equilibrium and can have closed or open boundaries.

Applications to Social Work

1. Social workers need to understand interactions between the micro, meso, and macro levels.

2. Problems at one part of a system may be manifested at another.

3. Ecomaps and genograms can help to understand system dynamics.

4. Understanding "person-in-environment" is essential to identifying barriers or opportunities for change.

5. Problems and change are viewed within larger contexts.

Some System Theory Terms

[handwritten: insensitive to env. deviations]

closed system	uses up its energy and dies
differentiation	becoming specialized in structure and function
entropy	closed, disorganized, stagnant; using up available energy
equifinality	arriving at the same end from different beginnings
homeostasis	steady state *[handwritten: effective systems]*
input	obtaining resources from the environment that are necessary to attain the goals of the system
negative entropy	exchange of energy and resources between systems that promote growth and transformation
open system	a system with cross-boundary exchange
output	a product of the system that exports to the environment
subsystem	a major component of a system made up of two or more interdependent components that interact in order to attain their own purpose(s) and the purpose(s) of the system in which they are embedded
suprasystem	an entity that is served by a number of component systems organized in interacting relationships
throughput	energy that is integrated into the system so it can be used by the system to accomplish its goals

[handwritten: Sensitive and responsive to env. deviations]

FAMILY THEORIES

Family theory provides a theoretical and therapeutic base for dealing with family-related situations; it is also useful in understanding and managing individual problems by determining the extent to which such problems are related to family issues. A family systems approach argues that in order to understand a family system, a social worker must look at the family as a whole, rather than focusing on its members.

People do not exist in a vacuum. They live, play, go to school, and work with other people. Most anthropologists agree that, next to their peculiar tendency to think and use tools, one of the distinguishing characteristics of human beings is that they are social creatures. The social group that seems to be most universal and pervasive in the way it shapes human behavior is the family. For social workers, the growing awareness of the crucial impact of families on clients has led to the development of family systems theory.

Family systems theory searches for the causes of behavior, not in the individual alone, but in the interactions among the members of a group. The basic rationale is that all parts of the family are interrelated. Further, the family has properties of its own that can be known only by looking at the relationships and interactions among all members.

The family systems approach is based on several basic assumptions:

- Each family is more than a sum of its members.
- Each family is unique, due to the infinite variations in personal characteristics and cultural and ideological styles.
- A healthy family has flexibility, consistent structure, and effective exchange of information.
- The family is an interactional system whose component parts have constantly shifting boundaries and varying degrees of resistance to change.
- Families must fulfill a variety of functions for each member, both collectively and individually, if each member is to grow and develop.
- Families strive for a sense of balance or **homeostasis.**
- Negative feedback loops are those patterns of interaction that maintain stability or constancy while minimizing change. Negative feedback loops help to maintain homeostasis. Positive feedback loops, in contrast, are patterns of interaction that facilitate change or movement toward either growth or dissolution.
- Families are seen as being goal oriented. The concept of **equifinality** refers to the ability of the family system to accomplish the same goals through different routes.
- The concept of hierarchies describes how families organize themselves into various smaller units or **subsystems** that are comprised by the larger family system. When the members or tasks associated with each subsystem become blurred with those of other subsystems, families have been viewed as having difficulties. For example, when a child becomes involved in marital issues, difficulties often emerge that require intervention.
- Boundaries occur at every level of the system and between subsystems. Boundaries influence the movement of people and the flow of information into and out of the system. Some families have very open boundaries where members and others are allowed to freely come and go without much restriction; in other families, there are tight restrictions on where family members can go and who may be brought into the family system. Boundaries also regulate the flow of information in a family. In more closed families, the rules strictly regulate what

information may be discussed and with whom. In contrast, information may flow more freely in families that have more permeable boundaries.

■ The concept of interdependence is critical in the study of family systems. Individual family members and the subsystems comprised by the family system are mutually influenced by and are mutually dependent upon one another. What happens to one family member, or what one family member does, influences other family members.

Genograms are diagrams of family relationships beyond a family tree allowing a social worker and client to visualize hereditary patterns and psychological factors. They include annotations about the medical history and major personality traits of each family member. Genograms help uncover intergenerational patterns of behavior, marriage choices, family alliances and conflicts, the existence of family secrets, and other information that will shed light on a family's present situation.

Family Therapy Approaches

Social workers use a variety of techniques to work with families. Family therapy treats the family as a unified whole—a system of interacting parts in which change in any part affects the functioning of the overall system. The family is the unit of attention for diagnosis and treatment. Social roles and interpersonal interaction are the focus of treatment. Real behaviors and communication that affect current life situations are addressed. The goal is to interrupt the circular pattern of pathological communication and behaviors and replace it with a new pattern that will sustain itself without the dysfunctional aspects of the original pattern.

Key clinical issues include:

■ Establishing a contract with the family
■ Examining alliances within the family
■ Identifying where power resides
■ Determining the relationship of each family member to the problem
■ Seeing how the family relates to the outside world
■ Assessing influence of family history on current family interactions
■ Ascertaining communication patterns
■ Identifying family rules that regulate patterns of interaction
■ Determining meaning of presenting symptom in maintaining family homeostasis
■ Examining flexibility of structure and accessibility of alternative action patterns
■ Finding out about sources of external stress and support

The following are some types of family therapy.

Strategic Family Therapy

In strategic family therapy, a social worker initiates what happens during therapy, designs a specific approach for each person's presenting problem, and takes responsibility for directly influencing people.

It has roots in structural family therapy and is built on communication theory.

It is active, brief, directive, and task-centered. Strategic family therapy is more interested in creating change in behavior than change in understanding.

Strategic family therapy is based on the assumption that families are flexible enough to modify solutions that do not work and adjust or develop. There is the assumption that all problems have multiple origins; a presenting problem is viewed as a symptom of and a response to current dysfunction in family interactions.

Therapy focuses on problem resolution by altering the feedback cycle or loop that maintains the symptomatic behavior. The social worker's task is to formulate the problem in solvable, behavioral terms and to design an intervention plan to change the dysfunctional family pattern.

Concepts/Techniques

- Pretend technique—encourage family members to "pretend" and encourage voluntary control of behavior
- First-order changes—superficial behavioral changes within a system that do not change the structure of the system
- Second-order changes—changes to the systematic interaction pattern so the system is reorganized and functions more effectively
- Family homeostasis—families tend to preserve familiar organization and communication patterns; resistant to change
- Relabeling—changing the label attached to a person or problem from negative to positive so the situation can be perceived differently; it is hoped that new responses will evolve
- Paradoxical directive or instruction—prescribe the symptomatic behavior so a client realizes he or she can control it; uses the strength of the resistance to change in order to move a client toward goals

Structural Family Therapy

This approach stresses the importance of family organization for the functioning of the group and the well-being of its members. A social worker "joins" (engages) the family in an effort to restructure it. Family structure is defined as the invisible set of functional demands organizing interaction among family members. Boundaries and rules determining who does what, where, and when are crucial in three ways.

1. Interpersonal boundaries define individual family members and promote their differentiation and autonomous, yet interdependent, functioning. *Dysfunctional families tend to be characterized by either a pattern of rigid enmeshment or disengagement.*

2. Boundaries with the outside world define the family unit, but boundaries must be permeable enough to maintain a well-functioning open system, allowing contact and reciprocal exchanges with the social world.

3. Hierarchical organization in families of all cultures is maintained by generational boundaries, the rules differentiating parent and child roles, rights, and obligations.

Restructuring is based on observing and manipulating interactions within therapy sessions, often by *enactments of situations* as a way to understand and diagnose the structure and provide an opportunity for restructuring.

Bowenian Family Therapy

Unlike other models of family therapy, the goal of this approach is not symptom reduction. Rather, a Bowenian-trained social worker is interested in improving the intergenerational transmission process. Thus, the focus within this approach is consistent whether a social worker is working with an individual, a couple, or the entire family. It is assumed that improvement in overall functioning will ultimately reduce a family member's symptomatology. Eight major theoretical constructs are essential to understanding Bowen's approach. These concepts are differentiation, emotional system, multigenerational transmission, emotional triangle, nuclear family, family projection process, sibling position, and societal regression. These constructs are interconnected.

Differentiation is the core concept of this approach. The more differentiated, the more a client can be an individual while in emotional contact with the family. This allows a client to think through a situation without being drawn to act by either internal or external emotional pressures.

Emotional fusion is the counterpart of differentiation and refers to the tendency for family members to share an emotional response. This is the result of poor interpersonal boundaries between family members. In a fused family, there is little room for emotional autonomy. If a member makes a move toward autonomy, it is experienced as abandonment by other members of the family.

Multigenerational transmission stresses the connection of current generations to past generations as a natural process. Multigenerational transmission gives the present a context in history. This context can focus a social worker on the differentiation in the system and on the transmission process.

An **emotional triangle** is the network of relationships among three people. Bowen's theory states that a relationship can remain stable until anxiety is introduced. However, when anxiety is introduced into the dyad, a third party is recruited into a triangle to reduce the overall anxiety. It is almost impossible for two people to interact without triangulation.

The **nuclear family** is the most basic unit in society and there is a concern over the degree to which emotional fusion can occur in a family system. Clients forming relationships outside of the nuclear family tend to pick mates with the same level of differentiation.

Sibling position is a factor in determining personality. Where a client is in birth order has an influence on how he or she relates to parents and siblings. Birth order determines the triangles that clients grow up in.

Societal regression, in contrast to progression, is manifested by problems such as the depletion of natural resources. Bowen's theory can be used to explain societal anxieties and social problems, because Bowen viewed society as a family—an emotional system complete with its own multigenerational transmission, chronic anxiety, emotional triangles, cutoffs, projection processes, and fusion/differentiation struggles.

GROUP THEORIES

Humans are small group beings. Group work is a method of social work that helps individuals to enhance their social functioning through purposeful group experiences, as well as to cope more effectively with their personal, group, or community problems. In group work, **individuals help each other** in order to influence and change personal, group, organizational, and community problems.

A social worker focuses on helping each member change his or her environment or behavior through interpersonal experience. Members help each other change or learn social roles in the particular positions held or desired in the social environment.

A therapeutic group provides a unique microcosm in which members, through the process of interacting with each other, gain more knowledge and insight into themselves for the purpose of making changes in their lives. The goal of the group may be a major or minor change in personality structure or changing a specific emotional or behavioral problem.

A social worker helps members come to agreement regarding the purpose, function, and structure of a group. A group is the major helping agent.

Individual self-actualization occurs through:

■ Release of feelings that block social performance

■ Support from others (not being alone)

- Orientation to reality and check out own reality with others
- Reappraisal of self

Some types of groups include:

- Groups centered on a shared problem
- Counseling groups
- Activity groups
- Action groups
- Self-help groups
- Natural groups
- Closed versus open groups
- Structured groups
- Crisis groups
- Reference groups (similar values)

Psychodrama is a treatment approach in which roles are enacted in a group context. Members of the group re-create their problems and devote themselves to the role dilemmas of each member.

Despite the differences in goals or purposes, all groups have common characteristics and processes.

The stages of group development are:

1. Preaffiliation—development of trust (known as forming)
2. Power and control—struggles for individual autonomy and group identification (known as storming)
3. Intimacy—utilizing self in service of the group (known as norming)
4. Differentiation—acceptance of each other as distinct individuals (known as performing)
5. Separation/termination—independence (known as adjourning)

Groups help through:

- Instillation of hope
- Universality
- Altruism
- Interpersonal learning
- Self-understanding and insight

Factors affecting group cohesion include:

- Group size
- Homogeneity: similarity of group members
- Participation in goal and norm setting for group
- Interdependence: dependent on one another for achievement of common goals
- Member stability: frequent change in membership results in less cohesiveness

Contraindications for group: **client** who is **in crisis; suicidal;** compulsively needy for attention; actively psychotic; and/or paranoid

Key Concepts

Groupthink is when a group makes faulty decisions because of group pressures. Groups affected by groupthink ignore alternatives and tend to take irrational actions that dehumanize other groups. A group is especially vulnerable to groupthink when its members are similar in background, when the group is insulated from outside opinions, and when there are no clear rules for decision making.

There are eight causes of groupthink:

1. Illusion of invulnerability—creates excessive optimism that encourages taking extreme risks

2. Collective rationalization—members discount warnings and do not reconsider their assumptions

3. Belief in inherent morality—members believe in the rightness of their cause and ignore the ethical or moral consequences of their decisions

4. Stereotyped views of those "on the out"—negative views of the "enemy" make conflict seem unnecessary

5. Direct pressure on dissenters—members are under pressure not to express arguments against any of the group's views

6. Self-censorship—doubts and deviations from the perceived group consensus are not expressed

7. Illusion of unanimity—the majority view and judgments are assumed to be unanimous

8. Self-appointed "mindguards"—members protect the group and the leader from information that is problematic or contradictory to the group's cohesiveness, views, and/or decisions

Group polarization occurs during group decision making when discussion strengthens a dominant point of view and results in a shift to a more extreme position than any of the members would adopt on their own. These more extreme decisions are toward greater risk if individuals' initial tendencies are to be risky and toward greater caution if individuals' initial tendencies are to be cautious.

PSYCHODYNAMIC THEORIES

Psychodynamic theories explain the origin of the personality. Although many different psychodynamic theories exist, they all emphasize unconscious motives and desires, as well as the importance of childhood experiences in shaping personality.

Psychoanalytic Theory

Originally developed by Sigmund Freud, a client is seen as the product of his past and treatment involves dealing with the repressed material in the unconscious. According to psychoanalytic theory, personalities arise because of attempts to resolve conflicts between unconscious sexual and aggressive impulses and societal demands to restrain these impulses.

Freud believed that behavior and personality derive from the constant and unique interaction of conflicting psychological forces that operate at **three different levels of awareness:** the preconscious, the conscious, and the unconscious.

The **conscious** contains all the information that a client is paying attention to at any given time.

The **preconscious** contains all the information outside of a client's attention but readily available if needed—thoughts and feelings that can be brought into consciousness easily.

The **unconscious** contains thoughts, feelings, desires, and memories of which clients have no awareness but that influence every aspect of their day-to-day lives.

Freud proposed that personalities have three components: the id, the ego, and the superego.

- **Id:** A reservoir of instinctual energy that contains biological urges such as impulses toward survival, sex, and aggression. The id is unconscious and operates according to the **pleasure principle**, the drive to achieve pleasure and avoid pain.
- **Ego:** The component that manages the conflict between the id and the constraints of the real world. Some parts of the ego are unconscious, whereas others are preconscious or conscious. The ego operates according to the reality principle—the awareness that gratification of

impulses has to be delayed in order to accommodate the demands of the real world. The ego's role is to prevent the id from gratifying its impulses in socially inappropriate ways.

Ego-Syntonic/Ego-Dystonic:

- syntonic = behaviors "insync" with the ego (no guilt)
- dystonic = behavior "dis-n-sync" with the ego (guilt)

The ego's job is to determine the best course of action based on information from the id, reality, and the superego. When the ego is comfortable with its conclusions and behaviors, a client is said to be ego-syntonic. However, if a client is bothered by some of his or her behaviors, he or she would be ego-dystonic (ego alien).

Inability of the ego to reconcile the demands of the id, the superego, and reality produces conflict that leads to a state of psychic distress known as anxiety.

Ego strength is the ability of the ego to effectively deal with the demands of the id, the superego, and reality. Those with little ego strength may feel torn between these competing demands, whereas those with too much ego strength can become too unyielding and rigid. Ego strength helps maintain emotional stability and cope with internal and external stress.

- **Superego:** the moral component of personality. It contains all the moral standards learned from parents and society. The superego forces the ego to conform not only to reality, but also to its ideals of morality. Hence, the superego causes clients to feel guilty when they go against society's rules.

Psychosexual Stages of Development

Freud believed that personality solidifies during childhood, largely before age 5. He proposed five stages of psychosexual development: the oral stage, the anal stage; the phallic stage, the latency stage, and the genital stage. He believed that at each stage of development, children gain sexual gratification or sensual pleasure from a particular part of their bodies. Each stage has special conflicts, and children's ways of managing these conflicts influence their personalities.

If a child's needs in a particular stage are gratified too much or frustrated too much, the child can become fixated at that stage of development. **Fixation** is an inability to progress normally from one stage into another. When the child becomes an adult, the fixation shows up as a tendency to focus on the needs that were overgratified or overfrustrated.

Freud believed that the crucially important **Oedipus complex** also developed during the phallic stage. The Oedipus complex refers to a male child's sexual desire for his mother and hostility toward his father, whom he considers

Stage	Age	Sources of pleasure	Result of fixation
Oral	Birth to roughly 12 months	Activities involving the mouth, such as sucking, biting, and chewing	Excessive smoking, overeating, or dependence on others
Anal	Age 2, when the child is being toilet trained	Bowel movements	An overly controlling (anal-retentive) personality or an easily angered (anal-expulsive) personality
Phallic	Age 3 to 5	Genitals	Guilt or anxiety about sex
Latency	Age 5 to puberty	Sexuality is latent, or dormant, during this period	No fixations at this stage
Genital	Begins at puberty	The genitals; sexual urges return	No fixations at this stage

to be a rival for his mother's love. Freud thought that a male child who sees a naked girl for the first time believes that her penis has been cut off. The child fears that his own father will do the same to him for desiring his mother—a fear called **castration anxiety**. Because of this fear, the child represses his longing for his mother and begins to identify with his father. The child's acceptance of his father's authority results in the emergence of the superego.

In psychoanalytic psychotherapy, the primary technique used is analysis (of dreams, resistances, transferences, and free associations).

Individual Psychology

Alfred Adler, a follower of Freud and a member of his inner circle, eventually broke away from Freud and developed his own school of thought, which he called individual psychology. Adler believed that the **main motivations for human behavior are not sexual or aggressive urges, but striving for perfection**. He pointed out that children naturally feel weak and inadequate in comparison to adults. This normal feeling of inferiority drives them to adapt, develop skills, and master challenges. Adler used the term **compensation** to refer to the attempt to shed normal feelings of inferiority.

However, some people suffer from an exaggerated sense of **inferiority**. Such people overcompensate, which means that, rather than try to master challenges, they try to cover up their sense of inferiority by focusing on outward signs of superiority such as status, wealth, and power.

Healthy individuals have a broad social concern and want to contribute to the welfare of others. Unhealthy people are those who are overwhelmed by feelings of inferiority.

The aim of therapy is to develop a more adaptive lifestyle by overcoming feelings of inferiority and self-centeredness and to contribute more toward the welfare of others.

Self Psychology

Defines the self as the central organizing and motivating force in personality. As a result of receiving empathic responses from early caretakers (self-objects), a child's needs are met and the child develops a strong sense of selfhood. "Empathic failures" by caretakers result in a lack of self-cohesion.

The objective of self psychology is to help a client develop a greater sense of self-cohesion. Through therapeutic regression, a client reexperiences frustrated self-object needs.

Three self-object needs are:

- **Mirroring:** *validates* the child's sense of a perfect self
- **Idealization:** child borrows strength from others and *identifies* with someone more capable
- **Twinship/Twinning:** child needs an alter ego for a *sense of belonging*

Ego Psychology

Ego psychology focuses on the *rational, conscious processes of the ego*. Ego psychology is based on an assessment of a client as presented in the *present (here and now)*. Treatment focuses on the ego functioning of a client, because healthy behavior is under the control of the ego. It addresses:

- How a client behaves in relation to the situation he or she finds himself or herself in
- Reality testing: a client's perception of the situation
- Coping abilities: ego strengths
- Capacity for relating to others

The *goal* is to maintain and enhance the ego's control and management of stress and its effects.

Stages of Psychosocial Development

Like Freud and others, Erik Erikson maintained that personality develops in a predetermined order. However, instead of focusing on sexual development, he was interested in how children socialize and how this affects their sense of self. He saw personality as developing throughout the life course and looked at identity crises as the focal point for each stage of human development.

According to Erikson, there are eight distinct stages, with two possible outcomes. Successful completion of each stage results in a healthy personality and successful interactions with others. Failure to successfully complete a stage can result in a reduced ability to complete further stages and, therefore, a more unhealthy personality and sense of self. These stages, however, can be resolved successfully at a later time.

Trust Versus Mistrust. From birth to 1 year of age, children begin to learn the ability to trust others based upon the consistency of their caregiver(s). If trust develops successfully, the child gains confidence and security in the world around him or her and is able to feel secure even when threatened. Unsuccessful completion of this stage can result in an inability to trust, and therefore a sense of fear about the inconsistent world. It may result in anxiety, heightened insecurities, and feelings of mistrust in the world around them.

Autonomy Versus Shame and Doubt. Between the ages of 1 and 3, children begin to assert their independence by walking away from their mother, picking which toy to play with, and making choices about what they like to wear, to eat, and so on. If children in this stage are encouraged and supported in their increased independence, they become more confident and secure in their own ability to survive in the world. If children are criticized, overly controlled, or not given the opportunity to assert themselves, they begin to feel inadequate in their ability to survive, and may then become overly dependent upon others while lacking self-esteem and feeling a sense of shame or doubt in their own abilities.

Initiative Versus Guilt. Around age 3 and continuing to age 6, children assert themselves more frequently. They begin to plan activities, make up games, and initiate activities with others. If given this opportunity, children develop a sense of initiative, and feel secure in their ability to lead others and make decisions. Conversely, if this tendency is squelched, either through criticism or control, children develop a sense of guilt. They may feel like nuisances to others and will therefore remain followers, lacking self-initiative.

Industry Versus Inferiority. From age 6 to puberty, children begin to develop a sense of pride in their accomplishments. They initiate projects, see them through to completion, and feel good about what they have achieved. If children are encouraged and reinforced for their initiative, they begin to feel industrious and feel confident in their ability to achieve goals. If this initiative is not encouraged but instead restricted, children begin to feel inferior, doubting their abilities and failing to reach their potential.

Identity Versus Role Confusion. During adolescence, the transition from childhood to adulthood is most important. Children are becoming more independent, and begin to look at the future in terms of career, relationships, families, housing, and so on. During this period, they explore possibilities and begin to form their own identities based upon the outcome of their explorations. This sense of who they are can be hindered, which results in a sense of confusion ("I don't know what I want to be when I grow up") about themselves and their role in the world.

Intimacy Versus Isolation. In young adulthood, individuals begin to share themselves more intimately with others and explore relationships leading toward longer term commitments with others outside the family. Successful completion can lead to comfortable relationships and a sense of commitment, safety, and care within a relationship. Avoiding intimacy and fearing commitment and relationships can lead to isolation, loneliness, and sometimes depression.

Generativity Versus Stagnation. During middle adulthood, individuals establish careers, settle down within relationships, begin families, and develop a sense of being a part of the bigger picture. They give back to society through raising children, being productive at work, and becoming involved in community activities and organizations. By failing to achieve these objectives, individuals become stagnant and feel unproductive.

Ego Integrity Versus Despair. As individuals grow older and become senior citizens, they tend to slow down and explore life as retired people. It is during this time that they contemplate accomplishments and are able to develop a sense of integrity if they are satisfied with the progression of their lives. If they see their lives as being unproductive and failing to accomplish life goals, they become dissatisfied with life and develop despair, often leading to depression and hopelessness.

Object Relations Theory

Object relations theory, which was a focus of Margaret Mahler's work, is centered on relationships with others. According to this theory, lifelong relationship skills are strongly rooted in early attachments with parents, especially mothers. Objects refer to people, parts of people, or physical items that symbolically represent either a person or part of a person. Object relations, then, are relationships to those people or items.

Age	Phase	Subphase	Characteristics
0–1 month	**Normal autism**		First few weeks of life. The infant is detached and self-absorbed. Spends most of his or her time sleeping. Mahler later abandoned this phase, based on new findings from her infant research.
1–5 months	**Normal symbiotic**		The child is now aware of his or her mother, but there is not a sense of individuality. The infant and the mother are one, and there is a barrier between them and the rest of the world.

(continued)

Age	Phase	Subphase	Characteristics
5–9 months	**Separation/ Individuation**	Differentiation/ Hatching	The infant ceases to be ignorant of the differentiation between him or her and the mother. Increased alertness and interest for the outside world. Using the mother as a point of orientation.
9–15 months		Practicing	Brought about by the infant's ability to crawl and then walk freely, the infant begins to explore actively and becomes more distant from the mother. The child experiences himself or herself as one with his or her mother.
15–24 months		**Rapprochement**	The infant once again becomes close to the mother. The child realizes that his or her physical mobility demonstrates psychic separateness from his or her mother. The toddler may become tentative, wanting the mother to be in sight so that, through eye contact and action, he or she can explore his or her world. The risk is that the mother will misread this need and respond with impatience or unavailability. This can lead to an anxious fear of abandonment in the toddler.
24–38 months	**Object Constancy**		Describes the phase when the child understands that the mother has a separate identity and is truly a separate individual. Provides the child with an image that helps supply him or her with an unconscious level of guiding support and comfort. Deficiencies in positive internalization could possibly lead to a sense of insecurity and low self-esteem issues in adulthood.

BEHAVIORAL, COGNITIVE, AND LEARNING THEORIES

Behavioral Theory

Behavioral theories suggest that personality is a result of interaction between the individual and the environment. Behavioral theorists study observable and measurable behaviors, rejecting theories that take internal thoughts and feelings into account.

These theories represent the systematic application of principles of learning to the *analysis and treatment of behaviors*. Behaviors determine feelings. Thus, changing behaviors will also change or eliminate undesired feelings. The goal is to modify behavior.

The focus is on *observable behavior*—a target symptom, a problem behavior, or an environmental condition, rather than on the personality of a client.

There are two fundamental classes of behavior: respondent and operant.

1. Respondent: involuntary behavior (anxiety, sexual response) that is automatically elicited by certain behavior. A stimulus elicits a response.

2. Operant: voluntary behavior (walking, talking) that is controlled by its consequences in the environment.

Best known applications of behavior modification are sexual dysfunction, phobic disorders, compulsive behaviors (i.e., overeating, smoking), and training of persons with intellectual disabilities and/or Autism Spectrum Disorder.

It is impractical for those using behavior modification to observe behavior when clients are not in residential inpatient settings offering 24-hour care. Thus, social workers train clients to observe and monitor their own behaviors. For example, clients can monitor their food intake or how many cigarettes they smoke. Client self-monitoring has advantages (i.e., inexpensive, practical, and therapeutic) and disadvantages (i.e., clients can collect inadequate and inaccurate information or can resist collecting any at all).

There are several behavioral paradigms.

A. RESPONDENT OR CLASSICAL CONDITIONING (Pavlov): Learning occurs as a result of pairing previously neutral (conditioned) stimulus with an unconditioned (involuntary) stimulus so that the conditioned stimulus eventually elicits the response normally elicited by the unconditioned stimulus.

Unconditioned Stimulus ——————————▶Unconditioned Response
Unconditioned Stimulus + Conditioned Stimulus ——————▶Unconditioned Response
Conditioned Stimulus ——————————▶ Conditioned Response

B. OPERANT CONDITIONING (B. F. Skinner): Antecedent events or stimuli precede behaviors, which, in turn, are followed by consequences. Consequences that increase the occurrence of the behavior are referred to as reinforcing consequences; consequences that decrease the occurrence of the behavior are referred to as punishing consequences. Reinforcement aims to increase behavior frequency, whereas punishment aims to decrease it.

Antecedent ⟶ Response/Behavior ⟶ Consequence

Operant Techniques:

1. **Positive reinforcement:** *Increases probability that behavior will occur*—praising, giving tokens, or otherwise rewarding positive behavior.

2. **Negative reinforcement:** Behavior increases because a negative (aversive) stimulus is removed (i.e., remove shock).

3. **Positive punishment:** Presentation of undesirable stimulus following a behavior for the purpose of *decreasing or eliminating that behavior* (i.e., hitting, shocking).

4. **Negative punishment:** Removal of a desirable stimulus following a behavior for the purpose of decreasing or eliminating that behavior (i.e., removing something positive, such as a token or dessert).

Specific Behavioral Terms:

1. **Aversion therapy:** Any treatment aimed at reducing the attractiveness of a stimulus or a behavior by repeated pairing of it with an aversive stimulus. **An example of this is treating alcoholism with Antabuse.**

2. **Biofeedback:** Behavior training program that teaches a person how to control certain functions such as heart rate, blood pressure, temperature, and muscular tension. Biofeedback is often used for ADHD and panic/anxiety disorders.

3. **Extinction:** Withholding a reinforcer that normally follows a behavior. Behavior that fails to produce reinforcement will eventually cease.

4. **Flooding:** A treatment procedure in which a client's anxiety is extinguished by prolonged real or imagined exposure to high-intensity feared stimuli.

5. **In vivo desensitization:** Pairing and movement through anxiety hierarchy from least to most anxiety provoking situation; *takes place in "real" setting.*

6. **Modeling:** Method of instruction that involves an individual (the model) demonstrating the behavior to be acquired by a client.

7. **Rational emotive therapy (RET):** A cognitively oriented therapy in which a social worker seeks to change a client's irrational beliefs by argument, persuasion, and rational reevaluation and by teaching a client to counter self-defeating thinking with new, nondistressing self-statements.

8. **Shaping:** Method used to train a new behavior by prompting and reinforcing successive approximations of the desired behavior.

9. **Systematic desensitization:** An anxiety-inhibiting response cannot occur at the same time as the anxiety response. *Anxiety-producing stimulus is paired with relaxation-producing response* so that eventually an anxiety-producing stimulus produces a relaxation response. At each step a client's reaction of fear or dread is overcome by pleasant feelings engendered as the new behavior is reinforced by receiving a reward. The reward could be a compliment, a gift, or relaxation.

10. **Time out:** Removal of something desirable—negative punishment technique.

11. **Token economy:** A client receives tokens as reinforcement for performing specified behaviors. The tokens function as currency within the environment and can be exchanged for desired goods, services, or privileges.

Cognitive Theory

Jean Piaget was a developmental psychologist best known for his theory of cognitive development. His stages address the acquisition of knowledge and how humans come to gradually acquire it. Piaget's theory holds that children learn though interaction with the environment and others.

Stage	Age	Characteristics
1. Sensorimotor	0–2 years	a. Retains image of objects b. Develops primitive logic in manipulating objects c. Begins intentional actions d. Play is imitative e. Signals meaning—infant invests meaning in event (i.e., babysitter arriving means mother is leaving) f. Symbol meaning (language) begins in last part of stage

(*continued*)

Stage	Age	Characteristics
2. Preoperational	2–7 years	a. Progress from concrete to abstract thinking b. Can comprehend past, present, future c. Night terrors d. Acquires words and symbols e. Magical thinking f. Thinking is not generalized g. Thinking is concrete, irreversible, egocentric h. Cannot see another point of view i. Thinking is centered on one detail or event Imaginary friends often emerge during this stage and may last into elementary school. Although children do interact with them, most know that their friends are not real and only pretend they are real. Thus, having an imaginary friend in childhood does *not* indicate the presence of a disorder. It is a normal part of development and social workers should normalize behavior with parents who are distressed about this activity during this developmental stage.
3. Concrete Operations	7–11 years	a. Beginnings of abstract thought b. Plays games with rules c. Cause and effect relationship understood d. Logical implications are understood e. Thinking is independent of experience f. Thinking is reversible g. Rules of logic are developed
4. Formal Operations	11 through maturity	a. Higher level of abstraction b. Planning for future c. Thinks hypothetically d. Assumes adult roles and responsibilities

Piaget also developed a theory of moral development, but the work by Lawrence Kohlberg is best known in this area. He agreed with Piaget's theory of moral development in principle, but wanted to develop the ideas further.

Kohlberg believed that moral development parallels cognitive development. Kohlberg's theory holds that moral reasoning, which is the basis for ethical behavior, has six identifiable developmental constructive stages—each more adequate at responding to moral dilemmas than the last. Kohlberg suggested that the higher stages of moral development provide the person with greater capacities or abilities in terms of decision making and that these stages allow people to handle increasingly complex dilemmas. He grouped his six stages of moral reasoning into three major levels. A person must pass through each successive stage of moral development without skipping a stage.

Level	Age	Stage	Orientation
Preconventional	Elementary school level (before age 9)	1	Child obeys an authority figure out of fear of punishment. *Obedience/punishment.*
		2	Child acts acceptably as it is in her or his best interests. Conforms to rules *to receive rewards.*
Conventional (follow stereotypic norms of morality)	Early adolescence	3	Person acts to gain approval from others. *"Good boy/good girl" orientation.*
		4	*Obeys laws* and fulfills obligations and duties to maintain social system. *Rules are rules.* Avoids censure and guilt.
Postconventional (this level is not reached by most adults)	Adult	5	Genuine interest in welfare of others; concerned with *individual rights* and being morally right.
		6	Guided *by individual principles based on broad, universal ethical principles.* Concern for larger universal issues of morality.

Learning Theory

Learning theory is a conceptual framework describing how information is absorbed, processed, and retained during learning. Cognitive, emotional, and environmental influences, as well as prior experience, all play a part in how understanding, or a worldview, is acquired or changed, as well as how knowledge and skills are retained.

There are many learning theories but all can be conceptualized as fitting into four distinct orientations:

1. Behaviorist (Pavlov, Skinner)—learning is viewed through change in behavior and the stimuli in the external environment are the locus of learning. Social workers aim to change the external environment in order to bring about desired change.

2. Cognitive (Piaget)—learning is viewed through internal mental processes (including insight, information processing, memory,

and perception) and the locus of learning is internal cognitive structures. Social workers aim to develop opportunities to foster capacity and skills to improve learning.

3. Humanistic (Maslow)—learning is viewed as a person's activities aimed at reaching his or her full potential, and the locus of learning is in meeting cognitive and other needs. Social workers aim to develop the whole person.

4. Social/Situational (Bandura)—learning is obtained between people and their environment and their interactions and observations in social contexts. Social workers establish opportunities for conversation and participation to occur.

COMMUNITY DEVELOPMENT THEORIES

There is no one way to define community development. Over the years, community development has been defined as an occupation, a movement, an approach, and a set of values. It has been labeled the responsibility of social workers because it is seen as the most practical framework for creating lasting change for clients.

Community development has been used to the benefit of communities of place, of interest, and of identity. But despite these differences, there are certain principles, characteristics, and values that underpin nearly every definition of community development—neighborhood work aimed at improving the quality of community life through the participation of a broad spectrum of people at the local level.

Community development is a **long-term** commitment. It is not a quick fix to address a community's problems, nor is it a time-limited process. It aims to address imbalances in power and bring about change founded on social justice, equality, and inclusion. Its key purpose is to build communities based on justice, equality, and mutual respect.

Community development is ultimately about getting community members **working together** in collective action to tackle problems that many individuals may be experiencing or to help in achieving a shared dream that many individuals will benefit from.

Similarly, **community organizing** is focused on harnessing the collective power of communities to tackle issues of shared concern. It challenges government, corporations, and other power-holding institutions in an effort to tip the power balance more in favor of communities.

It is essential for social workers to understand sources of power in order to access them for the betterment of the community. Organizing members to focus these sources of power on the problem(s) and mobilizing resources to assist is critical.

- *Coercive:* power from control of punishment
- *Reward:* power from control of rewards
- *Expert:* power from superior ability or knowledge
- *Referent:* power from having charisma or identification with others who have power
- *Legitimate:* power from having legitimate authority
- *Informational:* power from having information

Community organization *enhances participatory skills of local citizens* by working with and not for them, thus developing leadership with particular emphasis on the ability to conceptualize and act on problems. It strengthens communities so they can better deal with future problems; *community members can develop the capacity to resolve problems.*

PERSON-IN-ENVIRONMENT

The person-in-environment perspective highlights the importance of understanding individual behavior in light of the environmental contexts in which a client lives and acts. The perspective has historical roots in the social work profession.

The person-in-environment (PIE) classification system was developed as an alternative to the commonly used disease and moral models (i.e., *Diagnostic and Statistical Manual of Mental Disorders (DSM), International Statistical Classification of Diseases and Related Health Problems (ICD)*, civil or penal codes) to implement social work philosophy and area of expertise. PIE is client-centered, rather than agency-centered.

The PIE system is field-tested and examines social role functioning, the environment, mental health, and physical health.

ADDICTION THEORIES AND CONCEPTS

There are many *risk factors* for alcohol and other drug abuse, including, but not limited to:

1. *Family:* Parents, siblings, and/or spouse use substances; family dysfunction (i.e., inconsistent discipline, poor parenting skills, lack of positive family rituals and routine); family trauma (i.e., death, divorce)

2. *Social:* Peers use drugs and alcohol; social or cultural norms condone use of substances; expectations about positive effects of drugs and alcohol; drugs and alcohol are available and accessible

3. *Psychiatric:* Depression, anxiety, low self-esteem, low tolerance for stress; other mental health disorders; feelings of desperation; loss of control over one's life

4. *Behavioral:* Use of other substances; aggressive behavior in childhood; impulsivity and risk taking; rebelliousness; school-based academic or behavioral problems; poor interpersonal relationships

Different models are believed to explain the causes of substance abuse.

1. *Biopsychosocial model*: There are a wide variety of reasons why people start and continue using substances. This model provides the most comprehensive explanation for the complex nature of substance abuse disorders. It incorporates hereditary predisposition, emotional and psychological problems, social influences, and environmental problems.

2. *Medical model:* Addiction is considered a chronic, progressive, relapsing, and potentially fatal medical disease.

   ■ *Genetic causes:* Inherited vulnerability to addiction, particularly alcoholism
   ■ *Brain reward mechanisms:* Substances act on parts of the brain that reinforce continued use by producing pleasurable feelings
   ■ *Altered brain chemistry:* Habitual use of substances alters brain chemistry and continued use of substances is required to avoid feeling discomfort from a brain imbalance

3. *Self-medication model:* Substances relieve symptoms of a psychiatric disorder and continued use is reinforced by relief of symptoms.

4. *Family and environmental model:* Explanation for substance abuse can be found in family and environmental factors such as behaviors shaped by family and peers, personality factors, physical and sexual abuse, disorganized communities, and school factors.

5. *Social model:* Drug use is learned and reinforced from others who serve as role models. A potential substance abuser shares the same values and activities as those who use substances. There are no controls that prevent use of substances. Social, economic, and political factors, such as racism, poverty, sexism, and so on, contribute to the cause.

Whatever the root causes, a client's substance abuse problem must be addressed before other psychotherapeutic issues. A social worker should also rule out symptoms being related to a substance abuse problem before attributing them to a psychiatric issue.

Substance Use Disorder

Substance Use Disorder in *DSM-5* combines the *DSM-IV* categories of Substance Abuse and Substance Dependence into a single disorder measured on a continuum from mild to severe. Each specific substance (other than caffeine, which cannot be diagnosed as a substance use disorder) is addressed as a separate use disorder (Alcohol Use Disorder, Stimulant Use Disorder, etc.).

Mild Substance Use Disorder in *DSM-5* requires two to three symptoms from a list of 11. Drug craving is added to the list, and problems with law enforcement is eliminated because of cultural considerations that make the criteria difficult to apply.

Non-Substance-Related Disorders

Gambling Disorder is the sole condition in a new category on behavioral addictions. Its inclusion here reflects research findings that Gambling Disorder is similar to substance-related disorders in clinical expression, brain origin, comorbidity, physiology, and treatment.

Goals of Treatment:

1. Abstinence from substances

2. Maximizing life functioning

3. Preventing or reducing the frequency and severity of relapse

The *harm reduction model* refers to any program, policy, or intervention that seeks to reduce or minimize the adverse health and social consequences associated with substance use *without requiring a client to discontinue use*. This definition recognizes that many substance users are unwilling or unable to abstain from use at any given time and that there is a need to provide them with options that minimize the harm that continued drug use causes to themselves, to others, and to the community.

Recovery is an ongoing process, and relapse occurs when attitudes, behaviors, and values revert to what they were during active drug or alcohol use. *Relapse most frequently occurs during early stages of recovery*, but it can occur at any time. *Prevention of relapse is a critical part of treatment*.

Stages of Treatment

1. *Stabilization:* focus is on establishing abstinence, accepting a substance abuse problem, and committing oneself to making changes

2. *Rehabilitation/habilitation:* focus is on remaining substance-free by establishing a stable lifestyle, developing coping and living skills, increasing supports, and grieving loss of substance use

3. *Maintenance:* focus is on stabilizing gains made in treatment, relapse prevention, and termination

A social worker should be aware of the signs and symptoms of use, as well as withdrawal. For example, use of cocaine can be associated with dilated pupils, hyperactivity, restlessness, perspiration, anxiety, and impaired judgment.

Delirium tremens (DTs) is a symptom associated with alcohol withdrawal that includes hallucinations, rapid respiration, temperature abnormalities, and body tremors.

Wernicke's encephalopathy and Korsakoff's syndrome are disorders associated with chronic abuse of alcohol. They are caused by a thiamine (vitamin B$_1$) deficiency resulting from the chronic consumption of alcohol. A person with Korsakoff's syndrome has memory problems. Treatment is administration of thiamine.

Treatment Approaches

1. *Medication-assisted treatment interventions* assist with interfering with the symptoms associated with use. For example, methadone, a synthetic narcotic, can be legally prescribed. A client uses it to detox from opiates or on a daily basis as a substitute for heroin. Antabuse is a medication that produces highly unpleasant side effects (flushing, nausea, vomiting, hypotension, and anxiety) if a client drinks alcohol, it is a form of "aversion therapy." Naltrexone is a drug used to reduce cravings for alcohol; it also blocks the effects of opioids.

2. *Psychosocial or psychological interventions* modify maladaptive feelings, attitudes, and behaviors through individual, group, marital, or family therapy. These therapeutic interventions also examine the roles that are adopted within families in which substance abuse occurs. For example, the "family hero," "scapegoat," "lost child," or "mascot," (a family member who alleviates pain in the family by joking around).

3. *Behavioral therapies* ameliorate or extinguish undesirable behaviors and encourage desired ones through behavior modification.

4. *Self-help groups* (AA, NA) provide mutual support and encouragement while becoming abstinent or in remaining abstinent. Twelve-step groups are utilized throughout all phases of treatment. After completing formal treatment, the recovering person can continue attendance indefinitely as a means of maintaining sobriety.

COMMUNICATION THEORIES

Communication theory involves the ways in which information is transmitted; the effects of information on human systems; how people receive information from their own feelings, thoughts, memories, physical sensations, and environments; how they evaluate this information; and how they subsequently act in response to the information.

Effective communication skills are one of the most crucial components of a social worker's job. Every day, social workers must communicate with clients to gain information, convey critical information, and make important decisions. Without effective communication skills, a social worker may not be able to obtain or convey that information, thereby causing detrimental effects on clients.

The *NASW Code of Ethics* states that a social worker should only solicit information essential for providing services (minimum necessary to achieve purpose).

One cannot *not* communicate. Even when one is silent one is communicating, and another person is reacting to the silence. **Silence** is very effective when faced with a client who is experiencing a high degree of emotion, because the silence indicates acceptance of these feelings. On the other hand, silence on the part a client can indicate a reluctance to discuss a subject. A social worker should probe further with a client who is silent for an unusually long period of time. If persons do not communicate clearly, mutual understanding, acceptance, or rejection of the communication will not occur, and relationship problems can arise.

Some communication styles can serve to inhibit effective communication with clients.

1. Using "shoulds" and "oughts" may be perceived as moralizing or sermonizing by a client and elicit feelings of resentment, guilt, or obligation. In reaction to feeling judged, a client may oppose a social worker's pressure to change.

2. Offering advice or solutions prematurely, before thorough exploration of the problem, may cause resistance because a client is not ready to solve the problem.

3. Using logical arguments, lecturing, or arguing to convince a client to take another viewpoint may result in a power struggle with a client. A better way of helping a client is to assist him or her in exploring options in order to make an informed decision.

4. Judging, criticizing, and blaming are detrimental to a client, as well as to the therapeutic relationship. A client could respond by becoming defensive or, worse yet, internalizing the negative reflections about himself or herself.

5. Talking to a client in professional jargon and defining a client in terms of his or her diagnosis may result in a client viewing himself or herself in the same way (as "sick").

6. Providing reassurance prematurely or without a genuine basis is often for a social worker's benefit rather than a client's. *It is a social worker's responsibility to explore and acknowledge a client's feelings, no matter how painful they are.* A client may also feel that a social worker does not understand his or her situation.

7. Ill-timed or frequent interruptions disrupt the interview process and can annoy clients. Interruptions should be purposive, well-timed, and done in such a way that they do not disrupt the flow of communication.

8. It is counterproductive to permit excessive social interactions rather than therapeutic interactions. In order for a client to benefit

from the helping relationship, he or she has to self-disclose about problematic issues.

9. Social workers must provide structure and direction to the therapeutic process on a moment-to-moment basis in order to maximize the helping process. Passive or inactive social workers may miss fruitful moments that could be used for client benefit. Clients may lose confidence in social workers who are not actively involved in the helping process.

The following are some communication concepts that are critical to social work practice.

Acceptance: an acknowledgment of "what is." Acceptance does not pass judgment on a circumstance and allows clients to let go of frustration and disappointment, stress and anxiety, regret and false hopes. Acceptance is the practice of recognizing the limits of one's control. Acceptance is not giving up or excusing other people's behavior and allowing it to continue. Acceptance is not about giving in to circumstances that are unhealthy or uncomfortable. The main thing that gets in the way of acceptance is wanting to be in control.

Cognitive dissonance: arises when a person has to choose between two contradictory attitudes and beliefs. The most dissonance arises when two options are equally attractive. Three ways to reduce dissonance are to (1) reduce the importance of conflicting beliefs, (2) acquire new beliefs that change the balance, or (3) remove the conflicting attitude or behavior. This theory is relevant when making decisions or solving problems.

Congruence: matching of awareness, experience, and communication (essential for the vitality of a relationship)

Context: the circumstances surrounding human exchanges of information

Double bind: offering two contradictory messages and prohibiting the recipient from noticing the contradiction

Echolalia: repeating noises and phrases. It is associated with Catatonia, Autism Spectrum Disorder, Schizophrenia, and other disorders

Information: anything people perceive from their environments or from within themselves. People act in response to information

Information processing: responses to information that are mediated through one's perception and evaluation of knowledge received

Information processing block: failure to perceive and evaluate potentially useful new information

Metacommunication: the context within which to interpret the content of the message (i.e., nonverbal communication, body language, vocalizations)

Nonverbal communications: facial expression, body language, and posture can be potent forms of communication

DEFENSE MECHANISMS

To manage internal conflicts, people use defense mechanisms. **Defense mechanisms** are behaviors that protect people from anxiety. Defense mechanisms are automatic, involuntary, usually unconscious psychological activities to exclude unacceptable thoughts, urges, threats, and impulses from awareness for fear of disapproval, punishment, or other negative outcomes. Defense mechanisms are sometimes confused with coping strategies, which are voluntary.

The following are some defense mechanisms (the list of defense mechanisms is huge, and there is no theoretical consensus on the exact number).

1. **Acting Out**—emotional conflict is dealt with through actions rather than feelings (i.e., instead of talking about feeling neglected, a person will get into trouble to get attention).

2. **Compensation**—enables one to make up for real or fancied deficiencies (i.e., a person who stutters becomes a very expressive writer; a short man assumes a cocky, overbearing manner).

3. **Conversion**—repressed urge is expressed disguised as a disturbance of body function, usually of the sensory, voluntary nervous system (as pain, deafness, blindness, paralysis, convulsions, tics).

4. **Decompensation**—deterioration of existing defenses.

5. **Denial**—primitive defense; inability to acknowledge true significance of thoughts, feelings, wishes, behavior, or external reality factors that are consciously intolerable.

6. **Devaluation**—a defense mechanism frequently used by persons with borderline personality organization in which a person attributes exaggerated negative qualities to self or another. It is the split of primitive idealization.

7. **Dissociation**—a process that enables a person to split mental functions in a manner that allows him or her to express forbidden or unconscious impulses without taking responsibility for the action, either because he or she is unable to remember the disowned behavior, or because it is not experienced as his or her own (i.e., pathologically expressed as fugue states, amnesia, or dissociative neurosis, or normally expressed as daydreaming).

8. **Displacement**—directing an impulse, wish, or feeling toward a person or situation that is not its real object, thus permitting expression in a less threatening situation (i.e., a man angry at his boss kicks his dog).

9. **Idealization**—overestimation of an admired aspect or attribute of another.

10. **Identification**—universal mechanism whereby a person patterns himself or herself after a significant other. Plays a major role in personality development, especially superego development.

11. **Identification With the Aggressor**—mastering anxiety by identifying with a powerful aggressor (such as an abusing parent) to counteract feelings of helplessness and to feel powerful oneself. Usually involves behaving like the aggressor (i.e., abusing others after one has been abused oneself).

12. **Incorporation**—primitive mechanism in which psychic representation of a person (or parts of a person) is/are figuratively ingested.

13. **Inhibition**—loss of motivation to engage in (usually pleasurable) activity avoided because it might stir up conflict over forbidden impulses (i.e., writing, learning, or work blocks or social shyness).

14. **Introjection**—loved or hated external objects are symbolically absorbed within self (converse of projection) (i.e., in severe depression, unconscious unacceptable hatred is turned toward self).

15. **Intellectualization**—where the person avoids uncomfortable emotions by focusing on facts and logic. Emotional aspects are completely ignored as being irrelevant. Jargon is often used as a device of intellectualization. By using complex terminology, the focus is placed on the words rather than the emotions.

16. **Isolation of Affect**—unacceptable impulse, idea, or act is separated from its original memory source, thereby removing the original emotional charge associated with it.

17. **Projection**—primitive defense; attributing one's disowned attitudes, wishes, feelings, and urges to some external object or person.

18. **Projective Identification**—a form of projection utilized by persons with Borderline Personality Disorder—unconsciously perceiving others' behavior as a reflection of one's own identity.

19. **Rationalization**—third line of defense; not unconscious. Giving believable explanation for irrational behavior; motivated by unacceptable unconscious wishes or by defenses used to cope with such wishes.

20. **Reaction Formation**—person adopts affects, ideas, attitudes, or behaviors that are opposites of those he or she harbors consciously or unconsciously (i.e., excessive moral zeal masking strong, but repressed asocial impulses or being excessively sweet to mask unconscious anger).

21. **Regression**—partial or symbolic return to more infantile patterns of reacting or thinking. Can be in service to ego (i.e., as dependency during illness).

22. **Repression**—key mechanism; expressed clinically by amnesia or symptomatic forgetting serving to banish unacceptable ideas, fantasies, affects, or impulses from consciousness.

23. **Splitting**—defensive mechanism associated with Borderline Personality Disorder in which a person perceives self and others as "all good" or "all bad." Splitting serves to protect the good objects. *A person cannot integrate the good and bad in people.*

24. **Sublimation**—potentially maladaptive feelings or behaviors are diverted into socially acceptable, adaptive channels (i.e., a person who has angry feelings channels them into athletics).

25. **Substitution**—unattainable or unacceptable goal, emotion, or object is replaced by one more attainable or acceptable.

26. **Symbolization**—a mental representation stands for some other thing, class of things, or attribute. This mechanism underlies dream formation and some other symptoms (such as conversion reactions, obsessions, compulsions) with a link between the latent meaning of the symptom and the symbol; usually unconscious.

27. **Turning Against Self**—defense to deflect hostile aggression or other unacceptable impulses from another to self.

28. **Undoing**—a person uses words or actions to symbolically reverse or negate unacceptable thoughts, feelings, or actions (i.e., a person compulsively washing hands to deal with obsessive thoughts).

NORMAL AND ABNORMAL BEHAVIOR

"Normal" and "abnormal" depend on the person, place, and situation, and are largely shaped by social standards. Definitions of "normal" change with societal standards and norms. Normality is often viewed as good, whereas abnormality is seen as bad. When people do not conform to what is perceived as "normal," they are often given a number of negative labels, including unusual, sick, or disabled. These labels can lead to that individual being marginalized, or stigmatized.

The most comprehensive attempt to distinguish normality from abnormality is the *DSM*. The *DSM* shows how normality has changed throughout history and how it often involves value judgments. The *DSM* explicitly distinguishes mental disorders and non-disordered conditions.

INDICATORS OF NORMAL PHYSICAL GROWTH AND DEVELOPMENT

Human growth, development, and learning become progressively complex over time and are influenced through a variety of experiences and interactions. Growth, development, and learning proceed in predictable patterns reflecting increasingly complex levels of organization across the life course. Each developmental stage has distinctive characteristics; however, each builds from the experiences of earlier stages. The domains of development are integrated within the child, so when one area is affected, other areas are also affected. Development proceeds at varying rates from child to child, as well as across developmental domains for individual children, reflecting the unique nature of each. Because growth and development are generally predictable, social workers should know the milestones of healthy development and the signs of potential delay or disability.

ADULT DEVELOPMENT

Adult development refers to the changes that occur in biological, psychological, and interpersonal domains of human life from the end of adolescence until the end of life. These changes may be gradual or rapid, and can reflect positive, negative, or no change from previous levels of functioning.

Young Adults (Age 21–39)

Healthy Growth and Development

- *Physical*—reaches physical and sexual maturity, nutritional needs are for maintenance, not growth
- *Mental*—acquires new skills, information; uses these to solve problems
- *Social-Emotional*—Seeks closeness with others; sets career goals; chooses lifestyle, community; starts own family

Key Health Care Issues

- *Communication*—be supportive and honest; respect personal values
- *Health*—encourage regular checkups; promote healthy lifestyle (proper nutrition, exercise, weight, etc.); inform about health risks (heart disease, cancer, etc.); update immunizations
- *Safety*—provide information on hazards at home, work

Examples of age-specific care for young adults:

- Support the person in making health care decisions
- Encourage healthy and safe habits at work and home
- Recognize commitments to family, career, community (time, money, etc.)

Middle Age Adults (Age 40–64)

Healthy Growth and Development

- *Physical*—begins to age; experiences menopause (women); may develop chronic health problems
- *Mental*—uses life experiences to learn, create, solve problems
- *Social-Emotional*—hopes to contribute to future generations; stays productive, avoids feeling "stuck" in life; balances dreams with reality; plans retirement; may care for children and parents

Key Health Care Issues

- *Communication*—keep a hopeful attitude; focus on strengths, not limitations
- *Health*—encourage regular checkups and preventive exams; address age-related changes; monitor health risks; update immunizations
- *Safety*—address age-related changes (effects on sense, reflexes, etc.)

Examples of age-specific care for middle adults:

- Address worries about future—encourage talking about feelings, plans, and so on
- Recognize the person's physical, mental, and social abilities/ contributions
- Help with plans for a healthy active retirement

Older Adults (Age 65–79)

Healthy Growth and Development

- *Physical*—ages gradually; natural decline in some physical abilities, senses
- *Mental*—continues to be an active learner, thinker; memory skills may start to decline
- *Social-Emotional*—takes on new roles (grandparent, widow or widower, etc.); balances independence, dependence; reviews life

Key Health Care Issues

- *Communication*—give respect; prevent isolation; encourage acceptance of aging

- *Health*—monitor health closely; promote physical, mental, social activity; guard against depression, apathy, update immunizations
- *Safety*—promote home safety; especially preventing falls

Examples of age-specific care for older adults:

- Encourage the person to talk about feelings of loss, grief, and achievements
- Provide information, materials, and so on, to make medication use and home safe
- Provide support for coping with any impairments (avoid making assumptions about loss of abilities)
- Encourage social activity with peers, as a volunteer, and so on

Elders (Age 80 and Older)

Healthy Growth and Development

- *Physical*—continues to decline in physical abilities; at increasing risk for chronic illness, major health problems
- *Mental*—continues to learn; memory skills and/or speed of learning may decline; confusion often signals illness or medication problem
- *Social-Emotional*—accepts end of life and personal losses; lives as independently as possible

Key Health Care Issues

- *Communication*—encourage the person to express feelings, thoughts, avoid despair; use humor, stay positive
- *Health*—monitor health closely, promote self-care; ensure proper nutrition, activity level, rest; reduce stress, update immunizations
- *Safety*—prevent injury, ensure safe living environment

Examples of age-specific care for adults ages 80 and older:

- Encourage independence—provide physical, mental, and social activities
- Support end-of-life decisions—provide information, resources, and so on
- Assist the person in self-care—promote medication safety; provide safety grips, ramps, and so on

EFFECTS OF LIFE CRISES

Crisis is an essential component in the understanding of human growth and development. It has important implications for quality of life and subjective well-being. Crisis situations are viewed as unusual, mostly negative events that tend to disrupt the normal life of a person.

A crisis is an upset to a steady state. When a stressful event becomes a crisis, the individual or family is vulnerable and feels mounting anxiety, tension, and disequilibrium. A *precipitating event of a crisis does not have to be a major event*. It may be the "last straw" in a series of events that exceed a client's ability to cope.

An individual or family, at this point, may be emotionally overtaxed, hopeless, and *incapable of effective functioning or making good choices and decisions. The person or family is at a "critical turning point" of coping effectively or not effectively.*

The way in which life crises are addressed—whether surviving trauma, parental divorce, or a personal loss—has a very significant role to play in determining quality of life. When crises are understood, dealt with, and overcome, clients emerge as healthier and happier.

IMPACT OF STRESS, TRAUMA, AND VIOLENCE

Emotional and psychological trauma is the result of extraordinarily stressful events that destroy a sense of security, making a client feel helpless and vulnerable in a dangerous world.

Traumatic experiences often involve a threat to life or safety, but **any situation that leaves a client feeling overwhelmed and alone can be traumatic, even if it does not involve physical harm.** It is not the objective facts that determine whether an event is traumatic, but a subjective emotional experience of the event.

An event will most likely lead to emotional or psychological trauma if:

- It happened unexpectedly
- There was not preparation for it
- There is a feeling of having been powerless to prevent it
- It happens repeatedly
- Someone was intentionally cruel
- It happened in childhood

Emotional and psychological trauma can be caused by one-time events or ongoing, relentless stress.

Not all potentially traumatic events lead to lasting emotional and psychological damage. Some clients rebound quickly from even the most tragic and shocking experiences. Others are devastated by experiences that, on the surface, appear to be less upsetting.

A number of risk factors make clients susceptible to emotional and psychological trauma. Clients are more likely to be traumatized by a stressful experience if they are already under a heavy stress load or have recently suffered a series of losses.

Clients are also more likely to be traumatized by a new situation if they have been traumatized before—especially if the earlier trauma occurred in childhood. Experiencing trauma in childhood can have a severe and long-lasting effect. Children who have been traumatized see the world as a frightening and dangerous place. When childhood trauma is not resolved, this fundamental sense of fear and helplessness carries over into adulthood, setting the stage for further trauma.

Emotional and psychological symptoms of trauma include:

- Shock, denial, or disbelief
- Anger, irritability, mood swings
- Guilt, shame, self-blame
- Feeling sad or hopeless
- Confusion, difficulty concentrating
- Anxiety and fear
- Withdrawing from others
- Feeling disconnected or numb

Physical symptoms of trauma include:

- Insomnia or nightmares
- Being startled easily
- Racing heartbeat
- Aches and pains
- Fatigue
- Difficulty concentrating
- Edginess and agitation
- Muscle tension

One type of trauma is that resulting from **intimate partner abuse** (heterosexual, gay, lesbian, dating, married, cohabitating). The common thread in all abusive relationships is the abuser's need for power and control over his or her partner. Domestic violence *occurs across all racial, cultural, and socioeconomic groups* and can involve physical, sexual, psychological/ emotional, and economic/financial abuse.

Signs of abuse are varied.

- *Suspicious injury* (not consistent with history of injury, unusual locations, various stages of healing, bites, repeated minor injuries, delay in seeking treatment, old scars or new injuries from weapons)

- *Somatic complaints* without a specific diagnosis (such as chronic pain—head, abdomen, pelvis, back, or neck)

- *Behavioral presentation* (crying, minimizing, no emotional expression, anxious or angry, defensive, fearful eye contact)

- *Controlling/coercive behavior of partner* (partner hovers, overly concerned, won't leave client unattended, client defers to partner, fear of speaking in front of partner or disagreeing with him or her)

Cycle of Violence

Phase I: *Tension building*
Phase II: *Battering incident*—shortest period of the cycle, lasts a brief time
Phase III: *"Loving–contrition"* (absence of tension or "honeymoon" phase)—batterer offers profuse apologies; assures attacks will never happen again and declares love and caring

Batterers often learn abusive behavior from their families of origin, peers, and media, as well as from personal experience of being abused as children. Batterers view their victims as "possessions" and treat them like objects. Victims are dehumanized to justify the battering. Batterers are very self-centered and feel entitled to have their needs (physical, emotional, sexual) met "no matter what." Batterers have control over their impulses and give themselves permission to be abusive.

Some of the reasons that clients stay in abusive relationships are:

- Hope that the abuser will change. If the batterer is in a treatment program, the client hopes the behavior will change; leaving represents a loss of the committed relationship

- Isolation and lack of support systems

- Fears that no one will believe the seriousness of abuse experienced

- Abuser puts up barricades so client won't leave the relationship (escalates threats of violence, threatens to kill, withholds support, threatens to seek custody of children, threatens suicide, etc.)

- Dangers of leaving may pose a greater danger than remaining with the batterer

- Client may not have the economic resources to survive on his or her own

Leaving is a process. Over time, the client comes to the conclusion that the abuser will not change; each time the client tries to leave, he or she gathers more information that is helpful.

Social exchange theory is based on the idea of totaling potential benefits and losses to determine behavior. People make decisions about relationships based on the amount of rewards they receive from them. A client remains in an abusive relationship because the high cost of leaving lowers the attractiveness (outweighs the benefits) of the best alternative. A client will leave when the best alternative promises a better life (rewards outweigh the costs).

Guidelines for Interventions

- **According to most literature on domestic violence, traditional marital/couples therapy is not appropriate in addressing abuse in the family. It puts victims in greater danger of further abuse.**

■ *Medical needs and safety are priorities*. Note: Consider domestic violence in the context of Maslow's hierarchy of needs.

■ In working with a victim of abuse, *trust* is a major issue in establishing a therapeutic alliance.

EMOTIONAL DEVELOPMENT

Emotional milestones are often harder to pinpoint than signs of physical development. This area emphasizes many skills that increase self-awareness and self-regulation. Social skills and emotional development are reflected in the ability to pay attention, make transitions from one activity to another, and cooperate with others.

During childhood, there is a lot happening during playtime. Children are lifting, dropping, looking, pouring, bouncing, hiding, building, knocking down, and more. Children are busy learning when they are playing. Play is the true work of childhood.

During play, children are also learning that they are liked and fun to be around. These experiences give them the self-confidence they need to build loving and supportive relationships all their lives.

SEXUAL DEVELOPMENT

Many people cannot imagine that everyone—babies, children, teens, adults, and older adults—are sexual beings. Some inappropriately believe that sexual activity is reserved for early and middle adulthood. Teens often feel that adults are too old for sexual intercourse. Sexuality, though, is much more than sexual intercourse. Humans are sexual beings throughout life.

Sexuality in infants and toddlers—Children are sexual even before birth. Males can have erections while still in the uterus, and some boys are born with an erection. Infants touch and rub their genitals because it provides pleasure. Little boys and girls can experience orgasm from masturbation, although boys will not ejaculate until puberty. By about age 2, children know their own gender. They are aware of differences in the genitals of males and females and in how males and females urinate.

Sexuality in children (age 3 to 7)—Preschool children are interested in everything about their world, including sexuality. They may practice urinating in different positions. They are highly affectionate and enjoy hugging other children and adults. They begin to be more social and may imitate adult social and sexual behaviors, such as holding hands and kissing. Many young children play "doctor" during this stage, looking at other children's genitals and showing theirs. This is normal curiosity. By age 5 or 6, most children become more modest and private about dressing and bathing.

Children of this age are aware of marriage and understand living together, based on their family experience. They may role play about being married or having a partner while they "play house." Most young children talk about marrying and/or living with a person they love when they get older. Most sex play at this age happens because of curiosity.

Sexuality in preadolescent youth (age 8 to 12)—Puberty, the time when the body matures, begins between the ages of 9 and 12 for most children. Girls begin to grow breast buds and pubic hair as early as 9 or 10. Boys' development of the penis and testicles usually begins between 10 and 11. Children become more self-conscious about their bodies at this age and often feel uncomfortable undressing in front of others, even a same-sex parent.

Masturbation increases during these years. Preadolescent boys and girls do not usually have much sexual experience, but they often have many questions. They usually have heard about sexual intercourse, homosexuality, rape, and incest, and they want to know more about all these things. The idea of actually having sexual intercourse, however, is unpleasant to most preadolescent boys and girls.

Same-gender sexual behavior can occur at this age. Boys and girls tend to play with friends of the same gender and are likely to explore sexuality with them. *Same-gender sexual behavior is unrelated to a child's sexual orientation*.

Some group dating occurs at this age. Preadolescents may attend parties that have guests of both genders, and they may dance and play kissing games. By age 12 or 13, some young adolescents may pair off and begin dating and/ or "making out." Young women are usually older when they begin voluntary sexual intercourse. However, many very young teens do practice sexual behaviors other than vaginal intercourse, such as petting to orgasm and oral intercourse.

Sexuality in adolescent youth (age 13 to 19)—Once youth have reached puberty and beyond, they experience increased interest in romantic and sexual relationships and in genital sex behaviors. As youth mature, they experience strong emotional attachments to romantic partners and find it natural to express their feelings within sexual relationships. There is no way to predict how a particular teenager will act sexually. Overall, most adolescents explore relationships with one another, fall in and out of love, and participate in sexual intercourse before the age of 20.

Adult sexuality—Adult sexual behaviors are extremely varied and, in most cases, remain part of an adult's life until death. At around age 50, women experience menopause, which affects their sexuality in that their ovaries no longer release eggs and their bodies no longer produce estrogen. They may experience several physical changes. Vaginal walls become thinner and vaginal intercourse may be painful because there is less vaginal lubrication and the entrance to the vagina becomes smaller. Many women use estrogen replacement therapy to relieve physical and emotional side effects of menopause. Use of vaginal lubricants can also make vaginal intercourse easier. Most women are able to have pleasurable sexual intercourse and to experience orgasm for their entire lives.

Adult men also experience some changes in their sexuality, but not at such a predictable time as with menopause in women. Men's testicles slow testosterone production after age 25 or so. Erections may occur more slowly once testosterone production slows. Men also become less able to have another erection after an orgasm and may take up to 24 hours to achieve and sustain another erection. The amount of semen released during ejaculation also decreases, but men are capable of fathering a baby even when they are in their 80s and 90s. Some older men develop an enlarged or cancerous prostate gland. If the doctors deem it necessary to remove the prostate gland, a man's ability to have an erection or an orgasm is normally unaffected.

Although adult men and women go through some sexual changes as they age, they do not lose their desire or their ability for sexual expression. Even among the very old, the need for touch and intimacy remains, although the desire and ability to have sexual intercourse may lessen.

AGING PROCESSES

Aging is scientifically defined as the accumulation of diverse deleterious changes occurring in cells and tissues with advancing age that are responsible for an increased risk of disease and death. Life expectancy is defined as the average total number of years that a human expects to live. The lengthening of life expectancy is mainly due to the elimination of most infectious diseases occurring in youth, better hygiene, and the adoption of antibiotics and vaccines.

The notion that aging requires treatment is based on the false belief that becoming old is undesirable. Aging has at times received a negative connotation and become synonymous with deterioration, approaching pathology, and death. Society should learn to value old age to the same extent as it presently values youth.

There are physical changes that naturally occur. In older adulthood, age-related changes in stamina, strength, or sensory perception may be noticed and will vary based on personal health choices, medical history, and genetics.

Social workers understand that old age is a time of continued growth and that older adults contribute significantly to their families, communities, and society. At the same time, clients face multiple biopsychosocial-spiritual-cultural challenges as they age: changes in health and physical abilities; difficulty in accessing comprehensive, affordable, and high-quality health and behavioral health care; decreased economic security; increased vulnerability to abuse and exploitation; and loss of meaningful social roles and opportunities to remain engaged in society. Social workers are well positioned and trained to support and advocate for older adults and their caregivers.

FAMILY LIFE CYCLE

The emotional and intellectual stages from childhood to retirement as a member of a family are called the family life cycle. In each stage, clients face challenges in family life that allow the building or gaining of new skills.

Not everyone passes through these stages smoothly. Situations such as severe illness, financial problems, or the death of a loved one can have an effect. If skills are not learned in one stage, they can be learned in later stages.

Stage 1: **Family of origin experiences**
Main tasks
- Maintaining relationships with parents, siblings, and peers
- Completing education
- Developing the foundations of a family life

Stage 2: **Leaving home**
Main tasks
- Differentiating self from family of origin and parents and developing adult-to-adult relationships with parents
- Developing intimate peer relationships
- Beginning work, developing work identity, and financial independence

Stage 3: **Premarriage stage**
Main tasks
- Selecting partners
- Developing a relationship
- Deciding to establish own home with someone

Stage 4: **Childless couple stage**
Main tasks
- Developing a way to live together both practically and emotionally
- Adjusting relationships with families of origin and peers to include partner

Stage 5: **Family with young children**
Main tasks
- Realigning family system to make space for children
- Adopting and developing parenting roles
- Realigning relationships with families of origin to include parenting and grandparenting roles
- Facilitating children to develop peer relationships

Stage 6: **Family with adolescents**
Main tasks
- Adjusting parent-child relationships to allow adolescents more autonomy

■ Adjusting family relationships to focus on midlife relationship and career issues

■ Taking on responsibility of caring for families of origin

Stage 7: **Launching children**

Main tasks

■ Resolving midlife issues

■ Negotiating adult-to-adult relationships with children

■ Adjusting to living as a couple again

■ Adjusting to including in-laws and grandchildren within the family circle

■ Dealing with disabilities and death in the family of origin

Stage 8: **Later family life**

Main tasks

■ Coping with physiological decline in self and others

■ Adjusting to children taking a more central role in family maintenance

■ Valuing the wisdom and experience of the elderly

■ Dealing with loss of spouse and peers

■ Preparing for death, life review, and reminiscence

Mastering the skills and milestones of each stage allows successful movement from one stage of development to the next. If not mastered, clients are more likely to have difficulty with relationships and future transitions. Family life cycle theory suggests that successful transitioning may also help to prevent disease and emotional or stress-related disorders.

The stress of daily living, coping with a chronic medical condition, or other life crises can disrupt the normal life cycle. Ongoing stress or a crisis can delay the transition to the next phase of life.

FAMILY DYNAMICS AND FUNCTIONING

Family dynamics are the patterns of relating or interactions between family members. Each family system and its dynamics are unique, although there are some common patterns. All families have some helpful and some unhelpful dynamics.

Even where there is little or no present contact with family, there is almost always an influence on a client by dynamics in previous years. Family dynamics often have a strong influence on the way individuals see themselves, others, and the world, and influence their relationships, their behaviors, and their well-being.

An understanding of the impact of family dynamics on a client's self-perception may help social workers pinpoint and respond to the driving forces behind her or his current needs.

Healthy functioning is characterized by:

- Treating each family member as an individual
- Having regular routines and structure
- Being connected to extended family, friends, and the community
- Having realistic expectations
- Spending quality time, which is characterized by fun, relaxed, and conflict-free interactions
- Ensuring that members take care of their own needs and not just the family needs
- Helping one another through example and direct assistance

COGNITIVE DEVELOPMENT

Cognitive development focuses on development in terms of information processing, conceptual resources, perceptual skill, language learning, and other aspects of brain development. It is the emergence of the ability to think and understand.

A major controversy in cognitive development has been "nature and nurture," that is, the question of whether cognitive development is mainly determined by a client's innate qualities ("nature"), or by his or her personal experiences ("nurture"). However, it is now recognized by most experts that this is a false dichotomy: There is overwhelming evidence from biological and behavioral sciences that, from the earliest points in development, gene activity interacts with events and experiences in the environment.

SOCIAL DEVELOPMENT

Human beings are inherently social. Developing competencies in this domain enhances a person's mental health, success in work, and ability to achieve in life tasks.

On a micro level, social development is learning how to behave and interact well with others. Social development relies on emotional development or learning how to manage feelings so they are productive and not counterproductive.

On a macro level, social development is about a commitment that development processes need to benefit people, particularly, but not only, the poor. It also recognizes the way people interact in groups and society, and the norms that facilitate such interaction.

Social development implies a change in social institutions. Progress toward an inclusive society, for example, implies that individuals treat each other fairly in their daily lives, whether in the family, workplace, or public office. Social cohesion is enhanced when peaceful and safe environments within neighborhoods and communities are created. Social accountability exists to the extent that individuals' voices are expressed and heard. Reforms aimed at improving rights and more participatory governance are part of the process by which institutional change is achieved.

CHILD DEVELOPMENT

Child development refers to the physical, mental, and socioemotional changes that occur between birth and the end of adolescence, as a child progresses from dependency to increasing autonomy. It is a continuous process with a predictable sequence, yet having a unique course. Individuals do not progress at the same rate, and each stage is affected by the preceding types of development. Because these developmental changes may be strongly influenced by genetic factors and events during prenatal life, genetics and prenatal development are usually included as part of the study of child development.

Infants and Toddlers (Age 0–3 Years)

Healthy Growth and Development

- *Physical*—grows at a rapid rate, especially brain size
- *Mental*—learns through senses, exploring, playing, communicates by crying, babbling, then "baby talk," simple sentences
- *Social-emotional*—seeks to build trust in others, dependent, beginning to develop a sense of self

Key Health Care Issues

- *Communication*—provide security, physical closeness; promote healthy parent-child bonds
- *Health*—keep immunizations/checkups on schedule; provide proper nutrition, sleep, skin care, oral health, routine screenings
- *Safety*—ensure a safe environment for exploring, playing, sleeping

Examples of age-specific care for infants and toddlers:

- Involve child and parent(s) in care during feeding, diapering, and bathing
- Provide safe toys and opportunities for play
- Encourage child to communicate—smile, talk softly to him or her
- Help parent(s) learn about proper child care

Young Children (Age 4–6)

Healthy Growth and Development

- *Physical*—grows at a slower rate; improving motor skills; dresses self, toilet trained
- *Mental*—begins to use symbols; improving memory; vivid imagination, fears; likes stories
- *Social-Emotional*—identifies with parent(s); becomes more independent; sensitive to others' feelings

Key Health Care Issues

- *Communication*—give praise, rewards, clear rules
- *Health*—keep immunizations/checkups on schedule; promote healthy habits (good nutrition, personal hygiene, etc.)
- *Safety*—promote safety habits (use bike helmets, safety belts, etc.)

Examples of age-specific care for young children:

- Involve parent(s) and child in care—let child make some food choices
- Use toys and games to teach child and reduce fear
- Encourage child to ask questions, play with others, and talk about feelings
- Help parent(s) teach child safety rules

Older Children (Age 7–12)

Healthy Growth and Development

- *Physical*—grows slowly until a "spurt" at puberty
- *Mental*—understands cause and effect, can read, write, do math; active, eager learner
- *Social-Emotional*—develops greater sense of self; focuses on school activities, negotiates for greater independence

Key Health Care Issues

- *Communication*—help child to feel competent, useful
- *Health*—keep immunizations/checkups on schedule; give information on alcohol, tobacco, other drugs, sexuality
- *Safety*—promote safety habits (playground safety, resolving conflicts peacefully, etc.)

Examples of age-specific care for older children:

- Allow child to make some care decisions (in which arm do you want vaccination?)
- Build self-esteem—ask child to help you do a task, recognize his or her achievements, and so on
- Guide child in making healthy, safe, lifestyle choices
- Help parent(s) talk with child about peer pressure, sexuality, alcohol, tobacco, and other drugs

BASIC HUMAN NEEDS

Maslow's hierarchy of needs implies that clients are motivated to meet certain needs. When one need is fulfilled, a person seeks to fulfill the next one, and so on. This hierarchy is often depicted as a pyramid. This five stage model can be divided into basic (or deficiency) needs (i.e., physiological, safety, social, and esteem) and growth needs (self-actualization).

1. Deficiency needs—also known as D-Needs
2. Growth needs—also known as "being needs" or B-Needs

Deficiency Needs

- Physiological
- Safety
- Social
- Esteem

Maslow called these needs "deficiency needs" because he felt that these needs arise due to deprivation. The satisfaction of these needs helps to "avoid" unpleasant feelings or consequence.

Growth Needs

- Self-actualization

These needs fall on the highest level of Maslow's pyramid. They come from a place of growth rather than from a place of "lacking."

A client must satisfy lower-level basic needs before moving on to meet higher-level growth needs. After meeting lower levels of needs, a client can reach the highest level of self-actualization, but few people do so.

Every client is capable and has the desire to move up the hierarchy toward a level of self-actualization. Unfortunately, progress is often disrupted by failure to meet lower level needs. Life experiences, including divorce and loss of job, may cause a client to fluctuate between levels of the hierarchy.

Physiological needs: These needs maintain the physical organism. These are biological needs such as food, water, oxygen, and constant body temperature. If a person is deprived of these needs, he or she will die.

Safety needs: There is a need to feel safe from harm, danger, or threat of destruction. Clients need regularity and some predictability.

Social needs: Friendship, intimacy, affection, and love are needed—from one's work group, family, friends, or romantic relationships.

Esteem needs: People need a stable, firmly based level of self-respect and respect from others.

Self-actualization needs: There is a need to be oneself, to act consistently with whom one is. *Self-actualization is an ongoing process.* It involves developing potential, becoming, and being what one is capable of being. It makes possible true objectivity—dealing with the world as it is, rather than as one needs it to be. You are free to really do what you want to do. There are moments when everything is right (peak experience); a glimmer of what it is like to be complete. One is in a position to find one's true calling (i.e., being an artist, writer, musician). Only 1% of the population consistently operates at this level.

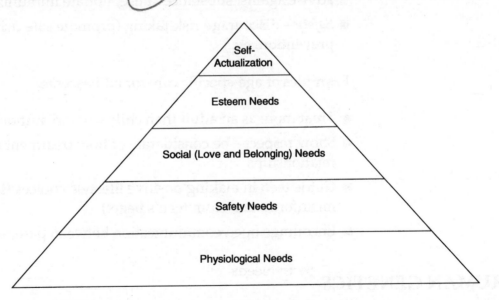

On the examination, Maslow's hierarchy of needs is often not explicitly asked about, but it can be applied when asked about the order of prioritizing problems or issues with a client. A client with an acute medical problem should focus on getting a medical evaluation first; a victim of domestic violence should prioritize medical and safety issues; and a refugee must initially meet basic survival needs (shelter, food, income, clothing, etc.) before working on fulfilling higher level needs.

ADOLESCENT DEVELOPMENT

The development of children ages 13 through 18 years old is a critical time as children develop the ability to understand abstract ideas, such as higher math concepts, and develop moral philosophies, including rights and privileges, and move toward a more mature sense of themselves and their purpose.

Healthy Growth and Development

- *Physical*—grows in spurts; matures physically; able to reproduce
- *Mental*—becomes an abstract thinker (goes beyond simple solutions, can consider many options, etc.); chooses own values
- *Social-Emotional*—develops own identity; builds close relationships; tries to balance peer group with family interests; concerned about appearances, challenges authority

Key Health Care Issues

- *Communication*—provide acceptance, privacy; build teamwork, respect
- *Health*—encourage regular checkups; promote sexual responsibility; advise against substance abuse; update immunizations
- *Safety*—discourage risk-taking (promote safe driving, violence prevention, etc.)

Examples of age-specific care for adolescents:

- Treat more as an adult than child—avoid authoritarian approaches
- Show respect—be considerate of how treatment may affect relationships
- Guide teen in making positive lifestyle choices (i.e., correct misinformation from teen's peers)
- Encourage open communication between parent(s), teen, and peers

HUMAN GENETICS

Social workers in all settings must educate themselves about the process of genetic inheritance and understand the primary reasons that clients seek genetic testing and counseling. Minimally, a social worker must understand the types of genetic conditions, including single gene disorders, chromosome anomalies, and multifactorial disorders, and the effect of harmful environmental toxins on development. Furthermore, an understanding of the patterns of inheritance between generations (autosomal dominant, autosomal recessive, and X-linked recessive) is essential in working with families.

It is important that social workers be educated about the specific application of skills to genetic cases. Social workers are already trained to view people from a biopsychosocial-spiritual-cultural perspective. In order to identify the patterns of disease in a family, a social worker may need to develop a genogram as part of the assessment.

Because a client's genetic test produces information about the whole family, the biology of a genetic condition must be thoroughly understood and explained to a client and his or her family in order to make informed decisions about whether or not to be tested. Sensitivity to the principle of self-determination is essential in the process of informing clients and family members.

Social workers must take care to ensure that clients are fully informed about all aspects of genetic testing. Social workers should provide counseling before and after the decision to have a genetic test and after the test itself.

GENDER ROLES

A gender role is a theoretical construct that refers to a set of social and behavioral norms that, within a specific culture, are widely considered to be socially appropriate for individuals of a specific sex. Socially accepted gender roles differ widely between different cultures. Gender role theory asserts that observed gender differences in behavior and personality characteristics are, at least in part, socially constructed, and therefore the product of socialization experiences; this contrasts with other models of gender, which assert that gender differences are "essential" to biological sex. Thus, there is a debate over the environmental or biological causes for the development of gender roles.

Gender role theory posits that boys and girls learn to perform one's biologically assigned gender through particular behaviors and attitudes. Gender role theory emphasizes the environmental causes of gender roles and the impact of socialization, or the process of transferring norms, values, beliefs, and behaviors to group members, in learning how to behave as a male or a female. Social role theory proposes that the social structure is the underlying force in distinguishing genders and that sex-differentiated behavior is driven by the division of labor between two sexes within a society. The division of labor creates gender roles, which, in turn, lead to gendered social behavior.

Gender has several definitions. It usually refers to a set of characteristics that are either seen to distinguish between male and female, one's biological sex, or one's gender identity. Gender identity is the gender(s), or lack thereof, a person self-identifies as; it is not based on biological sex, either real or perceived, nor is it always based on sexual orientation. There are two main genders, masculine (male) and feminine (female), although in some cultures there are more genders. Gender roles refer to the set of attitudes and behaviors socially expected from those with a particular gender identity.

IMPACT OF ENVIRONMENT ON INDIVIDUALS

Social workers must be knowledgeable about human behavior across the life course, the range of social systems in which people live, and the ways social systems promote or deter people in maintaining or achieving health and well-being. Social workers should apply theories and knowledge to understand biological, social, cultural, psychological, and spiritual development.

The ecological perspective is rooted in systems theory, which views coping as a transactional process that reflects the "person-in-environment" relationship. Using this perspective, the focus of intervention is the interface between a client (person, family, group, etc.) and a client's environment. The ecological perspective is also concerned with the issues of power and privilege and how they are withheld from some groups, imposing enormous stress on affected individuals.

Environmental factors can have strong positive or negative impacts on development.

IMPACT OF PHYSICAL, MENTAL, AND COGNITIVE DISABILITIES ON HUMAN DEVELOPMENT

The impacts of disabilities on human development are extremely varied depending upon the manifestations of the disability and when it occurs during the life course. Some disabilities are short-term, whereas others are lifelong. Critical to mitigating the negative impacts is the development of coping skills that strengthen a client's ability to deal with his or her limitations. Support (formal and informal) is also critical.

There may also be positive effects of disabilities because familial bonds may be stronger or individuals may develop skills to compensate for other tasks that cannot be performed.

Disability is a normal phenomenon in the sense that it exists in all societies. Although medical explanations remain primary in defining disability, the history of disability took an important turn in the latter half of the 20th century that has significantly influenced responses to it. Disability rights scholars and activists rejected the medical explanation for disability, since such explanations of permanent deficit did not advance social justice, equality of opportunity, and rights as citizens. Rather, these leaders proposed the intolerance and rigidity of social institutions, rather than medical conditions, as the explanation for disability. Words such as *inclusion*, *participation*, and *nondiscrimination* were introduced into the disability literature and reflected the notions that people who did not fit within the majority were disabled by stigma, prejudice, marginalization, segregation, and exclusion. This notion of disability requires the modification of societal structures to include all, rather than "fixing" individuals with varying abilities.

INTERPLAY OF BIOLOGICAL, PSYCHOLOGICAL, AND SOCIAL FACTORS

Human development is a lifelong process beginning before birth and extending to death. At each moment in life, every human being is in a state of personal evolution. Physical changes largely drive the process, as our cognitive abilities advance and decline in response to the brain's growth in childhood and reduced functioning in old age. Psychosocial development is also significantly influenced by physical growth, as changing body and brain, together with environment, shape a client's identity and relationships with other people.

Thus, development is the product of the elaborate interplay of biological, psychological, and social influences. As children develop physically, gaining greater psychomotor control and increased brain function, they become more sophisticated cognitively—that is, more adept at thinking about and acting upon their environment. These physical and cognitive changes, in turn, allow them to develop psychosocially, forming individual identities and relating effectively and appropriately with other people.

EFFECTS OF FAMILY DYNAMICS ON INDIVIDUALS

Family dynamics significantly impact on a client's biological, psychological, and social functioning in both positive and negative ways. Having a close-knit and supportive family provides emotional support, ensures economic well-being, and increases overall health. However, the opposite is also true. When family life is characterized by stress and conflict, well-being can be poor.

Social support is one of the main ways that family positively impacts well-being. Social relationships, such as those found in close families, have been demonstrated to decrease the likelihood of negative outcomes, such as chronic disease, disability, mental illness, and death.

Though good familial relations and social support serve as protective factors and improve overall well-being and health, studies have shown that not all familial relations positively impact these areas. Problematic and non-supportive familial interactions have a negative impact. For example, growing up in an unsupported, neglectful, or violent home is associated with poor physical health and development.

DYNAMICS OF GRIEF AND LOSS

Elisabeth Kübler-Ross outlined what has been the traditional five stages of grief. She originally developed this model based on her observations of people suffering from terminal illness. She later expanded her theory to apply to any form of personal loss, such as the death of a loved one, the loss of a job or income, major rejection, the end of a relationship or divorce, drug addiction, incarceration, the onset of a disease or chronic illness, and/or an infertility diagnosis, as well as many tragedies and disasters (and even minor losses).

Denial and isolation: Shock is replaced with the feeling of "this can't be happening to me."

Anger: The emotional confusion that results from this loss may lead to anger and finding someone or something to blame—"why me?"

Bargaining: The next stage may result in trying to negotiate with one's self (or a higher power) to attempt to change what has occurred.

Depression: A period of sadness and loneliness then will occur in which a person reflects on his or her grief and loss.

Acceptance: After time feeling depressed about the loss, a person will eventually be at peace with what happened.

Hope is not a separate stage, but is possible at any stage.

IMPACTS OF ECONOMIC CHANGE ON CLIENT SYSTEMS

Family income has selective but, in some instances, quite substantial impacts on child and adolescent well-being. Family income appears to be more strongly related to children's ability and achievement than to their emotional outcomes.

Children who live in extreme poverty or who live below the poverty line for multiple years appear, all other things being equal, to suffer the worst outcomes. The timing of poverty also seems to be important for certain outcomes. Children who experience poverty during their preschool and early school years have lower rates of school completion than children and adolescents who experience poverty only in later years. Although more research is needed, findings to date suggest that interventions during early childhood may be most important in reducing poverty's impact on children.

Social workers must also consider the implications on the biopsychosocial-spiritual-cultural aspects of well-being. Medical care may be neglected in order to meet other needs. Coping skills are needed when there are dramatic changes in income and opportunities to adapt and return to economic stability are critical.

EFFECTS OF BODY IMAGE ON SELF AND RELATIONSHIPS

Body image is the way one perceives and relates to his or her body, and how one thinks he or she is seen.

Body image affects nearly everyone from time to time. Body image is not only influenced by the perceptions of others, but by the media and cultural forces as well. Senses are bombarded by an onslaught of mixed messages about how one "should" look or think about his or her body.

Having a healthy body image is a key to well-being, both mentally and physically. A positive body image means that, most of the time, a client has a realistic perception of, and feels comfortable with, his or her looks.

Factors associated with *positive* body image:

- Acceptance and appreciation of natural body shape and body differences
- Self-worth not tied to appearance
- Confidence in and comfort with body
- An unreasonable amount of time is not spent worrying about food, weight, or calories
- Judgment of others is not made related to their body weight, shape, and/or eating or exercise habits
- Knowing physical appearance says very little about character and value as a person

Factors of *negative* body image:

- Distorted perception of shape or body parts, unlike what they really are
- Believing only other people are attractive and that body size or shape is a sign of personal failure
- Feeling body doesn't measure up to family, social, or media ideals
- Ashamed, self-conscious, and anxious about body
- Uncomfortable and awkward in body
- Constant negative thoughts about body and comparisons to others

Some possible *effects* of a negative body image:

- Emotional distress
- Low self-esteem
- Unhealthy dieting habits
- Anxiety
- Depression
- Eating disorders
- Social withdrawal or isolation

CULTURAL, RACIAL, AND ETHNIC IDENTITY DEVELOPMENT

Ethnicity refers to the idea that one is a member of a particular cultural, national, or racial group that may share culture, religion, race, language, or place of origin. Two people can share the same race but have different ethnicities.

The meaning of **race** is not fixed; it is related to a particular social, historical, and geographic context. The way races are classified has changed in the public mind over time; for example, at one time racial classifications were based on ethnicity or nationality, religion, or minority language groups. Today, society classifies people into different races primarily based on skin color.

Cultural identity is often defined as the identity of a group or culture of an individual who is influenced by his or her self-identification with that group or culture. Certain ethnic and racial identities may also bestow privilege.

Cultural, racial, and ethnic identities are important. They may instill feelings of shared commitment and values and a sense of belonging that may otherwise be missing.

Cultural, racial, and ethnic identities are passed from one generation to the next through customs, traditions, language, religious practice, and cultural values. Current events, mainstream media, and popular literature also influence cultural, racial, and ethnic identities.

Cultural, racial, and ethnic identities play a particularly large role among minority youth because they experience the contrasting and dominant culture of the majority ethnic group. Youth who belong to the majority ethnic culture may not even recognize or acknowledge their cultural, racial, and ethnic identities.

Following is a three-stage model for adolescent cultural and ethnic identity development. These stages do not correspond to specific ages, but can occur at any time. Individuals may spend their entire lives at a particular stage.

- The first stage, **unexamined cultural, racial, and ethnic identity**, is characterized by a lack of exploration of culture, race, and ethnicity and cultural, racial, and ethnic differences—they are rather taken for granted without much critical thinking. This is usually the stage reserved for childhood when cultural, racial, and ethnic ideas provided by parents, the community, or the media are easily accepted. Children at this stage tend not to be interested in culture, race, or ethnicity and are generally ready to take on the opinions of others.

- The second stage of the model is referred to as the **cultural, racial, and ethnic identity search** and is characterized by the exploration and questioning of culture, race, and ethnicity in order to learn more about them and to understand the implications of belonging. During this stage, there is questioning of where beliefs come from and why they are held. For some, this stage may arise from a turning point in their lives or from a growing awareness of other cultures, races, and ethnicities. It can also be a very emotional time.

- Finally, the third stage of the model is **cultural, racial, and ethnic identity achievement**. Ideally, people at this stage have a clear sense of their cultural, racial, and ethnic identity and are able to successfully navigate it in the contemporary world, which is undoubtedly very interconnected and intercultural. The acceptance of cultural, racial, and ethnic identity may play a significant role in important life decisions and choices, influencing attitudes and behavior. This usually leads to an increase in self-confidence and positive psychological development.

The classic model of cultural, racial, and ethnic identity development refers to identity statuses rather than stages, because stages imply a linear progression of steps that may not occur for all.

- **Pre-encounter:** At this point, the client may not be consciously aware of his or her culture, race, or ethnicity and how it may affect his or her life.

- **Encounter:** A client has an encounter that provokes thought about the role of cultural, racial, and ethnic identification in his or her life. This may be a negative or positive experience related to culture, race, and ethnicity. For minorities, this experience is often a negative one in which they experience discrimination for the first time.

- **Immersion-Emersion:** After an encounter that forces a client to confront cultural, racial, and ethnic identity, a period of exploration follows. A client may search for information and will also learn through interaction with others from the same cultural, racial, or ethnic groups.

- **Internalization and Commitment:** At this point, a client has developed a secure sense of identity and is comfortable socializing both within and outside the group he or she identifies with.

STRENGTHS PERSPECTIVE

The strengths perspective is based on the assumption that clients have the *capacity to grow, change, and adapt* (**humanistic approach**). Clients also have the knowledge that is important in defining and solving their problems (clients or families are experts about their own lives and situations); they are resilient and survive and thrive despite difficulties.

Strength is any ability that helps an individual (or family) to confront and deal with a stressful life situation and to use the challenging situation as a stimulus for growth. Individual strengths include, but are not limited to, cognitive abilities, coping mechanisms, personal attributes, interpersonal skills, or external resources. Families may have other strengths such as kinship bonds, community supports, religious connections, flexible roles, strong ethnic traditions, and so on.

Strengths vary from one situation to another and are contextual. What may be an appropriate strength or coping mechanism in one situation may not be appropriate in another. Ideally, in a given situation, a client selects an appropriate way to cope by drawing from a repertoire of coping mechanisms or strengths. The appropriateness of a particular coping mechanism may vary according to life course stage, developmental tasks, kinds of stressors, situation, and so on. Having a variety of coping mechanisms and resources enables flexibility in the way a client copes with stresses.

The strengths perspective focuses on understanding clients (or families) on the basis of their strengths and resources (internal and external) and mobilizing the resources to improve their situations. There is a systematic assessment of all the strengths and resources available to meet desired goals.

Methods to enhance strengths include:

- Collaboration and partnership between a social worker and client
- Creating opportunities for learning or displaying competencies
- Environmental modification—environment is both a resource and a target of intervention

Abuse and Neglect

ABUSE AND NEGLECT CONCEPTS

There are various forms of abuse and neglect: **physical abuse** (infliction of physical injury); **sexual abuse** (inappropriate exposure or sexual contact, activity, or behavior without consent); **psychological abuse** (emotional/verbal/mental injury); and **neglect** (failing to meet physical, emotional, or other needs).

Different forms of abuse occur separately, but are often seen in combinations. Psychological abuse almost always accompanies other forms of abuse. There is no single cause of abuse.

- *Stressors*: history of abuse; isolated with lack of social supports; low sense of self-competence and self-esteem; financial problems
- *Poor skills*: rigid, authoritarian; low IQ; poor self-control; poor communication, problem-solving, and interpersonal skills
- *Family issues*: marital discord, imbalanced relationship with marital partner (dominant or noninvolved); domestic violence; substance abuse

The victim is often blamed for the abuse by the perpetrator.

INDICATORS AND DYNAMICS OF SEXUAL ABUSE

Physical or anatomical signs/injuries associated with the genital and rectal areas are signs of physical or sexual abuse. Behavioral signs include any extreme changes in behavior, including regression, fears and anxieties, withdrawal, sleep disturbances, and/or recurrent nightmares. If the victim is a child, he or she may also show an unusual interest in sexual matters or know sexual information inappropriate for his or her age group. Sexual promiscuity, sexual victimization, and prostitution can also be signs.

Some factors influencing the effect of sexual abuse include:

- Age of the victim (at time of abuse and time of assessment)
- Extent and duration of sexual abuse
- Relationship of offender to victim
- Reaction of others to the abuse
- Other life experiences

Immediately after disclosing the abuse, an individual is at risk for:

- Disbelief by others (especially if victim is a child or perpetrator is a spouse/partner of an adult)
- Being rejected by others
- Being blamed for the abuse and the consequences of disclosing the sexual abuse

For a child, one of the most significant factors contributing to adjustment after sexual abuse is the level of parental support.

Some of the effects of sexual abuse can be:

- Aversive feelings about sex; overvaluing sex; sexual identity problems; and/or hypersexual behaviors
- Feelings of shame and guilt or feeling responsible for the abuse, which are reflected in self-destructive behaviors (such as substance abuse, self-mutilation, suicidal ideation and gestures, and acts that aim to provoke punishment)
- Lack of trust, unwillingness to invest in others; involvement in exploitive relationships; angry and acting-out behaviors
- Perceived vulnerability and victimization; phobias; sleep and eating problems

INDICATORS AND DYNAMICS OF PSYCHOLOGICAL ABUSE AND NEGLECT

Psychological abuse/neglect is sustained, repetitive, and inappropriate behavior aimed at threatening, isolating, discrediting, belittling, teasing, humiliating, bullying, confusing, and/or ignoring. Psychological abuse/neglect can be seen in constant criticism, belittling, teasing, ignoring or withholding of praise or affection, and placing excessive or unreasonable demands, including expectations above what is appropriate.

It can impact intelligence, memory, recognition, perception, attention, imagination, and moral development. Individuals who have been psychologically abused are likely to be fearful, withdrawn, and/or resentful, distressed, and despairing. They are likely to feel unloved, worthless, and unwanted, or only valued in meeting another's needs.

Those who are victims of psychological abuse and neglect often:

- Avoid eye contact and experience deep loneliness, anxiety, and/or despair
- Have a flat and superficial way of relating, with little empathy toward others
- Have a lowered capacity to engage appropriately with others
- Engage in bullying, disruptive, or aggressive behaviors toward others
- Engage in self-harming and/or self-destructive behaviors (i.e., cutting, physical aggression, reckless behavior showing a disregard for self and safety, drug taking)

INDICATORS OF PHYSICAL ABUSE AND NEGLECT

Physical abuse is defined as nonaccidental trauma or physical injury caused by punching, beating, kicking, biting, or burning. It is the most visible form of abuse because there are usually physical signs.

With a child, physical abuse can result from inappropriate or excessive physical discipline.

Indicators of physical abuse include:

- Unexplained bruises or welts on the face, lips, mouth, torso, back, buttocks, or thighs, sometimes reflecting the shape of the article used to inflict them (electric cord, belt buckle, etc.)
- Unexplained burns from a cigar or cigarette, especially on soles, palms, back, or buttocks—sometimes patterned like an electric burner, iron, or similar
- Unexplained fractures to the skull, nose, or facial structure
- Unexplained lacerations or abrasions to the mouth, lips, gums, eyes, and/or external genitalia

Behavioral indicators include being wary of individuals (parent or caretaker if a child is being abused) and behavioral extremes (aggressiveness or withdrawal), as well as fear related to reporting injury.

CHARACTERISTICS OF ABUSE PERPETRATORS

Many individuals with these characteristics do not commit acts of abuse. However, some factors are more likely to be present in those who commit abusive acts. Thus, having one of these risk factors does not mean that an individual will become an abuser, but an abuser is likely to have one or more of these risk factors.

A past history of violent behavior is the best predictor of future violence. Each prior act of violence increases the chance of future episodes of violence. In addition, those who suffered some form of abuse as children are more likely to be perpetrators of abuse as adults.

Risk Factors:

1. History of owning weapons and using them against others
2. Criminal history; repetitive antisocial behavior
3. Drug and alcohol use (substance use is associated with the most violent crimes)
4. Psychiatric disorder with coexisting substance abuse
5. Certain psychiatric symptoms such as psychosis, intense suspiciousness, anger, and/or unhappiness
6. Personality disorders (Borderline and Antisocial Personality disorders)
7. History of impulsivity; low frustration tolerance; recklessness; inability to tolerate criticism; entitlement
8. Angry affect without empathy for others—high anger scores associated with increased chance of violence
9. Environmental stressors: lower socioeconomic status or poverty; job termination

A social worker should take all reports of abuse and all threats for harm seriously.

A social worker can distinguish between static and dynamic risk factors.

Static risk factors: such as past history of violent behavior or demographic information.

Dynamic risk factors: factors that can be changed by interventions such as change in living situation, treatment of psychiatric symptoms, abstaining from drug and alcohol use, access to weapons, and so on. Each client presents with a unique set of risk factors that require an individualized plan.

Interventions to reduce dynamic risk factors include:

- Pharmacological interventions
- Substance use treatment
- Psychosocial interventions
- Removal of weapons
- Increased level of supervision

INDICATORS AND DYNAMICS OF EXPLOITATION

Exploitation is treating someone badly in order to benefit from his or her resources or work. It is when someone uses a situation to gain unfair advantage for himself or herself. Exploitation is more common when there is a power differential between parties due to social status, abilities, income, education, job position, and so on.

Social workers have ethical mandates not to exploit clients, supervisees, students, and others who they come in contact with in their work.

They also may be asked to assess exploitation of clients by others and intervene when needed. For example, a form of maltreatment sometimes seen with older adults is financial/material exploitation or unauthorized use of an older person's resources. Individuals may befriend an older person to gain his or her trust so that the older adult's money or items of value can be inappropriately used for the individual's wants or needs and not the care of the older adult.

On a macro level, it is also important to see the relationship between discrimination and exploitation of individuals. When individuals are not provided the same access to social rewards, they are inherently exploited. Most social problems are aggravated by the status of particular groups in the society, including that:

- There is a greater prevalence of poverty among people of color and female household heads
- Poverty decreasing the opportunities for employment, education, goods, and so on
- Poverty creating greater stresses that lead to physical and mental illnesses, family breakdown, inability to work, and other problems
- Discrimination creating deficits in social power

Diversity, Social/Economic Justice, and Oppression

INFLUENCES OF CULTURE, RACE, AND/OR ETHNICITY ON BEHAVIORS AND ATTITUDES

The United States has a racially and ethnically diverse population. The Census officially recognizes six ethnic and racial categories: White American; American Indian and Alaska Native; Asian; African American; Native Hawaiian and Other Pacific Islander; and people of two or more races. The U.S. Census Bureau also classifies Americans as "Hispanic or Latino" and "Not Hispanic or Latino," which identifies Hispanic and Latino Americans as a racially diverse ethnicity that comprises the largest minority group in the nation.

A social worker must remember that there is tremendous intragroup diversity. In fact, the differences between racial and ethnic groups (intergroup) are often less profound than those found within these groups (intragroup). It is important to view a client as the expert and to not stereotype or make assumptions about values, behaviors, or attitudes based on a client's racial or ethnic group.

The following is an overview of some characteristics recognized as being more prevalent within each of the Census categories/classifications:

White American

■ Family: parents with young children; divorce common; personal desires put over family; parents try to be friends with their children; avoid physical punishment

- Communication: language—American Standard English; communication can be long-winded and impersonal

- Spirituality: religion is a private affair, but mainly Protestant and Bible-based

- Values: capitalism (i.e., the future is what you make it); poverty is a moral failing and wealth is held in high esteem; physical beauty is valued with white skin, blond hair, and thin body being the ideal; sports are an important part of life (baseball, American football, basketball); democracy and freedom; individual rights

American Indian/Alaska Native

- Family: complex family organizations that include relatives without blood ties; strong kinship bonds (multigenerational, extended families); group takes preference over individual; husband and wife show a tendency to communicate more with their gender group than with each other; harmony within the group is very important; common sharing of material goods; group decision making

- Communication: indirectness; being still and quiet; comfortable with silence; value listening and nonverbal communication; may avoid making direct eye contact as a show of respect when talking to a higher status person

- Spirituality: fundamental part of life; interconnectedness of all living things; sacredness of all creation; use of traditional and Western healing practices; medicine man, shaman, or spiritual leaders are traditional healers

- Values: holistic; interconnectedness of mind, body, spirit, and heart; time is viewed as a circular flow that is always with us; follow nature's rhythms rather than linear time

Asian

- Family: patriarchal system in which a wife has lower status and is subservient to her father, husband, and oldest son; obligation to parents and respect for elders; hierarchical family structure with strictly prescribed roles and rules of behavior and conduct

- Communication: often indirect in order to avoid direct confrontation and maintain highly valued harmonious relationships; less emotional expressiveness (reserved) and demonstration of affection

- Spirituality: cultures influenced by Confucian and Buddhist philosophies

- Values: shaming and obligation to others are mechanisms for reinforcing cultural norms; adhering to rules of conduct reflects not only on the individual, but also on the family and extended kinship network, including past and future generations; usually seek help from the family or cultural community

Asian clients may respond to psychotropic drugs differently than clients from other ethnic groups. They typically require lower doses of medications and may experience more severe side effects from the same doses given to other clients. It is sometimes recommended to start Asian clients on less than the normally prescribed dosage. They are also sometimes resistant and view treatment of symptoms via homeopathic methods as more acceptable.

African American

- Family: multigenerational family systems; strong kinship bonds, including extended families and relatives without blood ties; informal adoption of children by extended family members; flexible family roles; women are often viewed as being "all sacrificing" and the "strength of the family"

- Communication: animated; individuals try to get their opinions heard; often includes physical touch; direct; show respect at all times; history of racism and sense of powerlessness impacts interactions

- Spirituality: turn to community and/or religious leaders if assistance is needed; church is seen as a central part of community life

- Values: strong kinship bonds; strong work orientation; strong religious orientation; use informal support network—church or community; distrust of government and social services—feel "big brother" doesn't care; don't like to admit they need help—strong sense of pride

Native Hawaiian and Other Pacific Islander

- Family: Western concept of "immediate family" is completely alien to indigenous Hawaiians; family is not restricted to those related by blood; "we are all related"; ties that bind cannot be broken, even by death; cherish their ancestors, with generation upon generation of lineage committed to memory and beautiful chants composed to herald their ancestors' abilities

- Communication: many native Hawaiian and Pacific Islander subgroups, representing different languages and customs; ability to speak English has a tremendous impact on access to health information, public services; Hawaii is the only state in the United States that has designated a native language, Hawaiian, as one of its two official state languages

- Spirituality: polytheistic, believing in many deities; belief that spirits are found in nonhuman beings and objects such as animals, waves, and the sky

- Values: importance of culture and welfare of all living in a community; focus on ensuring the health of the community as a whole; everyone has a responsibility to use his or her talents to the benefit of the whole; sharing is central

Hispanic/Latino

- Family: extended family system incorporates godparents and informally adopted children; deep sense of commitment and obligation to family; family unity, welfare, and honor are important; emphasis on group rather than individual; male has greater power and authority

- Communication: often speak Spanish (but do not assume that they wish to receive services in native language); display varied emotional expressiveness depending on language being spoken; when speaking Spanish, client may be very expansive/expressive, friendly, playful, but in switching to English, speech may be more businesslike and guarded

- Spirituality: most are Roman Catholic; emphasis on spiritual values; strong church and community orientation/interdependence

- Values: wish to improve their life circumstances; belief in the innate worth of all individuals and that people are born into their lot in life; respect for dignity of self and others; respect for elders; respect for authority; very proud of heritage—never forget where they came from

INFLUENCE OF SEXUAL ORIENTATION AND/OR GENDER IDENTITY ON BEHAVIOR AND ATTITUDES

Sexual orientation refers to an individual's pattern of physical and emotional arousal toward other persons. Heterosexual individuals are attracted to persons of the opposite sex, homosexual individuals are attracted to persons of the same sex, and bisexual individuals are attracted to persons of both sexes. Homosexual males are often referred to as "gay"; homosexual females are often referred to as "lesbian." *It is important to not use labels.*

In contrast, **gender identity** is the knowledge of oneself as being male or female. Gender identity usually conforms to anatomic sex in both heterosexual and homosexual individuals. However, individuals who identify as transgender feel themselves to be of a gender different from their biological sex; their gender identity does not match their anatomic or chromosomal sex. Transvestite should not be confused with transgender or transsexual ("person who lives as a member of a sex different from his or her birth sex"). Transvestites simply enjoy being able to cross-dress and do not view themselves as a gender different from their biological sex.

People who are transgender may identify as heterosexual, homosexual, bisexual, pansexual (attracted to individuals outside or independent of gender—blind to gender), polysexual (attracted to many genders), or asexual.

It is important to let individuals define their own sexual orientation and gender identity.

INFLUENCE OF DISABILITY ON BEHAVIOR AND ATTITUDES

Disability places a set of extra demands on the family system. A disability can consume a lot of a family's resources of time, energy, and money, so that other individual and family needs may go unmet.

Day-to-day assistance may lead to exhaustion and fatigue, taxing the physical and emotional energy of family members. There can be emotional strain, including worry, guilt, anxiety, anger, and uncertainty about the cause or prognosis of the disability, about the future, about the needs of other family members, and about whether the individual is getting enough assistance.

There can be a financial burden associated with getting health, education, and social services; buying or renting equipment and devices; making accommodations to the home; transportation; and acquiring medications and/or special food. The person or family may be eligible for payment or reimbursement from an insurance company and/or a publicly funded program such as Medicaid or Supplemental Security Income. However, knowing about services and programs and then working to become eligible is another major challenge faced by families.

Working through eligibility issues and coordinating among different providers is a challenge faced by families for which they may want a social worker to assist.

Many communities still lack programs, facilities, and resources that allow for the full inclusion of persons with disabilities. Families often report that one burden comes from dealing with people in the community whose attitudes and behaviors are judgmental, stigmatizing, and rejecting.

There are differential impacts, depending upon several factors. For example, a disability in which cognitive ability is limited may be difficult because it may limit the person's ability to complete major life tasks or live independently. In addition, the degree to which a physical disability limits activities or functions of daily living or the ages of individuals or parents when a disability emerges are important factors that may impact on adjustment.

EFFECTS OF DIFFERENCES IN VALUES

Values are linked to both behaviors and attitudes. For example, extrinsic values—such as wealth or preservation of public image—tend to influence our levels of personal well-being. In general, the esteem of others or pursuit of material goods seem to drive people toward their pursuit, though more inherently rewarding motivations and self-direction values seem to provide more self-satisfaction.

It is common to see people segmented into distinct groups or dichotomies based upon their values.

People who hold strong traditional values are more likely to observe national holidays and customs. Stronger achievement values are associated with stress-related behaviors (such as taking on too many commitments).

However, values are not the sole determinant of behavior: In fact, actions can at times be fairly divergent from dominant values. For example, despite proenvironmental and prosocial values, a client may not always protect either people or the environment.

Aspects of our society may constrain people from expressing the intrinsic values they hold. Education, the media, and social pressures are likely to influence the kinds of values seen as relevant to particular situations.

Given the importance of values on actions, it is important for a social worker to look at what influences values and how they develop and change over time.

IMPACTS OF CULTURAL HERITAGE ON SELF-IMAGE

Although experiences will differ, many individuals have experienced racism, oppression, or discrimination in some form and are very sensitive to being treated with disrespect or to being exploited. They will be skeptical and cautious about seeking help for fear of being mistreated or misunderstood.

Trust is an important element in establishing a therapeutic alliance. Clients want to know if a social worker can be trusted and is competent to help them solve their problems. Clients regard and treat social workers as experts and authority figures.

Matching clients and social workers of the same race and ethnicity may decrease dropout rates and increase utilization of services, but the quality of the therapeutic relationship remains the most important factor in predicting the outcome of treatment.

Clients will ascribe credibility to a social worker using their cultural norms as a reference point (role, age, education, gender, etc.).

Understanding the cultural heritage of a client is important to working with him or her. Conflict between older and younger generations is often a common occurrence. Younger members assume the values and traditions of the majority, which can conflict with the more traditional values of the original culture that are held by an older generation.

Power and role reversals that threaten and undermine parental authority and leadership can also occur in families when parents rely on younger members of the family to become cultural interpreters. Role reversals may also occur if a woman becomes the main breadwinner because her husband cannot find employment. In a traditional marital relationship with strict gender roles, men may have difficulty dealing with this role reversal.

Members of ethnic minority groups must adapt to being members of two cultures ("bicultural") and learn to function in relationship to their culture of origin and the majority culture. Factors that influence the degree of "bicultural" socialization include:

1. The degree to which the two cultures are alike (i.e., values, beliefs, norms)—less dissonance between cultural factors makes adjustment easier

2. The degree to which bicultural socialization is supported and valued (help in accessing resources and intervening with other social systems, lend assistance in times of crisis, advocate for client, etc.)

3. The degree to which the majority culture and culture of origin provide positive or negative feedback regarding attempts to adapt to the majority culture

4. Language barriers

5. The degree to which a client appears the same in physical characteristics to those members of the majority culture (skin color, facial characteristics, etc.)

A higher degree of psychological well-being, self-esteem, and marital adjustment is reported in subjects with higher levels of bicultural socialization.

Although no culture condones child abuse or neglect, there are cultural variations about what constitutes child abuse and neglect, as well as acceptable disciplinary measures.

There are greater incidences of domestic violence in cultures where women have lower status than men.

Cultural groups have various explanations for an illness, particularly mental illness, and also have different ideas on what will help (often depends on the identified cause of the illness)—some illnesses are culture-bound syndromes.

IMPACTS OF SPIRITUALITY AND/OR RELIGIOUS BELIEFS ON BEHAVIOR AND ATTITUDES

Many models attempt to explain the impact of spirituality and/or religious beliefs on behavior. Many of them describe this impact along a continuum as follows, with some individuals changing during their life course and others remaining at the same point.

Individuals are unwilling to accept a will greater than their own.

Behavior is chaotic, disordered, and reckless. Individuals tend to defy and disobey, and are extremely egoistic. They lack empathy for others. Very young children can be at this stage. Adults who do not move beyond this point in the continuum may engage in criminal activity because they cannot obey rules.

Individuals have blind faith in authority figures and see the world as divided simply into good and evil and right and wrong.

Children who learn to obey their parents and other authority figures move to this point in the continuum. Many "religious" people who have blind faith in a spiritual being and do not question its existence may also be at this point. Individuals who are good, law-abiding citizens may never move further in the continuum.

Scientific skepticism and questioning are critical, because an individual does not accept things on faith, but only if convinced logically.

Many people working in a scientific and technical field may question spiritual or supernatural forces because they are difficult to measure or prove scientifically. Those who do engage in this skepticism move away from the simple, official doctrines.

The individual starts enjoying the mystery and beauty of nature and existence.

The individual develops a deeper understanding of good and evil, forgiveness and mercy, compassion and love. Religiousness and spirituality differ significantly from other points in the continuum and things are not accepted on blind faith or out of fear. The individual does not judge people harshly or seek to inflict punishment on them for their transgressions. This is the stage of loving others as one loves oneself, losing attachment to ego, and forgiving enemies.

Basic principles of all models move from the "egocentric," which are associated particularly with childhood, to "conformist," and eventually to "integration" or "universal."

EFFECTS OF DISCRIMINATION

The negative impacts of discrimination can be seen on both the micro and macro levels. Exposure to discrimination is linked to anxiety and depression as well as other mental health and behavioral problems. In addition, there may be physical effects such as diabetes, obesity, and high blood pressure.

These health problems may be caused by not maintaining healthy behaviors (such as physical activity) or engaging in unhealthy ones (such as smoking and alcohol or drug abuse).

On a macro level, discrimination also restricts access to the resources and systems needed for good health, education, employment, social support, and participation in sports, cultural, and civic activities. Discrimination and intolerance can also create a climate of despondence, apprehension, and fear within a community. The social and economic effects of discrimination on one generation may flow on to affect future generations, which can lead to cycles of poverty and disadvantage for future generations.

SYSTEMATIC (INSTITUTIONALIZED) DISCRIMINATION

Social workers should not practice, condone, facilitate, or collaborate with any form of discrimination on the basis of race, ethnicity, national origin, color, sex, sexual orientation, gender identity or expression, age, marital status, political belief, religion, immigration status, or mental or physical disability (*NASW Code of Ethics, 1999–4.02 Discrimination*).

Discrimination can occur at the individual or institutional level. Individual discrimination is when an individual is treated differently whereas institutionalized discrimination refers to policies or practices that discriminate against a group of people based on these characteristics (achievement gaps in education, residential segregation, etc.).

PROFESSIONAL COMMITMENT TO PROMOTING JUSTICE

One of the most important values of the social work profession is social justice.

Social workers promote social justice and social change with and on behalf of clients who are individuals, families, groups, organizations, and/or communities.

Social workers should engage in social and political action that seeks to ensure that all people have equal access to the resources, employment, services, and opportunities they require to meet their basic human needs and to develop fully. Social workers should be aware of the impact of the political arena on practice and should advocate for changes in policy and legislation to improve social conditions in order to meet basic human needs and promote social justice (*NASW Code of Ethics, 1999–6.04 Social and Political Action*).

IMPACT OF SOCIAL INSTITUTIONS ON SOCIETY

Many social institutions exist within our society. They have many functions including satisfying individuals' basic needs, defining and promoting dominant social values, defining and promoting individual roles, creating permanent patterns of social behavior, and supporting other social institutions.

The five basic institutions are family, religion, government, education, and economics.

Some of the functions of each of these institutions include the following.

Family

- To control and regulate sexual behavior
- To provide for new members of society (children)
- To provide for the economic and emotional maintenance of individuals
- To provide for primary socialization of children

Religion

- To provide solutions for the unexplained
- To support the normative structure of the society
- To provide a psychological diversion from unwanted life situations
- To sustain the existing class structure
- To promote and prevent social change

Government

- To create norms via laws and enforce them
- To adjudicate conflict via the courts
- To provide for the welfare of members of society
- To protect society from external threats

Education

- To transmit culture
- To prepare for jobs and roles
- To evaluate and select competent individuals
- To transmit functional skills

Economics

- To provide methods for the production and distribution of goods and services
- To enable individuals to acquire goods and services that are produced

IMPACT OF DIVERSITY ON STYLES OF COMMUNICATING

Communication styles may be strongly influenced by culture, race, and/or ethnicity.

Communication is far more than an exchange of words. Facial expressions, hand gestures, posture, eye contact, and even silence are constantly sending messages about attitudes, emotions, status, and relationships.

Nonverbal cues are critical. For example, personal space or the distance two people keep between themselves in order to feel comfortable is culturally based. Personal space may be influenced by gender or status. It can also be influenced by intimacy of a relationship.

Eye contact is also influenced by culture. For some, direct eye contact is very brief, with the gaze then sliding away to the side, especially with superiors or members of the opposite sex. In contrast, others may engage in more direct eye contact.

Speaking volume can be nearly as important as the words themselves. Normal baseline volumes vary among cultures and among individuals in these cultures.

The appropriateness of physical touch is also important to understand. In some cultures, individuals rarely touch each other, limiting themselves to handshakes and occasional pats on the shoulder or arm in business relationships, or hugs in closer friendships. In other cultures, however, physical touch, such as hugging, is part of many interactions, even those that are casual.

Smiling, facial expressions, time, and silence are other communication factors that vary among those from different cultures, races, or ethnic groups.

In order to be effective with those from diverse cultural, racial, and/or ethnic groups, a social worker must:

1. Recognize direct and indirect communication styles

2. Demonstrate sensitivity to nonverbal cues

3. Generate a wide variety of verbal responses, nonverbal responses, and strategies

4. Use language that is culturally appropriate

5. Identify his or her own professional style and recognize limitations and strengths

6. Identify and reduce barriers that will inhibit engagement with persons who are culturally different

INFLUENCE OF AGE ON BEHAVIOR AND ATTITUDES

Clearly, age has a profound impact on behavior and attitudes. Most developmental theorists trace physical, psychosocial, and other changes across the life course, marking distinctions in these areas by age. Interestingly, although behavior analysts have contributed to research on aging, the focus has largely been on remedying age-related deficits, rather than a concern with aging as a developmental process. Thus, although there is much documented that confirms that behavior changes with advancing years, there is less known about the sources of those changes.

Age can influence health behaviors, social/emotional patterns, mobility, cognitive functioning, economic well-being, independence, and other areas of life.

Assessment and Intervention Planning (24%)

4

Biopsychosocial History and Collateral Data

PSYCHOPHARMACOLOGY

Psychotropic medications affect brain chemicals associated with mood and behavior. Psychotropic drugs are prescribed to treat a variety of mental health problems and typically work by changing the amounts of important chemicals in the brain called neurotransmitters. Psychotropic drugs are usually prescribed by psychiatrists, though other physicians and professionals may be allowed to prescribe them in certain jurisdictions. Psychotropic drugs may be needed to treat disorders such as Schizophrenia or Bipolar Disorder, but are often combined with other supports, such as that from family and friends, therapy, lifestyle changes, and other treatment protocols, to ensure healthy everyday living.

Antipsychotics

Used for the treatment of Schizophrenia and mania

Typical
Haldol (haloperidol)
Haldol Decanoate (long-acting injectable)
Loxitane (loxapine)
Mellaril (thioridazine)
Moban (molindone)
Navane (thiothixene)
Prolixin (fluphenazine)
Serentil (mesoridazine)
Stelazine (trifluoperazine)

Thorazine (chlorpromazine)
Trilafon (perphenazine)

Atypical

Abilify (aripiprazole)
Clozaril (clozapine)
Geodon (ziprasidone)
Risperdal (risperidone)
Seroquel (quetiapine)
Zyprexa (olanzapine)

With Clozaril, there is an increased risk of agranulocytosis that requires blood monitoring.

Some antipsychotics are available in injectable forms; these are useful for clients who are noncompliant with oral medications.

Tardive dyskinesia (abnormal, involuntary movements of the tongue, lips, jaw, and face, as well as twitching and snakelike movement of the extremities and occasionally the trunk) may result from taking high doses of antipsychotic medications over a long period of time. Symptoms may persist indefinitely after discontinuation of these medications. Thus, antipsychotic use should be closely monitored and prescribed at low doses if possible.

Antimanic Agents (Mood Stabilizers)

Used for the treatment of Bipolar Disorder

Depakene (valproic acid, sodium divalproex), Depakote sprinkles
Lamictal (lamotrigine)
Lithium (lithium carbonate), Eskalith, Lithobid
Tegretol (carbamazepine), Carbotrol
Topamax (topiramate)

There is a small difference between toxic and therapeutic levels (narrow therapeutic index) that necessitates periodic checks of blood levels of lithium. Also, there is a need for periodic checks of thyroid and kidney functions, because lithium can affect the functioning of these organs.

Antidepressants

Used for the treatment of depression

Selective Serotonin Reuptake Inhibitors (SSRIs)

Celexa (citalopram)
Lexapro (escitalopram)

Luvox (fluvoxamine)
Paxil (paroxetine)
Prozac (fluoxetine)
Zoloft (sertraline)

Tricyclics

Anafranil (clomipramine)
Asendin (amoxapine)
Elavil (amitriptyline)
Norpramin (desipramine)
Pamelor (nortriptyline)
Aventyl Sinequan (doxepin)
Surmontil (trimipramine)
Tofranil (imipramine)
Vivactil (protriptyline)

Monoamine Oxidase Inhibitors (MAOIs)

Nardil (phenelzine)
Parnate (tranylcypromine)

There are dietary restrictions of foods that contain high levels of tyramine (generally food that has been aged). Foods to avoid may include beer, ale, wine (particularly Chianti), cheese (except cottage and cream cheese), smoked or pickled fish (herring), beef or chicken liver, summer (dry) sausage, fava or broad bean pods (Italian green beans), and yeast vitamin supplements (brewer's yeast).

Others

Effexor (venlafaxine)
Desyrel (trazodone)
Remeron (mirtazapine)
Serzone (nefazodone)
Wellbutrin (bupropion), Zyban

Antianxiety Drugs

Used for the treatment of Anxiety and Panic disorders

Ativan (lorazepam)
Buspar (buspirone)
Klonopin (clonazepam)

Valium (diazepam)
Xanax (alprazolam)

There is a high abuse potential of these drugs and they can be dangerous when combined with alcohol or illicit substances. It is critical to look for signs of impaired motor or other functioning.

Stimulants

Used for the treatment of Attention-Deficit/Hyperactivity Disorder

Adderall (amphetamine, mixed salts)
Concerta (methylphenidate, long acting)
Dexedrine (dextroamphetamine), Dextrostat
Dexedrine Spansules (dextroamphetamine, long acting)
Metadate (methylphenidate, long acting), Ritalin SR
Ritalin (methylphenidate), Methylin

COMPONENTS OF A BIOPSYCHOSOCIAL HISTORY

The biopsychosocial-spiritual-cultural history is a tool that provides information on the current/presenting issue or issues; a client's past and present physical health, including developmental milestones; a client's emotional functioning; educational or vocational background; cultural issues; spiritual and religious beliefs; environmental issues; and social functioning. Each issue may be reviewed for its relationship and/or impact with the presenting issue.

The *biological section* assesses a client's medical history, developmental history, current medications, substance abuse history, and family history of medical illnesses. Issues related to medical problems should be explored because mental health symptoms can exacerbate them. Referrals should be made to address medical concerns that are not being treated. Clients who are on medications should have care coordinated with the treating provider, and more should be known about the medications because side effects can also mask or exacerbate psychiatric symptoms or illnesses.

The *psychological section* assesses a client's present psychiatric illness or symptoms, history of the current psychiatric illness or symptoms, past or current psychosocial stressors, and mental status. Exploration of how the problem has been treated in the past, past or present psychiatric medications, and the family history of psychiatric and substance-related issues is also included.

The *social section* focuses on client systems and unique client context, and may identify strengths and/or resources available for treatment planning. Included are sexual identity issues or concerns, personal history, family of

origin history, support system, abuse history, education, legal history, marital/
relationship status and concerns, work history, and risks.

The assessment should also include information about a client's spiritual
beliefs, as well as his or her cultural traditions.

COMPONENTS OF A SEXUAL HISTORY

Some clients may not be comfortable talking about their sexual history, sex
partners, or sexual practices. It is critical that social workers try to put clients
at ease and let them know that taking a sexual history may be an important
part of the assessment process. A history is usually obtained through a face-
to-face interview, but can also be gotten from a pencil-and-paper document.

Questions included in a sexual history may vary depending upon client issues. However, they usually involve collecting information about partners (number, gender, risk factors, length of relationships), practices (risk
behaviors, oral/vaginal/anal intercourse, satisfaction with practices, desire/
arousal/organism), protection from and past history of STDs (condom use),
and prevention of pregnancy (if desired)/reproductive history.

If clients are experiencing dissatisfaction or dysfunction, social workers
will need to understand the reasons for dissatisfaction and/or dysfunction.
Medical explanations must be ruled out before psychological factors are considered as causes. A systems perspective should be used to understand issues
in this area. For example, a medical/biological condition that decreases satisfaction or causes dysfunction may heavily impact on psychological and social
functioning. In addition, a psychological or social issue can lead to a lack of
desire, inability to become aroused, or failure to attain orgasm.

Alcohol and/or drug use should also be considered related to concerns
about desire, arousal, or orgasm because they can cause decreased interest or
abilities in these areas.

COMMON PRESCRIPTION MEDICATIONS

The vast majority of Americans take at least one prescription medication, with
more than half of Americans taking two or more. The most commonly prescribed include the following medications.

Hydrocodone/acetaminophen is the most popular painkiller used to treat
moderate to severe pain. Hydrocodone, a narcotic analgesic, relieves pain
through the central nervous system, and it also is used to stop or prevent
coughing. This drug can become habit-forming when used over an extended
period of time.

Levothyroxine sodium is used to treat hypothyroidism, a condition where
the thyroid gland does not produce enough of the thyroid hormone. This

drug also is used to treat thyroid cancer and to help shrink an enlarged thyroid gland.

Lisinopril (which used to be sold under the brand names Zestril and Prinivil) is a high blood pressure medication. Its main function is to block chemicals in the body that trigger the tightening of blood vessels. Lisinopril also is used to help treat heart failure.

Metoprolol, the generic version of Lopressor, is used to treat high blood pressure and also helps reduce the risk of repeated heart attacks. Metoprolol also treats heart failure and heart pain or angina.

Simvastatin (generic Zocor) is prescribed to treat high cholesterol and is typically recommended in conjunction with diet changes. This drug is believed to have a variety of benefits including helping to prevent heart attacks and strokes.

Other Commonly Prescribed Medications

Synthroid is a prescription, man-made thyroid hormone that is used to treat hypothyroidism.

Crestor is a lipid-lowering agent taken orally.

Nexium is used to treat symptoms of gastroesophageal reflux disease (GERD) and other conditions involving excessive stomach acid.

Ventolin solution is used in inhalers for asthma.

Advair Diskus is a prescription used to treat asthma and chronic obstructive pulmonary disease (COPD).

Diovan is used to treat heart disease or heart failure.

Lantus is a sterile solution of insulin glargine for use as a subcutaneous injection for diabetes.

Cymbalta is a selective serotonin and norepinephrine reuptake inhibitor (SSNRI) for oral administration.

Vyvanse is used to treat hyperactivity and impulse control disorders.

Lyrica is used to control seizures, as well as treat nerve pain and fibromyalgia.

COMPONENTS OF A FAMILY HISTORY

Understanding a client's family history is an important part of the assessment process. A client is part of a larger family system. Thus, gaining a better understanding of the experiences of other family members may prove useful in understanding influences imposed on a client throughout his or her life course.

One tool used by social workers to depict a client as part of a larger family system is a **genogram**. A genogram is a graphic representation of a family tree that displays the interaction of generations within a family. It goes beyond a traditional family tree by allowing the user to analyze family, emotional, and social relationships within a group. It is used to identify repetitive patterns of behavior and to recognize hereditary tendencies. A social worker can also ask about these relationships, behaviors, and tendencies without using a genogram.

There are no set questions that must be included in a family history; often, they relate to the problem or issue experienced by a client at the time. However, they may include identifying family members':

- Ethnic backgrounds (including immigration) and traditions
- Biological ties (adoption, blended family structures, foster children)
- Occupations and educational levels
- Unusual life events or achievements
- Psychological and social histories, as well as current well-being
- Past and present substance use behaviors
- Relationships with other family members
- Roles within the immediate and larger family unit
- Losses such as those from death, divorce, or physical separation
- Current and past significant problems, including those due to medical, financial, and other issues
- Values related to economic status, educational attainment, and employment
- Coping skills or defense mechanisms

Finding out which adults and/or children get the most attention or recognition and which get the least may also provide insight.

BASIC MEDICAL TERMINOLOGY

Social workers must recognize the relationship between physical well-being and mental status. Social workers should always rule out medical etiology before making psychiatric diagnoses. A **differential diagnosis** is a systematic diagnostic method used to identify the presence of an entity where multiple alternatives are possible.

Social workers must know the major body systems and medical conditions associated with them that can affect psychological functioning and mood.

1. *Circulatory System*

   The circulatory system is the body's transport system. It is made up of a group of organs that transport blood throughout the body. The heart pumps the blood and the arteries and veins transport it.

2. *Digestive System*

The digestive system is made up of organs that break down food into protein, vitamins, minerals, carbohydrates, and fats, which the body needs for energy, growth, and repair.

3. *Endocrine System*

The endocrine system is made up of a group of glands that produce the body's long-distance messengers, or hormones. Hormones are chemicals that control body functions, such as metabolism, growth, and sexual development.

4. *Immune System*

The immune system is a body's defense system against infections and diseases. Organs, tissues, cells, and cell products work together to respond to dangerous organisms (like viruses or bacteria) and substances that may enter the body from the environment.

5. *Lymphatic System*

The lymphatic system is also a defense system for the body. It filters out organisms that cause disease, produces white blood cells, and generates disease-fighting antibodies. It also distributes fluids and nutrients in the body and drains excess fluids and protein so that tissues do not swell.

6. *Muscular System*

The muscular system is made up of tissues that work with the skeletal system to control movement of the body. Some muscles—like those in arms and legs—are voluntary, meaning that an individual decides when to move them. Other muscles, like the ones in the stomach, heart, intestines, and other organs, are involuntary. This means that they are controlled automatically by the nervous system and hormones—one often does not realize they are at work.

7. *Nervous System*

The nervous system is made up of the brain, the spinal cord, and nerves. One of the most important systems in the body, the nervous system is the body's control system. It sends, receives, and processes nerve impulses throughout the body. These nerve impulses tell muscles and organs what to do and how to respond to the environment.

8. *Reproductive System*

The reproductive system allows humans to produce children. Sperm from the male fertilizes the female's egg, or ovum, in the fallopian tube. The fertilized egg travels from the fallopian tube to the uterus, where the fetus develops over a period of nine months.

9. *Respiratory System*

The respiratory system brings air into the body and removes carbon dioxide. It includes the nose, trachea, and lungs.

10. *Skeletal System*

The skeletal system is made up of bones, ligaments, and tendons. It shapes the body and protects organs. The skeletal system works with the muscular system to help the body move.

11. *Urinary System*

The urinary system eliminates waste from the body in the form of urine. The kidneys remove waste from the blood. The waste combines with water to form urine.

SYMPTOMS OF NEUROLOGIC AND ORGANIC PROCESSES

Neurologic and organic symptoms are those that are caused by disorders that affect part or all of the nervous system or are biologically based. These symptoms can vary greatly. For example, the nervous system controls many different body functions. Symptoms can, but do not have to, be associated with pain, including headache and back pain. Neurologic symptoms can also include muscle weakness or lack of coordination, abnormal sensations in the skin, and disturbances of vision, taste, smell, and hearing.

They may be minor (such as a foot that has fallen asleep) or life threatening (such as coma due to stroke).

Some Common Neurologic Symptoms

Pain

- Back pain
- Neck pain
- Headache
- Pain along a nerve pathway (as sciatica)

Muscle malfunction

- Weakness
- Tremor (rhythmic shaking of a body part)
- Paralysis
- Involuntary (unintended) movements (such as tics)
- Clumsiness or poor coordination
- Muscle spasms

Changes in sensation

- Numbness of the skin
- Tingling or a "pins-and-needles" sensation
- Hypersensitivity to light touch
- Loss of sensation for touch, cold, heat, or pain

Changes in the senses

- Disturbances of smell and taste
- Partial or complete loss of vision
- Double vision
- Deafness
- Ringing or other sounds originating in the ears (tinnitus)

Other symptoms

- Vertigo
- Loss of balance
- Slurred speech (dysarthria)

Changes in consciousness

- Fainting
- Confusion or delirium
- Seizures (ranging from brief lapses in consciousness to severe muscle contractions and jerking throughout the body)

Changes in cognition (mental ability)

- Difficulty understanding language or using language to speak or write (aphasia)
- Poor memory
- Inability to recognize familiar objects (agnosia) or familiar faces (prosopagnosia)
- Inability to do simple arithmetic (acalculia)

Organic brain syndrome is a term used to describe physical disorders that impair mental function. The most common symptoms are confusion; impairment of memory, judgment, and intellectual function; and agitation. Disorders that cause injury or damage to the brain and contribute to organic

	Delirium	Dementia	Depression
Alertness	Altered level of consciousness; alertness may fluctuate	May vary	May vary
Motor behavior	Fluctuates; lethargy or hyperactivity	May vary	Psychomotor behavior may be agitated or unaffected
Attention	Impaired and fluctuates	Usually normal	Usually normal, but may be distractible
Awareness	Impaired, reduced	Clear	Clear
Course	Acute; responds to treatment	Chronic, with deterioration over time	Chronic; responds to treatment
Progression	Abrupt	Slow but stable	Varies
Orientation	Fluctuates in severity; usually impaired	May be impaired	May be selective disorientation
Memory	Recent and immediate impaired	Recent and remote impaired	Selective or patchy impairment
Thinking	Disorganized, distorted, incoherent; slow or accelerated	Difficulty with abstraction; thoughts impoverished; difficulty finding words; poor judgment	Intact, but may voice hopelessness and self-depreciation
Instrumental activities of daily living (IADLs)	May be intact or impaired	May be intact early; impaired ADLs as disease progresses	May be intact or impaired
Stability	Variable, hour-to-hour	Fairly stable	Some variability
Emotions	Irritable, aggressive, fearful	Labile, apathetic, irritable	Flat, unresponsive, or sad; may be irritable
Activities of daily living (ADLs)	May be intact or impaired	May be intact early, impaired as disease progresses	May neglect basic self-care

brain syndrome include, but are not limited to, alcoholism, Alzheimer's disease, Fetal Alcohol Spectrum Disorders (FASDs), Parkinson's disease, and stroke.

Elderly clients are at high risk for depression, as well as cognitive disorders, the latter of which can be chronic (as in Dementia) or acute (as in Delirium). Some patients have both affective (mood) and cognitive disorders. Clarifying the diagnosis is the first step to effective treatment, but this can be particularly difficult because elderly clients often have medical comorbidities that can contribute to cognitive and affective changes.

INDICATORS OF SEXUAL DYSFUNCTION

Sexual dysfunction is a problem associated with sexual desire or response. Many issues can be included under the term *sexual dysfunction*. For example, for men, sexual dysfunction may include erectile dysfunction and premature or delayed ejaculation. For women, sexual dysfunction may refer to pain during sexual intercourse.

Problems may be caused by psychological factors, physical conditions, or a combination of both. It is essential that a medical examination be the first step in treating sexual dysfunction in order to identify medications or medical conditions that are the causes of the problems. Many of the symptoms can be addressed medically. However, sexual dysfunction can also be due to childhood sexual abuse, depression, anxiety, stressful life events, and/or other psychological issues. Treatment may also be needed to assist with coping with the signs and symptoms; these include, but are not limited to:

- Premature or delayed ejaculation in men
- Erectile disorder or dysfunction (not being able to get or keep an erection)
- Pain during sex
- Lack or loss of sexual desire
- Difficulty having an orgasm
- Vaginal dryness

INDICATORS OF PSYCHOSOCIAL STRESS

Psychosocial stress results when there is a perceived threat (real or imagined). Examples of psychosocial stress include threats to social status, social esteem, respect, and/or acceptance within a group; threats to self-worth; or threats that are perceived as uncontrollable.

Psychosocial stress can be caused by upsetting events, such as natural disasters, sudden health problems or death, and/or breakups or divorce.

Although current upsetting events certainly create stress, events from the past can also still affect clients. Social workers should assess the impacts of events such as childhood abuse, bullying, discrimination, violence, and/or trauma.

Often, psychosocial stress is not caused by single events, but by ongoing problems such as caring for a parent or child with disabilities.

Stress may manifest itself in many different ways, such as high blood pressure, sweating, rapid heart rate, dizziness, and/or feelings of irritability or sadness.

When psychosocial stress triggers a stress response, the body releases a group of stress hormones that lead to a burst of energy, as well as other changes in the body. The changes brought about by stress hormones can be helpful in the short-term, but can be damaging in the long run.

It is essential that clients learn to manage psychosocial stress so that the stress response is only triggered when necessary and not for prolonged states of chronic stress.

INDICATORS OF TRAUMATIC STRESS AND VIOLENCE

Stress is a typical response to feeling overwhelmed or threatened. Fight, flight, and freeze are survival responses to protect individuals from danger. Individuals react and respond to stress in different ways. There are many disadvantages to a stressful lifestyle that creates constant feelings of being overwhelmed, as well as physiological stimulation. Interventions aimed at social and lifestyle changes can usually restore physiological and psychological balance in order to address stress.

This is not the case when traumatization occurs. Traumatization is when a client experiences neurological distress that does not go away or when he or she is not able to return to a state of equilibrium. Traumatization can lead to mental, social, emotional, and physical disability. Like stress, trauma is also experienced differently by different individuals.

There are many indicators of traumatic stress and violence, including:

1. Addictive behaviors related to drugs, alcohol, sex, shopping, and gambling

2. An inability to tolerate conflicts with others or intense feelings

3. A belief of being bad, worthless, without value or importance

4. Dichotomous "all or nothing" thinking

5. Chronic and repeated suicidal thoughts/feelings

6. Poor attachment

7. Dissociation

8. Eating disorders—anorexia, bulimia, and obesity

9. Self-blame

10. Intense anxiety and repeated panic attacks

11. Depression

12. Self-harm, self-mutilation, self-injury, or self-destruction

13. Unexplained, but intense, fears of people, places, or things

When trauma or violence occurs during childhood, children may have problems regulating their behaviors and emotions. They may be clingy and fearful of new situations, easily frightened, difficult to console, aggressive, impulsive, sleepless, delayed in developmental milestones, and/or regressing in functioning and behavior.

In order to practice competently in this area, social workers must:

1. Realize the widespread impact of trauma and understand potential paths for recovery

2. Recognize the signs and symptoms of trauma in clients, families, staff, and other systems

3. Respond by fully integrating knowledge about trauma into social work policies, procedures, and practices

4. Seek to actively resist retraumatization

INDICATORS OF SUBSTANCE ABUSE AND OTHER ADDICTIONS

Some people are able to engage in behaviors or use substances without abusing them and/or becoming addicted.

There are signs when clients are addicted to behaviors and/or substances are being abused. These include, but are not limited to, indications that the behavior or substance use is:

■ Causing problems at work, home, school, and in relationships

■ Resulting in neglected responsibilities at school, work, or home (i.e., flunking classes, skipping work, neglecting children)

■ Dangerous (i.e., driving while on drugs, using dirty needles, having unprotected sex, binging/purging despite medical conditions)

■ Causing financial and/or legal trouble (i.e., arrests, stealing to support shopping, gambling, or drug habit)

■ Causing problems in relationships, such as fights with partner or family members or loss of old friends

■ Creating tolerance (more of the behavior or substance is needed to produce the same impact)

■ Out of control or causing a feeling of being powerless

- Life-consuming, resulting in abandoned activities that used to be enjoyed
- Resulting in psychological issues such as mood swings, attitude changes, depression, and/or paranoia

Signs of Drug Use

- *Marijuana*: glassy, red eyes; loud talking, inappropriate laughter followed by sleepiness; loss of interest, motivation; weight gain or loss
- *Cocaine*: dilated pupils; hyperactivity; euphoria; irritability; anxiety; excessive talking followed by depression or excessive sleeping at odd times; may go long periods of time without eating or sleeping; weight loss; dry mouth and nose
- *Heroin*: contracted pupils; no response of pupils to light; needle marks; sleeping at unusual times; sweating; vomiting; coughing, sniffling; twitching; loss of appetite

5

Use of Assessment Methods and Techniques

USE OF COLLATERAL SOURCES TO OBTAIN RELEVANT INFORMATION

Social workers often use collateral sources—family, friends, other agencies, physicians, and so on—as informants when collecting information to effectively treat clients. These sources can provide vital information because other professionals or agencies may have treated clients in the past. Family members and friends may also provide important information about the length or severity of issues or problems.

It is essential that a social worker get a client's informed consent prior to reaching out to collateral sources. However, they can be a valuable source of data to supplement that obtained directly from a client, as well as provide contextual or background information that a client may not know.

METHODS TO EVALUATE COLLATERAL INFORMATION

Collateral information is often used when the credibility and validity of information obtained from a client or others is questionable. For example, child custody cases are inherently characterized by biased data within an adversarial process. Thus, it is often necessary to evaluate the integrity of information gathered through use of collateral information.

However, social workers should always assess the credibility of collateral informants, because data from more neutral parties has higher integrity. In addition, informants who have greater access to key information may produce more valid data.

When an account by a collateral informant agrees with information gathered from a client, it enhances the trustworthiness of the data collected.

Using multiple information sources (or triangulation) is an excellent method for social workers to have accurate accounts upon which to make assessments or base interventions.

PROCESS USED IN PROBLEM IDENTIFICATION

In both micro and macro practice, social workers must work with clients to identify the problem(s) to be addressed. Problem identification concerns determining the problem targeted for intervention. Although this seems straightforward, it is often difficult to isolate the issue that, when addressed, will result in a change in the symptomology of a client and/or client system.

Part of problem identification is determining the issue in exact definable terms, when it occurs, and its magnitude. When doing macro practice, a social worker may often need to get consensus from the group regarding whether there is agreement as to the nature of the problem and its occurrence and magnitude.

It is often useful in problem identification to determine that which is *not* the problem. Such a technique will ensure that these elements are not grouped in with those that are targeted and will assist in narrowing down the focus.

The problem should always be considered within the person-in-environment perspective and using a strengths-based approach. It should not blame a client and/or client system for its existence.

METHODS OF INVOLVING CLIENT'S COMMUNICATION SKILLS

Social workers must involve clients in every aspect of treatment. In order to do so, social workers must assess clients' communication skills and determine effective methods to gather needed information, as well as to ensure that clients understand data that is presented to them. Thus, the expressive and receptive communication of clients must be considered.

Communication can be verbal and nonverbal, so an assessment of clients' communication skills must involve both. Role-playing is a good way to assess and enhance clients' communication skills. It also allows a social worker to see if there is congruence between nonverbal and verbal communication.

As many clients may have experienced trauma, it is essential that social workers understand how such experiences may impact on clients' communication styles and patterns. Much of communication is also cultural and should be viewed within the context of clients' backgrounds and experiences.

Silence is a form of communication and should be considered by a social worker when used by a client.

Social workers should understand how to communicate with client, who are upset and angry, as well as how some wording choices and tones can be upsetting to clients based on their ethnic backgrounds and/or past experiences, such as victimization.

USE OF OBSERVATION

Although most information that a social worker uses during assessment comes from the social work interview, direct observation of interactions between family members and the client's nonverbal behavior can produce a lot of information about emotional states and interaction patterns.

Social workers also may use observation as part of macro-level intervention in order to assess the extent of a problem/issue, driving and restraining forces for change, key policy influencers, and community members who can work as part of a task group for reform.

When functioning as an observer, a social worker can take many roles, including complete participant (living the experience as a participant), participant as observer (interacting with those who are participating), observer as participant (limited relationship with others participating—primarily observer), or complete observer (removed from activity—observer only). Observation is also a method used in scientific inquiry to collect data.

METHODS OF INVOLVING CLIENTS IN IDENTIFYING PROBLEMS

Social workers focus on assisting clients to identify problems and areas of strength, as well as increasing problem-solving strategies.

It is essential that, throughout the problem-solving process, social workers view clients as experts in their lives.

Clients should be asked about what they would like to see changed in their lives and clients' definitions of problems should be accepted.

Clients should be asked about what will be different in their lives when their problems are solved. Social workers should listen carefully for, and work hard to respect, the directions in which clients want to go with their lives (their goals) and the words they use to express these directions.

Clients should be asked about the paths that they would like to take to make desired changes. Clients' perceptions should be respected and clients' inner resources (strengths) should be maximized as part of treatment.

INDICATORS OF CLIENT'S STRENGTHS AND CHALLENGES

Strength is the capacity to cope with difficulties, to maintain functioning under stress, to return to equilibrium in the face of significant trauma, to use external challenges to promote growth, and to be resilient by using social supports.

There is not a single approach to the assessment of strengths. However, social workers can view all of these areas as strengths or protective factors that can assist clients when they experience challenges. These characteristics can also be abilities that need to be bolstered as a focus of treatment.

1. *Cognitive and appraisal skills*
   - Intellectual/cognitive ability
   - Creativity, curiosity
   - Initiative, perseverance, patience
   - Common sense
   - Ability to anticipate problems
   - Realistic appraisal of demands and capacities
   - Ability to use feedback

2. *Defenses and coping mechanisms*
   - Ability to regulate impulses and affect
   - Self-soothing
   - Flexible; can handle stressors

3. *Temperamental and dispositional factors*
   - Belief in trustworthiness of others
   - Belief in justice
   - Self-esteem, self-worth
   - Sense of mastery, confidence, optimism
   - Ability to tolerate ambiguity and uncertainty
   - Ability to make sense of negative events
   - Sense of humor
   - Lack of hostility, anger, anxiety
   - Optimistic, open
   - Ability to grieve
   - Lack of helplessness
   - Responsibility for decisions
   - Sense of direction, mission, purpose

4. *Interpersonal skills and supports*
   - Ability to develop/maintain good relationships
   - Ability to confide in others
   - Problem-solving skills
   - Capacity for empathy
   - Presence of an intimate relationship
   - Sense of security

5. *Other factors*
   - Supportive social institutions, such as church
   - Good physical health
   - Adequate income
   - Supportive family and friends

USE OF ASSESSMENT/DIAGNOSTIC INSTRUMENTS IN PRACTICE

There are many psychological tests in existence for assessment and diagnostic purposes. The following are a few of the most well-known.

Beck Depression Inventory

The Beck Depression Inventory (BDI) is a 21-item test, presented in multiple choice formats, that assesses the presence and degree of depression in adolescents and adults.

The Minnesota Multiphasic Personality Inventory

The Minnesota Multiphasic Personality Inventory (MMPI) is an objective verbal inventory designed as a personality test for the assessment of psychopathology consisting of 550 statements, 16 of which are repeated.

Myers–Briggs Type Indicator

The Myers–Briggs Type Indicator (MBTI) is a forced-choice, self-report inventory that attempts to classify individuals along four theoretically independent dimensions. The first dimension is a general attitude toward the world, either extraverted (E) or introverted (I). The second dimension, perception, is divided between sensation (S) and intuition (N). The third dimension is that of processing. Once information is received, it is processed in either a thinking (T) or feeling (F) style. The final dimension is judging (J) versus perceiving (P).

Rorschach Inkblot Test

Client responses to inkblots are used to assess perceptual reactions and other psychological functioning. It is one of the most widely used projective tests.

Stanford–Binet Intelligence Scale

The Stanford–Binet Intelligence Scale is designed for the testing of cognitive abilities. It provides verbal, performance, and full scale scores for children and adults.

Thematic Apperception Test

The Thematic Apperception Test (TAT) is another widely used projective test. It consists of a series of pictures of ambiguous scenes. Clients are asked to make up stories or fantasies concerning what is happening, has happened, and is going to happen in the scenes, along with a description of their thoughts and feelings. The TAT provides information on a client's perceptions and imagination for use in the understanding of a client's current needs, motives, emotions, and conflicts, both conscious and unconscious. Its use in clinical assessment is generally part of a larger battery of tests and interview data.

Wechsler Intelligence Scale

The Wechsler Intelligence Scale (WISC) is designed as a measure of a child's intellectual and cognitive ability. It has four index scales and a full scale score.

METHODS TO ORGANIZE INFORMATION

There is no one way to organize information or client files. Some client information and files are obtained and stored in paper format. However, increasingly client records are kept electronically with software to assist professionals in organizing and accessing data.

Whether paper or electronic, client files are usually stored with the following in separate sections or folders:

1. Demographic information and intake materials
2. Assessments, quarterly reviews, and reassessments
3. Service plan(s) with goals
4. Discharge plan
5. Releases of information and referrals
6. Correspondence

Social workers should keep psychotherapy notes in a secure location outside of client files to provide added confidentiality protection.

Often agency policies or requirements imposed by funders dictate the organizational structure for client files. However, regardless of the schema, it is essential that files are secure, up-to-date, and complete, with a format that makes locating information easy and evident.

In health care, client records are often organized in a SOAP format.

S (Subjective): The subjective component is a client's report of how he or she has been doing since the last visit and/or what brought a client into treatment.

O (Objective): In health care, the objective component includes vital signs (temperature, blood pressure, pulse, and respiration), documentation of any physical examinations, and results of laboratory tests. In other settings, this section may include other objective indicators of problems such as disorientation, failing school, legal issues, and so on.

A (Assessment): A social worker pulls together the subjective and objective findings and consolidates them into a short assessment.

P (Plan): The plan includes what will be done as a consequence of the assessment.

CURRENT *DSM*® DIAGNOSTIC FRAMEWORK AND CRITERIA

The *Diagnostic and Statistical Manual of Mental Disorders*, 5th Edition (*DSM-5*), was published in 2013 and is the current diagnostic framework used by social workers. It has many revisions in content and format from the *DSM-IV-TR*, which was used previously.

The *DSM-5* deleted a separate section for "Disorders Usually First Diagnosed in Infancy, Childhood, or Adolescence" and now lists them in other chapters.

The *DSM-5* replaces the NOS categories with two options: Other Specified Disorder and Unspecified Disorder. The first allows a social worker to specify the reason that the criteria for a specific disorder is not met whereas the second allows a social worker the option to forgo specification.

The *DSM-5* has discarded the multiaxial system of diagnosis (formerly Axis I, Axis II, and Axis III) and combines the first three axes outlined in past editions of the *DSM* into one axis with all mental and other medical diagnoses.

It has replaced Axis IV with significant psychosocial and contextual features and dropped Axis V (Global Assessment of Functioning, known as GAF).

The World Health Organization's (WHO) Disability Assessment Schedule (WHODAS) is added to Section III, Emerging Measures and Models, under Assessment Measures.

1. Neurodevelopmental Disorders

This is a new chapter.

Intellectual Disabilities
Intellectual Disability (Intellectual Developmental Disorder)

"Mental retardation" is now Intellectual Disability (Intellectual Developmental Disorder)

Intelligence quotient (IQ) scores and adaptive functioning are both used in determining a client's ability.

Global Developmental Delay

Unspecified Intellectual Disability (Intellectual Developmental Disorder)

Communication Disorders
Language Disorder

Speech Sound Disorder (previously Phonological Disorder)

Childhood-Onset Fluency Disorder (Stuttering)

Social (Pragmatic) Communication Disorder
This is a new condition that has impaired social verbal and nonverbal communication.

Unspecified Communication Disorder

Autism Spectrum Disorder
Autism Spectrum Disorder
Autism Spectrum Disorder incorporates Asperger Disorder, Childhood Disintegrative Disorder, and Pervasive Developmental Disorder Not Otherwise Specified (PDD-NOS).

Attention-Deficit/Hyperactivity Disorder
Attention-Deficit/Hyperactivity Disorder
Must appear by age 12.

Other Specified Attention-Deficit/Hyperactivity Disorder

Unspecified Attention-Deficit/Hyperactivity Disorder

Specific Learning Disorder
Specific Learning Disorder
Motor Disorders (new subcategory)

Developmental Coordination Disorder

Stereotypic Movement Disorder

Tic Disorders

    Tourette's Disorder

    Persistent (Chronic) Motor or Vocal Tic Disorder

    Provisional Tic Disorder

    Other Specified Tic Disorder

    Unspecified Tic Disorder

Other Neurodevelopmental Disorders
Other Specified Neurodevelopmental Disorder

Unspecified Neurodevelopmental Disorder

2. *Schizophrenia Spectrum and Other Psychotic Disorders*

Schizophrenia (all subtypes of Schizophrenia were deleted—
paranoid, disorganized, catatonic, undifferentiated, and residual)

Schizotypal (Personality) Disorder
Delusional Disorder (has new criteria and is no longer separate from
Shared Delusional Disorder)

Brief Psychotic Disorder

Schizophreniform Disorder

Schizoaffective Disorder
Requires a major mood episode.

Substance/Medication-Induced Psychotic Disorder

Psychotic Disorder Due to Another Medical Condition

Catatonia 3/12
Requires 3 of a total of 12 symptoms. Catatonia may be a specifier
for Depressive, Bipolar, and Psychotic disorders; part of another
medical condition; or of another specified diagnosis.

Catatonia Associated With Another Mental Disorder (Catatonia
Specifier)

Catatonic Disorder Due to Another Medical Condition

Unspecified Catatonia

Other Specified Schizophrenia Spectrum and Other Psychotic Disorders

Unspecified Schizophrenia Spectrum and Other Psychotic Disorder

3. *Bipolar and Related Disorders*

New specifier "with mixed features" can be applied to Bipolar I
Disorder, Bipolar II Disorder, Bipolar Disorder NED (Not Elsewhere
Defined, previously called "NOS"/Not Otherwise Specified).
Anxiety symptoms are a specifier (called "anxious distress") added
to Bipolar Disorder and to Depressive Disorders (but are not part of
the bipolar diagnostic criteria).

Bipolar I Disorder

Bipolar II Disorder

Cyclothymic Disorder

Substance/Medication-Induced Bipolar and Related Disorder

Bipolar and Related Disorder Due to Another Medical Condition

Other Specified Bipolar and Related Disorder (allowed for particular conditions)

Unspecified Bipolar and Related Disorder

4. *Depressive Disorders*

Anxiety symptoms are a specifier (called "anxious distress"). The bereavement exclusion was removed.

Disruptive Mood Dysregulation Disorder (DMDD; this is a new disorder for children up to age 18 years)

Major Depressive Disorder, Single and Recurrent Episodes (new specifier "with mixed features" can be applied)

Persistent Depressive Disorder (previously Dysthymia)

Premenstrual Dysphoric Disorder (new disorder)

Substance/Medication-Induced Depressive Disorder

Depressive Disorder Due to Another Medical Condition

Other Specified Depressive Disorder

Unspecified Depressive Disorder

5. *Anxiety Disorders*

Requirement that clients "must recognize that their fear and anxiety are excessive or unreasonable" is removed. The duration of at least 6 months now applies to everyone (not only to children).

Separation Anxiety Disorder (previously a Disorder of Early Onset)

Selective Mutism (previously a Disorder of Early Onset)

Specific Phobia

Social Anxiety Disorder (Social Phobia)

Panic Disorder (it is separated from Agoraphobia)

Panic Attack (Specifier; applies to all *DSM-5* diagnoses)

Agoraphobia

Generalized Anxiety Disorder

Substance/Medication-Induced Anxiety Disorder

Anxiety Disorder Due to Another Medical Condition

Other Specified Anxiety Disorder

Unspecified Anxiety Disorder

6. *Obsessive-Compulsive and Related Disorders*

Obsessive-Compulsive Disorder

Body Dysmorphic Disorder (new criteria were added that describes repetitive behaviors or mental acts that may arise with perceived defects or flaws in physical appearance)

  A specifier was expanded to allow for good or fair insight, poor insight, and "absent insight/delusional" (i.e., complete conviction that obsessive-compulsive disorder beliefs are true).

Hoarding Disorder (new disorder defined as a persistent difficulty discarding or parting with possessions due to a perceived need to save the items and distress associated with discarding them)

  A specifier was expanded to allow for good or fair insight, poor insight, and "absent insight/delusional" (i.e., complete conviction that obsessive-compulsive disorder beliefs are true).

Trichotillomania (Hair-Pulling Disorder; was moved from "Impulse-Control Disorders Not Elsewhere Classified.")

Excoriation (Skin-Picking) Disorder (new disorder)

Substance/Medication-Induced Obsessive-Compulsive and Related Disorder (new disorder)

Obsessive-Compulsive and Related Disorder Due to Another Medical Condition (new disorder)

Other Specified Obsessive-Compulsive and Related Disorder (new disorder)

  Includes body-focused repetitive behavior disorder (behaviors like nail biting, lip biting, and cheek chewing, other than hair pulling and skin picking) or obsessional jealousy.

Unspecified Obsessive-Compulsive and Related Disorder (new disorder)

7. *Trauma- and Stressor-Related Disorders*

Separate criteria were added for children 6 years old or younger.

Reactive Attachment Disorder (previously a subtype, but now a separate disorder)

Disinhibited Social Engagement Disorder (previously a subtype, but now a separate disorder)

Posttraumatic Stress Disorder (criteria were modified and now has four clusters)

Acute Stress Disorder (criteria were modified)

Adjustment Disorders (moved, and now recognized as a stress-response syndrome)

Other Specified Trauma- and Stressor-Related Disorder

Unspecified Trauma- and Stressor-Related Disorder

8. *Dissociative Disorders*

Dissociative Identity Disorder (the criteria were expanded to include "possession-form phenomena and functional neurological symptoms")

   It is made clear that "transitions in identity may be observable by others or self-reported"; criterion was also modified for clients who experience gaps in recall of everyday events—not only trauma.

Dissociative Amnesia (Dissociative Fugue became a specifier)

Depersonalization/Derealization Disorder (previously Depersonalization Disorder)

Other Specified Dissociative Disorder

Unspecified Dissociative Disorder

9. *Somatic Symptom and Related Disorders*

   Somatoform Disorders are now called Somatic Symptom and Related Disorders. Somatization Disorder, Hypochondriasis, Pain Disorder, and Undifferentiated Somatoform Disorder were deleted. They are defined by positive symptoms, and the use of medically unexplained symptoms is minimized, except in the cases of Conversion Disorder and Pseudocyesis (false pregnancy). People with chronic pain can now be diagnosed with Somatic Symptom Disorder With Predominant Pain; or Psychological Factors That Affect Other Medical Conditions; or an Adjustment Disorder.

   Somatic Symptom Disorder (Somatization Disorder and Undifferentiated Somatoform Disorder were combined to become Somatic Symptom Disorder, a diagnosis that no longer requires a specific number of somatic symptoms)

   Illness Anxiety Disorder

   Conversion Disorder (Functional Neurological Symptom Disorder; criteria were changed)

Psychological Factors Affecting Other Medical Conditions (new disorder)

Factitious Disorder

Other Specified Somatic Symptom and Related Disorder

Unspecified Somatic Symptom and Related Disorder

10. *Feeding and Eating Disorders*

Pica (criteria now refer to clients of any age)

Rumination Disorder (criteria now refer to clients of any age)

Avoidant/Restrictive Food Intake Disorder (previously "Feeding Disorder of Infancy or Early Childhood" and the criteria were expanded)

Anorexia Nervosa (criteria changed and there is no longer a requirement of amenorrhea)

Bulimia Nervosa (requirements were changed from "at least twice weekly for 6 months" to "at least once weekly over the last 3 months")

Binge-Eating Disorder (new disorder)

Other Specified Feeding or Eating Disorder

Unspecified Feeding or Eating Disorder

11. *Elimination Disorders*

Enuresis
Social worker needs to rule out medical reasons for bed-wetting—infection, physiological abnormalities.

Encopresis
Involves repeated passage of feces in inappropriate places, causing embarrassment, and client may avoid situations that lead to embarrassment—camp or sleepovers.

Other Specified Elimination Disorder

Unspecified Elimination Disorder

12. *Sleep–Wake Disorders*

"Sleep Disorders Related to Another Mental Disorder" and "Sleep Disorders Related to a General Medical Condition" were deleted.

Insomnia Disorder (previously Primary Insomnia)

Hypersomnolence Disorder

Narcolepsy

Breathing-Related Sleep Disorders
Obstructive Sleep Apnea Hypopnea (new disorder)

Central Sleep Apnea (new disorder)

Sleep-Related Hypoventilation (new disorder)

Circadian Rhythm Sleep–Wake Disorders
Includes advanced sleep phase syndrome, irregular sleep–wake type, and non-24-hour sleep–wake type. Jet lag was removed.

Parasomnias
Non-Rapid Eye Movement Sleep Arousal Disorders

Sleepwalking

Sleep Terrors

Nightmare Disorder

Rapid Eye Movement Sleep Behavior Disorder (a separate disorder instead of being listed under "Dyssomnia Not Otherwise Specified")

Restless Legs Syndrome (a separate disorder instead of being listed under "Dyssomnia Not Otherwise Specified")

Substance/Medication-Induced Sleep Disorder

Other Specified Insomnia Disorder

Unspecified Insomnia Disorder

Other Specified Hypersomnolence Disorder

Unspecified Hypersomnolence Disorder

Other Specified Sleep–Wake Disorder

Unspecified Sleep–Wake Disorder

13. *Sexual Dysfunctions*

DSM-5 has sex-specific sexual dysfunctions. Sexual Aversion Disorder was deleted. Sexual Dysfunctions (except Substance-/Medication-Induced Sexual Dysfunction) now require a duration of approximately 6 months and more exact severity criteria. Subtypes for all disorders include only "lifelong versus acquired" and "generalized versus situational."

Two subtypes were deleted: "Sexual Dysfunction Due to a General Medical Condition" and "Due to Psychological Versus Combined Factors."

Delayed Ejaculation

Erectile Disorder

Female Orgasmic Disorder

Female Sexual Interest/Arousal Disorder (for females, Sexual Desire and Arousal Disorders are combined into this single disorder)

Genito-Pelvic Pain/Penetration Disorder (a new diagnosis, combines Vaginismus and Dyspareunia)

Male Hypoactive Sexual Desire Disorder

Premature (Early) Ejaculation

Substance/Medication-Induced Sexual Dysfunction

Other Specified Sexual Dysfunction

Unspecified Sexual Dysfunction

14. *Gender Dysphoria* (It is now its own category.)

> Separate criteria for children, adolescents, and adults that are appropriate for varying developmental states are added. Subtypes of Gender Identity Disorder based on sexual orientation were deleted. Among other wording changes, Criterion A and Criterion B (cross-gender identification and aversion toward one's gender) were combined. The creation of a separate Gender Dysphoria in children, as well as one for adults and adolescents.

Gender Dysphoria

Other Specified Gender Dysphoria

Unspecified Gender Dysphoria

15. *Disruptive, Impulse-Control, and Conduct Disorders*

Oppositional Defiant Disorder (there are three types: angry/irritable mood, argumentative/defiant behavior, and vindictiveness; the Conduct Disorder exclusion is deleted; the criteria were also changed, with a note on frequency requirements and a measure of severity)

Intermittent Explosive Disorder (a specifier was added for people with limited "prosocial emotion," showing callous and unemotional traits)

Conduct Disorder

Antisocial Personality Disorder .

Pyromania

Kleptomania

Other Specified Disruptive, Impulse-Control, and Conduct Disorder
  Oppositional Defiant Disorder, Conduct Disorder, and Disruptive Behavior Disorder Not Otherwise Specified became Other Specified and Unspecified Disruptive Disorder, Impulse-Control, and Conduct Disorders.

Unspecified Disruptive, Impulse-Control, and Conduct Disorder

16. *Substance-Related and Addictive Disorders*

Substance Abuse and Substance Dependence have been combined into the single Substance Use Disorders specific to each substance of abuse.

"Recurrent legal problems" was deleted and "craving or a strong desire or urge to use a substance" was added to the criteria.

The threshold of the number of criteria that must be met was changed. Severity from mild to severe is based on the number of criteria endorsed.

New specifiers were added for early and sustained remission along with new specifiers for "in a controlled environment" and "on maintenance therapy."

Substance-Related Disorders

Substance Use Disorders

Substance-Induced Disorders

Substance Intoxication and Withdrawal

Substance/Medication-Induced Mental Disorders

Alcohol-Related Disorders
Alcohol Use Disorder

Alcohol Intoxication

Alcohol Withdrawal

Other Alcohol-Induced Disorders

Unspecified Alcohol-Related Disorder

Caffeine-Related Disorders
Caffeine Intoxication

Caffeine Withdrawal (criteria added)

Other Caffeine-Induced Disorders

Unspecified Caffeine-Related Disorder

Cannabis-Related Disorders
Cannabis Use Disorder

Cannabis Intoxication

Cannabis Withdrawal (criteria added)

Other Cannabis-Induced Disorders

Unspecified Cannabis-Related Disorder

Hallucinogen-Related Disorders
Phencyclidine Use Disorder

Other Hallucinogen Use Disorder

Phencyclidine Intoxication

Other Hallucinogen Intoxication

Hallucinogen Persisting Perception Disorder

Other Phencyclidine-Induced Disorders

Other Hallucinogen-Induced Disorders

Unspecified Phencyclidine-Related Disorder

Unspecified Hallucinogen-Related Disorder

Inhalant-Related Disorders
Inhalant Use Disorder

Inhalant Intoxication

Other Inhalant-Induced Disorders

Unspecified Inhalant-Related Disorder

Opioid-Related Disorders
Opioid Use Disorder

Opioid Intoxication

Opioid Withdrawal

Other Opioid-Induced Disorders

Unspecified Opioid-Related Disorder

Sedative-, Hypnotic-, or Anxiolytic-Related Disorders
Sedative, Hypnotic, or Anxiolytic Use Disorder

Sedative, Hypnotic, or Anxiolytic Intoxication

Sedative, Hypnotic, or Anxiolytic Withdrawal

Other Sedative-, Hypnotic-, or Anxiolytic-Induced Disorders

Unspecified Sedative-, Hypnotic-, or Anxiolytic-Related Disorder

Stimulant-Related Disorders
Stimulant Use Disorder

Stimulant Intoxication

Stimulant Withdrawal

Other Stimulant-Induced Disorders

Unspecified Stimulant-Related Disorder

Tobacco-Related Disorders (new category of disorders)
Tobacco Use Disorder

Tobacco Withdrawal

Other Tobacco-Induced Disorders

Unspecified Tobacco-Related Disorder

Other (or *Unknown*) *Substance-Related Disorders*

Other (or Unknown) Substance Use Disorder

Other (or Unknown) Substance Intoxication

Other (or Unknown) Substance Withdrawal

Other (or Unknown) Substance-Induced Disorders

Unspecified Other (or Unknown) Substance-Related Disorder

Non-Substance-Related Disorders

Gambling Disorder (new disorder)

17. *Neurocognitive Disorders*

Delirium

Other Specified Delirium

Unspecified Delirium

Major and Mild Neurocognitive Disorders
  Dementia and Amnestic Disorder became Major or Mild Neurocognitive Disorder (Major NCD or Mild NCD). New separate criteria are now presented for Major or Mild NCD due to various conditions.

Major Neurocognitive Disorder

Mild Neurocognitive Disorder

Major or Mild Neurocognitive Disorder Due to Alzheimer's Disease

Major or Mild Frontotemporal Neurocognitive Disorder

Major or Mild Neurocognitive Disorder With Lewy Bodies

Major or Mild Vascular Neurocognitive Disorder

Major or Mild Neurocognitive Disorder Due to Traumatic Brain Injury

Substance/Medication-Induced Major or Mild Neurocognitive Disorder (new disorder)

Major or Mild Neurocognitive Disorder Due to HIV Infection

Major or Mild Neurocognitive Disorder Due to Prion Disease

Major or Mild Neurocognitive Disorder Due to Parkinson's Disease

Major or Mild Neurocognitive Disorder Due to Huntington's Disease

Major or Mild Neurocognitive Disorder Due to Another Medical Condition

Major or Mild Neurocognitive Disorder Due to Multiple Etiologies

Unspecified Neurocognitive Disorder (new disorder)

Personality Disorders

Personality Disorders are associated with ways of thinking and feeling that significantly and adversely affect how a client functions in many aspects of life.

A personality disorder is an enduring pattern of inner experience and behavior that deviates from the expectations of a client's culture. The pattern is manifested in cognition, affect, interpersonal functioning, and/or impulse control.

Personality Disorders previously belonged on a different axis than almost all other disorders, but they are now with all mental and other medical diagnoses.

General Personality Disorder

Cluster A: Odd and Eccentric

Schizoid Personality Disorder

Introverted, withdrawn, solitary, emotionally cold, and distant; absorbed with own thoughts and feelings and fearful of closeness and intimacy with others.

Paranoid Personality Disorder

Interpreting the actions of others as deliberately threatening or demeaning; untrusting, unforgiving, and prone to angry or aggressive outbursts.

Schizotypal Personality Disorder

A pattern of peculiarities—odd or eccentric manners of speaking or dressing; strange, outlandish, or paranoid beliefs; display signs of "magical thinking."

Cluster B: Dramatic, emotional, and erratic

Antisocial Personality Disorder

Impulsive, irresponsible, and callous; history of legal difficulties; belligerent and irresponsible behavior; aggressive and even violent relationships; no respect for others.

Borderline Personality Disorder

Unstable in interpersonal relationships, behavior, mood, and self-image; abrupt and extreme mood changes; stormy interpersonal relationships; fluctuating self-image; self-destructive actions.

Narcissistic Personality Disorder

Exaggerated sense of self-importance; absorbed by fantasies of unlimited success; seek constant attention; oversensitive to failure.

Histrionic Personality Disorder

Behave melodramatically or "over the top," constantly displaying an excessive level of emotionality; attention seeking.

Cluster C: Anxious and fearful

Avoidant Personality Disorder

Hypersensitive to rejection and unwilling to become involved with others unless sure of being liked; avoidance of social events or work that involves interpersonal contact.

Dependent Personality Disorder

Pattern of dependent and submissive behavior; relying on others to make personal decisions; require excessive reassurance and advice.

Obsessive-Compulsive Personality Disorder

Conscientious, with high levels of aspiration; strive for perfection; never satisfied with achievements.

Other Personality Disorders

Personality change due to another medical condition.

Other Specified Personality Disorder

Unspecified Personality Disorder

18. *Paraphilic Disorders*

New specifiers "in a controlled environment" and "in remission" were added to criteria for all Paraphilic Disorders.

Disorder added to names to distinguish between behavior and disorder. Must have both qualitative criteria and negative consequences to have the disorder and be diagnosed.

Voyeuristic Disorder

Exhibitionistic Disorder

Frotteuristic Disorder

Sexual Masochism Disorder

Sexual Sadism Disorder

Pedophilic Disorder

Fetishistic Disorder

Transvestic Disorder

Other Specified Paraphilic Disorder

Unspecified Paraphilic Disorder

19. *Other Mental Disorders*

Other Specified Mental Disorder Due to Another Medical Condition

Unspecified Mental Disorder Due to Another Medical Condition

Other Specified Mental Disorder

Unspecified Mental Disorder

20. *Medication-Induced Movement Disorders and Other Adverse Effects of Medication*

21. *Other Conditions That May Be a Focus of Clinical Attention*

COMPONENTS AND FUNCTION OF THE MENTAL STATUS EXAMINATION

A mental status examination is a structured way of observing and describing a client's current state of mind under the domains of appearance, attitude, behavior, mood and affect, speech, thought process, thought content, perception, cognition, insight, and judgment. A mental status examination is a necessary part of any client assessment no matter what the presenting problem. It should be documented in the record either in list form or in narrative form. The following client functions should be included:

1. *Appearance*—facial expression, grooming, dress, gait, and so on
2. *Orientation*—awareness of time and place, events, and so on
3. *Speech pattern*—slurred, pressured, slow, flat tone, calm, and so on
4. *Affect/mood*—mood as evidenced in both behavior and client's statements (sad, jittery, manic, placid, and so on)
5. *Impulsive/potential for harm*—impulse control with special attention to potential suicidality and/or harm to others
6. *Judgment/insight*—ability to predict the consequences of her or his behavior, to make "sensible" decisions, to recognize her or his contribution to her or his problem
7. *Thought processes/reality testing*—thinking style and ability to know reality, including the difference between stimuli that are coming from inside herself or himself and those that are coming from outside herself or himself (statements about delusions, hallucinations, and conclusions about whether or not a client is psychotic would appear here)
8. *Intellectual functioning/memory*—level of intelligence and of recent and remote memory functions

A paragraph about mental status in the record might read as follows:

"Client is a 43-year-old woman who looks older than her stated age. She is well groomed and appropriately dressed for a professional interview. She is well oriented. Her speech is slow as if it is painful to talk. She has had occasional thoughts of 'ending it all,' but has not made any suicidal plans or preparations. She talks about future events with expectation to be alive. She is aware that she is 'depressed' and recognizes that the source of some of the feeling comes from 'inside moods' although she often refers to the difficulties of her situation. Her thoughts are organized. She is not psychotic."

PROCESS OF SOCIAL WORK ASSESSMENT/DIAGNOSIS

Although the *Diagnostic and Statistical Manual of Mental Disorders (DSM)* provides a framework and criteria for applying uniform labels to psychiatric dysfunction, the process of social work assessment and diagnosis is much broader.

Diagnosis refers to the process of identifying problems, with their underlying causes and practical solutions.

A diagnosis is generally obtained after a social worker utilizes information gained through the assessment. Diagnosing includes drawing inferences and reaching conclusions based on the data available. A social worker should *not* diagnose if adequate information or data is not available.

A social worker must consider biological, psychological, and social factors when identifying the root causes of client problems.

Diagnostic information should always be shared with clients and used to facilitate the establishment of intervention plans.

Assessment and diagnosis must be a continual part of the problem-solving process.

The assessment process must focus on client strengths and resources for addressing problems.

There are some terms and concepts that a social worker should be familiar with when making assessments and/or diagnosing.

1. *Comorbid*: existing with or at the same time; for instance, having two different illnesses at the same time

2. *Contraindicated*: not recommended or safe to use (a medication or treatment that is contraindicated would not be prescribed because it could have serious consequences)

3. *Delusion*: false, fixed belief despite evidence to the contrary (believing something that is not true)

4. *Disorientation*: confusion with regard to person, time, or place

5. *Dissociation*: disturbance or change in the usually integrative functions of memory, identity, perception, or consciousness (often seen in clients with a history of trauma)

6. *Endogenous depression*: depression caused by a biochemical imbalance rather than a psychosocial stressor or external factors

7. *Exogenous depression*: depression caused by external events or psychosocial stressors

8. *Folie à deux*: shared delusion

9. *Hallucinations*: hearing, seeing, smelling, or feeling something that is not real (auditory most common)

10. *Hypomanic*: elevated, expansive, or irritable mood that is less severe than full-blown manic symptoms (not severe enough to interfere with functioning and not accompanied by psychotic symptoms)

11. *Postmorbid*: subsequent to the onset of an illness

12. *Premorbid*: prior to the onset of an illness

13. *Psychotic*: experiencing delusions or hallucinations

METHODS USED IN ASSESSING EGO STRENGTH

Ego strength is the ability of the ego to effectively deal with the demands of the id, the superego, and reality. It is a basis for resilience and helps maintain emotional stability by coping with internal and external stress.

Traits usually considered to be indicators of positive ego strengths include tolerance of pain associated with loss, disappointment, shame, or guilt; forgiveness of others, with feelings of compassion rather than anger; persistence and perseverance in the pursuit of goals; and/or openness, flexibility, and creativity in learning to adapt. Those with positive ego strength are less likely to have psychiatric crises.

Other indicators of positive ego strength include clients:

- Acknowledging their feelings—including grief, insecurity, loneliness, and anxiety
- Not getting overwhelmed by their moods
- Pushing forward after loss and not being paralyzed by self-pity or resentment
- Using painful events to strengthen themselves
- Knowing that painful feelings will eventually fade
- Empathizing with others without trying to reduce or eliminate their pain
- Being self-disciplined and fighting addictive urges
- Taking responsibility for actions
- Holding themselves accountable
- Not blaming others
- Accepting themselves with their limitations
- Setting firm limits even if it means disappointing others or risking rejection
- Avoiding people who drain them physically and/or emotionally

METHODS USED TO ASSESS COMMUNITY STRENGTHS AND CHALLENGES

When conducting community assessments, it is essential for social workers to identify strengths and challenges. Strengths are positive features of the community that can be leveraged to develop solutions to problems. Strengths can include organizations, people, partnerships, facilities, funding, policies, regulations, and culture.

A social worker should consider the current assets that are already in existence to promote the quality of life of community members. For example, organizations that provide after-school programs that help youth graduate on time would be included in a community assessment focused on keeping kids in school. In some instances, a social worker may want to look at experiences of other communities with similar demographics that have successfully addressed similar problems. Examining the presence and utilization of strengths in these communities can assist a social worker in determining if similar assets can be found in its target community.

A social worker must also develop an informed understanding of the gaps or needs that exist within a community. These needs serve as challenges that can affect a large or small number of community members. If community needs affect a large number of community members, there may be more support for addressing them. Collaboration and community building are essential in addressing community challenges.

There are a number of methods for data collection related to community strengths and challenges including interviews, observation, and surveys. Ensuring that the data collection procedures are robust is essential in conducting a complete and accurate community assessment.

METHODS USED IN RISK ASSESSMENT

Social workers are often called upon to assess risks of clients to themselves and others. Such assessments are not easy, because there are no indicators that definitively predict whether a client will act on his or her feelings or desires to hurt himself or herself. A social worker must review all assessment data in order to determine the appropriate level of care and a treatment plan. Such an assessment must include examining risk and protective factors, as well as the presence of behavioral warning signs. Such an assessment may include examining:

- Frequency, intensity, and duration of suicidal or violent thoughts
- Access to or availability of method(s)
- Ability or inability to control suicidal/violent thoughts

- Ability *not* to act on thoughts
- Factors making a client feel better or worse
- Consequences of actions
- Deterrents to acting on thoughts
- Whether client has been using drugs or alcohol to cope
- Measures a client requires to maintain safety

In situations where a client is seen to be a danger to self or others, a social worker may limit a client's right to self-determination and seek involuntary treatment such as commitment to an inpatient setting. If a client is deemed to be a danger to an identifiable third party, a social worker should consider this as a "duty to warn" situation (under the Tarasoff decision), as well as the party in danger.

INDICATORS OF CLIENT DANGER TO SELF OR OTHERS

There are risk factors that must be considered in any assessment, because they are linked to a risk of suicide or violence.

Danger to Self: Suicide

Risk Factors

- History of previous suicide attempt (*best predictor of future attempt*; medical seriousness of attempt is also significant)
- Lives alone; lack of social supports
- Presence of psychiatric disorder—depression (feeling hopeless), anxiety disorder, personality disorder (*A client is also at greater risk after being discharged from the hospital or after being started on antidepressants as he or she may now have the energy to implement a suicide plan.*)
- Substance abuse
- Family history of suicide
- Exposure to suicidal behavior of others through media or peers
- Losses—relationship, job, financial, social
- Presence of firearm or easy access to other lethal methods

Some Protective Factors

- Effective and appropriate clinical care for mental, physical, and substance use disorders
- Easy access to a variety of clinical interventions and support (i.e., medical and mental health care)
- Restricted access to highly lethal methods
- Family and community support

■ Learned coping and stress reduction skills
■ Cultural and religious beliefs that discourage suicide and support self-preservation

Some Behavioral Warning Signs

■ Change in eating and sleeping habits
■ Drug and alcohol use
■ Unusual neglect of personal appearance
■ Marked personality change
■ Loss of interest in pleasurable activities
■ Not tolerating praise or rewards
■ Giving away belongings
■ Isolation from others
■ Taking care of legal and other issues
■ *Dramatic increase in mood (might indicate a client has made a decision to end his or her life)*
■ Verbalizes threats to commit suicide or feelings of despair and hope-
■ lessness
  ● "I'm going to kill myself."
  ● "I wish I were dead."
  ● "My family would be better off without me."
  ● "The only way out for me is to die."
  ● "It's just too much for me to put up with."
  ● "Nobody needs me anymore."

Danger to Others: Violence

Risk Factors

■ Youth who become violent before age 13 generally commit more crimes, and more serious crimes, for a longer time; these youth exhibit a pattern of escalating violence throughout childhood, sometimes continuing into adulthood
■ Most highly aggressive children or children with behavioral disorders do not become serious violent offenders
■ Serious violence is associated with *drugs, guns, and other risky behaviors*
■ *Involvement with delinquent peers and gang membership are two of the most powerful predictors of violence*

Some Protective Factors

■ Effective programs combine components that address both *individual risks and environmental conditions;* building individual skills and competencies; changes in peer groups
■ Interventions that target *change in social context* appear to be more effective, on average, than those that attempt to change individual attitudes, skills, and risk behaviors

- Effective and appropriate clinical care for mental, physical, and substance abuse disorders
- Easy access to a variety of clinical interventions and support (i.e., medical and mental health care)
- Restricted access to highly lethal methods
- Family and community support
- Learned coping and stress reduction skills

Some Behavioral Warning Signs

- Drug and alcohol use
- Marked personality changes
- Angry outbursts
- Preoccupation with killing, war, violence, weapons, and so on
- Isolation from others
- Obtaining guns or other lethal methods

INDICATORS OF MOTIVATION AND RESISTANCE

Motivation and resistance exist along a continuum of readiness. When assessing motivation and resistance of a client, it is important to determine what stage of change a client is in. This will provide a social worker with appropriate clinical strategies to use to address these issues. If social workers push clients at a faster pace than they are ready to take, the therapeutic alliance may break down.

A lack of motivation and resistance are often found in *precontemplation and contemplation* before making the decision to change. There can also be motivational challenges during preparation, action, and maintenance, but they are more easily addressed. When resistance occurs in these latter stages of change, a social worker should reassess the problem and appropriateness of the intervention to ensure that there have not been new developments in a client's life that need to be considered. They may be distracting a client from making progress or serving as barriers to making real change.

In *precontemplation*, a client is unaware, unable, and/or unwilling to change. In this stage, there is the greatest resistance and lack of motivation. It can be characterized by arguing, interrupting, denial, ignoring the problem, and/or avoiding talking or thinking about it. A client may not even show up for appointments and does not agree that change is needed.

A social worker can best deal with lack of motivation and resistance in this stage by establishing a rapport, acknowledging resistance or ambivalence, keeping conversation informal, trying to engage a client, and recognizing a client's thoughts, feelings, fears, and concerns.

In *contemplation*, a client is ambivalent or uncertain regarding behavior change; thus, his or her behaviors are unpredictable. In this stage, a client may be willing to look at the pros and cons of behavior change, but is not committed to working toward it.

A social worker can best deal with lack of motivation and resistance in this stage by emphasizing a client's free choice and responsibility, as well as discussing the pros and cons of changing. It is also useful to discuss how change will assist a client in achieving his or her goals in life. Fear can be reduced by producing examples of change and clarifying what change is and is not.

METHODS TO IDENTIFY SERVICE NEEDS OF CLIENTS

Often, clients have multiple service needs that must be prioritized. Social workers should consider Maslow's hierarchy of needs when working with clients. Clients will need services that address clients' "deficiency needs" (such as those related to physiological, security, social, and esteem needs) prior to accessing support to promote their "growth needs" (such as self-actualization).

In addition, making sure that psychological and social issues are not caused, and cannot be subsequently addressed, by medical and/or substance use issues is paramount. Social workers should always address these problems first.

Interventions and services are intended to aid clients in alleviating problems impeding their well-being. The interventions used by social workers and the services available to clients are those that are identified as potentially helpful on the basis of the ongoing assessment of clients.

The selection and prioritization of service needs may be driven by many factors including client desires and motivation, treatment modality selected, agency setting, available resources, funding and time constraints, and so on. A social worker should focus on ensuring that service needs chosen are outlined in the intervention or treatment plan and are reevaluated on a regular basis. A social worker should also make sure that the needs are based on an unbiased assessment and client wishes. They should *not* be solely driven by funding and time constraints.

Social workers should *not* recommend only services that are familiar or provided by their employing agencies, because this is a "cookie cutter" or "one size fits all" approach.

USE OF INTERVIEWING TECHNIQUES

In social work, an interview is always purposeful and involves verbal and nonverbal communication between a social worker and client, during which ideas, attitudes and feelings are exchanged. The actions of a social worker aim to gather important information and keep a client focused on the achievement of the goal.

A social work interview is designed to serve *the interest of a client*; therefore, the actions of a social worker during the interview must be planned and focused. Questions in a social work interview should be tailored to the specifics of a client, not generic, "one size fits all" inquiries. The focus is on the uniqueness of a client and his or her unique situation.

The purpose of the social work interview can be informational, diagnostic, or therapeutic. The same interview may serve more than one purpose.

Communication during a social work interview is interactive and interrelational. A social worker's questions will result in specific responses by a client that, in turn, lead to other inquiries. The message is formulated by a client, encoded, transmitted, received, processed, and decoded. The importance of words and messages may be implicit (implied) or explicit (evident).

There are a number of techniques that a social worker may use during an interview to assist clients.

- *Universalization*—the generalization or normalization of behavior
- *Clarification*—reformulate problem in a client's words to make sure that you are on the same wavelength
- *Confrontation*—calling attention to something
- *Interpretation*—pulling together patterns of behavior to get a new understanding
- *Reframing and relabeling*—stating problem in a different way so a client can see possible solutions

PROCESS OF ASSESSING THE CLIENT'S NEEDED LEVEL OF CARE

Social workers must assess the client's needed level of care, with the belief that there should be a continuum of intensity depending upon the level of crisis. Clients should enter treatment at a level appropriate to their needs and then step up to more intense treatment or down to less intense treatment as needed. An effective continuum of care features successful transfer of a client between levels of care.

Levels of care for behavioral health services, for example, vary from early intervention services/outpatient services to intensive outpatient/partial hospitalization to residential/inpatient services.

Early intervention or outpatient services are appropriate unless a client is experiencing crisis or at risk for residential/inpatient services, which may then warrant a step up to intensive outpatient or partial hospitalization. The goal is to serve clients in the least restrictive environment, while ensuring health and safety.

Intervention Planning

FACTORS USED IN DETERMINING THE CLIENT'S READINESS/ ABILITY TO PARTICIPATE IN SERVICES

Social workers should not assume that clients are ready or have the skills needed to make changes in their lives. Clients may be oppositional, reactionary, noncompliant, and/or unmotivated. These attitudes or behaviors are often referred to as resistance.

There are indicators that a social worker should use as evidence that a client may be resistant or not ready/able to fully participate in services. These indicators include:

- Limiting the amount of information communicated to a social worker
- Silence/minimal talking during sessions
- Engaging in small talk with a social worker about irrelevant topics
- Engaging in intellectual talk by using technical terms/abstract concepts or asking questions of a social worker that are not related to client issues or problems
- Being preoccupied with past events, instead of current issues
- Discounting, censoring, or editing thoughts when asked about them by a social worker
- False promising
- Flattering a social worker in an attempt to "soften" him or her so as not to be pushed
- Not keeping appointments
- Payment delays or refusals

It is essential to determine the extent to which this resistance or these inabilities are caused by a client, a social worker, and/or the conditions present.

A client may be resistant due to feelings of guilt or shame and may not be ready to recognize or address the feelings and behaviors being brought up by a social worker. Clients may be frightened of change and may be getting some benefit from the problems that they are experiencing.

Social workers may experience a lack of readiness, as they have not developed sufficient rapport with clients. There also may not be clear expectations by clients of their role versus those of social workers. Social workers need to use interventions that are appropriate for clients.

Sometimes a lack of readiness or ability is a result of external factors, such as changes in clients' living situations, physical health problems, lack of social support, and/or financial problems.

Whatever the causes, a social worker must address these barriers as clients will not make changes until they are ready and able.

CRITERIA USED IN SELECTING INTERVENTION MODALITIES

Evidence-based social work practice combines research knowledge, professional/clinical expertise, social work values, and client preferences/circumstances. It is a dynamic and fluid process whereby social workers seek, interpret, use, and evaluate the best available information in an effort to make the best practice decisions.

Decisions are based on the use of many sources, ranging from systematic reviews and meta-analyses to less rigorous research designs.

Social workers often use "evidence-based practice" to refer to programs that have a proven track record. However, it takes a long time for a program or intervention to be "evidence-based." Thus, most interventions in social work need more empirically supported research in order to accurately apply the term. "Evidence-informed practice" may be more appropriate.

Some questions guide the selection of intervention modalities:

- How will the recommended modality assist with the achievement of the treatment goal and will it help get the outcomes desired?

- How does the recommended treatment modality promote client strengths, capabilities, and interests?

- What are the risks and benefits associated with the recommended modality?

- Is there research or evidence to support the use of this modality for this target problem?

- Is this modality appropriate and tested on those with the same or similar cultural background as the client?
- What training and experience does a social worker have with the recommended modality?
- Is the recommended modality evidence-based or consistent with available research? If not, why?
- Was the recommended modality discussed with and selected by a client?
- Will the use of the recommended modality be assessed periodically? When? How?
- Is the recommended treatment modality covered by insurance? What is the cost? How does it compare to the use of other options?

COMPONENTS OF AN INTERVENTION OR SERVICE PLAN

The goals of intervention and means used to achieve these goals are incorporated in a contractual agreement between a client and a social worker. The contract (also called an intervention or service plan) may be informal or written. The contract specifies problem(s) to be worked on; the goals to reduce the problem(s); client and social worker roles in the process; the interventions or techniques to be employed; the means of monitoring progress; stipulations for renegotiating the contract; and the time, place, fee, and frequency of meetings.

HUMAN DEVELOPMENT CONSIDERATIONS IN THE CREATION OF AN INTERVENTION PLAN

A social worker develops an intervention plan by consulting the relevant practice research and then flexibly implementing an approach to fit a client's needs and circumstances. The intervention plan is driven by the data collected as part of assessment. Assessment is informed by current human behavior and development research that provides key information about how clients behave and research about risk and resilience factors that affect human functioning. These theories inform social workers about what skills, techniques, and strategies must be used by social workers, clients, and others for the purpose of improving well-being. These techniques and strategies are outlined in an intervention plan.

An intervention plan should be reviewed during the intervention, at termination, and, if possible, following the termination of services to make adjustments, ensure progress, and determine the sustainability of change after treatment.

METHODS USED TO DEVELOP AN INTERVENTION PLAN

The problem-solving process drives the methods used to develop an intervention plan. The steps that precede planning include engagement and assessment, which are both essential to ensuring that a social worker and client have created a therapeutic alliance and collected the information needed to move into planning, the third stage.

In planning, a social worker and client should be:

1. Defining the problem (in a well defined, clear, and data-driven format)

2. Examining the causes of the problem and how it relates to other positive or negative aspects of a client's life

3. Generating possible solutions that will impact on the problem

4. Identifying the driving and restraining forces related to implementation of each of the possible solutions

5. Rating the driving and restraining forces related to consistency and potency

6. Prioritizing these solutions based on these ratings;

7. Developing SMART objectives—Specific, Measurable, Achievable, Relevant, and Time-specific—related to the chosen solutions

8. Creating strategies and activities related to the objectives

TECHNIQUES USED TO ESTABLISH MEASURABLE INTERVENTION OR SERVICE PLANS

When social workers are creating intervention or service plans, it is essential that goals are written in observable and measurable terms. In order to achieve this aim, the following should be included in each goal contained in the intervention or service plan.

- *Criteria*: What behavior must be exhibited, how often, over what period of time, and under what conditions to demonstrate achievement of the goal?
- *Method for evaluation*: How will progress be measured?
- *Schedule for evaluation*: When, how often, and on what dates or intervals of time will progress be measured?

There may also be benchmarks or the intermediate knowledge, skills, and/or behaviors that must be learned/achieved in order for a client to reach his or her ultimate goal.

Objectives break down the goals into discrete components or subparts, which are steps toward the final desired outcome.

METHODS USED TO INVOLVE CLIENTS IN INTERVENTION PLANNING

The participation of clients in the process of identifying what is important to them now and in the future, and acting upon these priorities, is paramount. Clients' participation in the process will reduce resistance, increase motivation to change, and ensure sustainability of progress made.

In order to involve clients, social workers must continually listen to, learn about, and facilitate opportunities with clients who they are serving. Client involvement should not just occur during intervention planning, but instead during the entire problem-solving process.

In *engagement*, a social worker should be actively involved with a client in determining why treatment was sought; what has precipitated the desire to change now; the parameters of the helping relationship, including defining the roles of a social worker and client; and the expectations for treatment (what will occur and when it will happen). Client involvement is essential in determining what is important to a client now and in the future.

In *assessment*, a client is the source of providing essential information upon which to define the problem and solutions, as well as identifying collateral contacts from which gaps in data can be collected.

In *planning*, a client and social worker must develop a common understanding of a client's preferred lifestyle. Goals are developed from this common understanding in order to provide a direction to help a client move toward this lifestyle. Specific action plans are developed and agreed upon in order to specify who will do what, what and how resources will be needed and used, and timelines for implementation and review.

In *intervention*, a client must be actively involved in mobilizing his or her support network to realize continued progress and sustainable change. A client must bring to the attention of a social worker issues that arise which may threaten goal attainment. Progress, based upon client reports, must be tracked and plans/timelines adjusted accordingly.

In *evaluation*, subjective reports of a client, in conjunction with objective indicators of progress, should be used to determine when goals or objectives have been met and whether new goals or objectives should be set. Client self-monitoring is a good way to involve a client so he or she can see and track progress himself or herself.

In *termination*, a client should reflect on what has been achieved and anticipate what supports are in place if problems arise again. Although this is the last step in the problem-solving process, it still requires active involvement by both a social worker and client.

METHODS FOR PLANNING INTERVENTIONS WITH GROUPS

Group work can be used for many purposes, including, but not limited to, helping clients:

- Achieve personal change
- Achieve social, environmental, or political change
- Foster relationships/gain support
- Maximize resources
- Facilitate learning

There are a number of different types of groups, such as action-based groups, task groups, psychotherapeutic groups, and so on.

In order to be effective, social workers must be familiar with:

- Theories related to group work and group dynamics
- Different kinds of groups and group work approaches
- The advantage and limitations of group work versus individual interventions
- Boundary issues in group work
- Logistics such as venue, duration, membership, size of the group, format, and activities
- Facilitation styles and approaches
- Group member roles
- Dealing with difficult situations and behaviors
- Evaluating the effectiveness of group intervention

When working with groups, **a social worker should use the group as the major helping agent and not make decisions for the group**. A social worker should only intervene when interactions or the communication pattern within a group is becoming fragmented or dysfunctional in some way.

Social workers' interventions may involve assisting to:

- Maintain a group's structure, boundary (ground rules), and/or purpose
- Open up new possibilities or avenues of exploration

■ Guide the direction of the group away from—or toward—certain themes

■ Interpret the assumptions, attitudes, or behavior of the group or its unconscious communication

■ Model a way of dealing with dilemmas or situations

METHODS FOR PLANNING INTERVENTIONS WITH ORGANIZATIONS AND COMMUNITIES

Organizational and community interventions are essential within social work practice. Clients may have a hard time achieving their goals if barriers exist within their larger environment (such as in organizations like work or school) or in their communities. In addition, if organizational and/or community factors have contributed to client distress, they must be changed to prevent them from affecting others in the same way.

Thus, organizational and community interventions are critical in accordance with viewing client behavior as a result of an interaction between a client and his or her environment. In addition, social workers must not only assist with individual problems, but also must make changes on a systemic level to achieve broader outcomes.

The problem-solving process can be used with organizations and communities. With these larger units of intervention, it includes:

1. Acknowledging the problem

2. Analyzing/defining the problem

3. Generating possible solutions—"brainstorming"

4. Evaluating each option

5. Implementing the option of choice

6. Evaluating the outcome

Thus, a social worker should use the same process of engagement, assessment, planning, intervention, evaluation, and termination. A social worker should collaborate with organizations and communities to build leadership within these entities so future problems can be addressed internally. A social worker should not serve as an "expert," telling them what is wrong and what to do. Instead, a strengths perspective should be employed, with a social worker serving as a resource to make changes in collaboration with organizational or community members based on their identified priorities and goals.

CULTURAL CONSIDERATIONS IN THE CREATION OF AN INTERVENTION PLAN

It is essential that a social worker address cultural considerations into treatment or intervention planning. These considerations should include the identification of cross-cultural barriers, which may hinder a client's engagement and/or progress in treatment.

Social workers also have an ethical mandate to take information learned when working with individual clients and adapt agency resources to meet others who may also have similar cultural considerations and/or language assistance needs.

A social worker should understand and validate each client's cultural norms, beliefs, and values. Areas in treatment or intervention planning that can be greatly influenced by cultural factors include identification of client strengths and problems, goals and objectives, and modalities of treatment.

For example, a client's culture can provide him or her with strengths that can be brought to the intervention process. These strengths can include, but are not limited to:

- Supportive family and community relations
- Community and cultural events and activities
- Faith and spiritual or religious beliefs
- Multilingual capabilities
- Healing practices and beliefs
- Participation in rituals (religious, cultural, familial, spiritual, community)
- Dreams and aspirations

A culturally informed intervention plan must be based on a therapeutic relationship in which a client feels safe to explore his or her problems within his or her cultural context.

Intervention will be most effective when it is consistent with a consumer's culture. A social worker should consider the following given their cultural appropriateness:

- Individual versus group treatment
- Alternative treatment approaches (yoga, aromatherapy, music, writing)
- Medication (western, traditional, and/or alternative)
- Family involvement
- Location/duration of intervention

The *DSM-5* incorporates a greater cultural sensitivity throughout the manual rather than a simple list of culture-bound syndromes.

Different cultures and communities exhibit or explain symptoms in various ways. Because of this, it is important for social workers to be aware of relevant contextual information stemming from clients' cultures, races, ethnicities, religious affiliations, and/or geographical origins so social workers can more accurately diagnose client problems, as well as more effectively treat them.

In the *DSM-5*, specific diagnostic criteria were changed to better apply across diverse cultures. The Cultural Formulation Interview Guide is included to help social workers assess cultural factors influencing clients' perspectives of their symptoms and treatment options. It includes questions about clients' backgrounds in terms of their culture, race, ethnicity, religion, or geographical origin. The Interview provides an opportunity for clients to define their distress in their own words and then relate this distress to how others, who may not share their culture, see their problems.

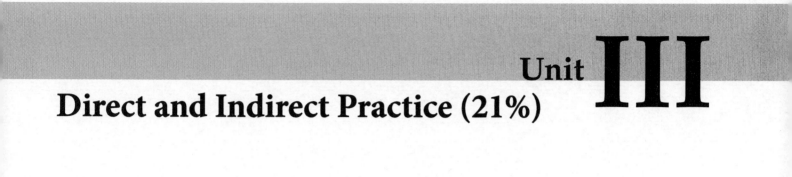

Direct and Indirect Practice (21%)

Unit **III**

7

Direct (Micro)

CLIENT ADVOCACY

Advocacy by social workers can occur on the micro or macro levels. It is a process for affecting or initiating change either with or on behalf of an individual client or group to (a) obtain services or resources that would not otherwise be provided; (b) modify or influence policies or practices that adversely affect groups or communities; and/or (c) promote legislation or policies that will result in the provision of requisite resources or services.

Social workers in direct practice fight for the rights of clients on a daily basis. Social workers are particularly concerned for those who are vulnerable or are unable to speak up for themselves. Advocacy can occur both within and outside the agency in which a social worker is employed. It can also focus on meeting a specific client's need or the needs of a larger group who are experiencing the same problem. Advocacy can occur on all organizational and governmental levels.

Advocacy can also be performed by social work managers and community organizers or developers. The role of advocacy by these social workers is to persuade others that something needs to be done and to gain support for their view of how systems, such as organizations and communities, should develop and function.

Advocacy focuses on obtaining public support by convincing those who have access to or control of resources (power, financial, etc.) that it is essential to make change. Advocacy can result in the acquisition of needed financial resources or, more importantly, the agreement or "buy in" of others to the identified cause.

EMPOWERMENT PROCESS

The primary mission of the social work profession is to enhance human well-being and help meet the basic human needs of all people, with particular attention to the needs and empowerment of people who are vulnerable, oppressed, and living in poverty (*NASW Code of Ethics, 1999 - Preamble*).

Empowerment aims to ensure a sense of control over well-being and that change is possible. A social worker can help to empower individuals, groups, communities, and institutions.

On an individual level, social workers can engage in a process with a client aimed at strengthening his or her self-worth by making a change in life that is based on his or her desires (self-determination).

To facilitate empowerment, a social worker should:

- Establish a relationship aimed at meeting a client's needs and wishes such as access to social services and benefits or to other sources of information

- Educate a client to improve his or her skills, thereby increasing the ability for self-help

- Help a client to secure resources, such as those from other organizations or agencies, as well as natural support networks, to meet needs

- Unite a client with others who are experiencing the same issues when needed to enable social and political action

Social workers should also use an empowerment process with groups, communities, and institutions so they may gain or regain the capacity to meet human needs, enhance overall well-being and potential, and provide individuals control over their lives to the extent possible.

A social worker needs many skills that focus on the activation of resources, the creation of alliances, and the expansion of opportunities in order to facilitate empowerment.

METHODS USED IN WORKING WITH INVOLUNTARY CLIENTS

Social workers often may find themselves providing services to those who did not choose to receive them, but instead have to do so as mandated by law, including families in the child protection system, people in the criminal justice system, and so on. Working with involuntary clients can be challenging, because they may want to have no contact or may only participate because they feel that they have no other choice.

Often these situations require social workers to receive peer support or supervision to process struggles encountered, as well as reassert their professionalism, because clients may try to test and exhibit anger at social workers, who represent the mandates placed upon them.

Some methods that can be helpful in working with involuntary clients include:

- Acknowledging clients' circumstances and understanding how they came about given clients' histories

- Listening to clients' experiences in order to try to understand how they feel about intervention

- Engaging in clear communication because involuntary clients struggle to understand what is happening to them

- Making clear what the purpose of the intervention is, what clients have control over and what they do not, what is going to happen next, and what the likely consequences will be if they do not participate

- Assisting at an appropriate pace as progress may be slow

- Building trust, even on the smallest scale, by consistently being honest and up-front about the situation and why a social worker is involved

- Giving clients practical assistance when needed to help them fight for their rights

- Paying attention to what is positive in clients' behavior and celebrating achievements

- Showing empathy and viewing clients as more than the problems that brought them into services

PSYCHOSOCIAL APPROACH

Psychosocial approaches within social work draw on psychoanalytic theory and practice derived from the work of Freud and his followers. They stress the importance of both internal and external factors in relation to client capacity to cope with the everyday stresses of modern living. As such, it contradicts the myth that psychosocial approaches are only concerned with clients' inner, emotional life: The external world is also an important area of analysis and concern.

This approach considers a client in the context of his or her interactions or transactions with the external world. Treatment focuses on the inner emotional needs of a client and results in a modification of the person, the environment, or both, and of the exchange between them (incorporates a systems approach).

COMPONENTS OF THE PROBLEM-SOLVING PROCESS

The problem-solving approach is based on the belief that an inability to cope with a problem is due to some lack of motivation, capacity, or opportunity to solve problems in an appropriate way. Clients' problem-solving capacities or resources are maladaptive or impaired.

The goal of the problem-solving process is to enhance client mental, emotional, and action capacities for coping with problems and/or making accessible the opportunities and resources necessary to generate solutions to problems.

A social worker engages in the problem-solving process via the following steps:

1. Engaging
2. Assessing*
3. Planning
4. Intervening
5. Evaluating
6. Terminating

CRISIS INTERVENTION APPROACH

A state of crisis is time limited. Brief intervention during a crisis usually provides maximum therapeutic effect. Crisis intervention is a process of actively influencing the psychosocial functioning of clients during a period of disequilibrium or crisis. The goals are to alleviate stress and mobilize psychological capabilities and social resources.

The goals of crisis intervention are to (a) relieve the impact of stress with emotional and social resources, (b) return a client to a previous level of functioning (regain equilibrium), (c) help strengthen coping mechanisms during the crisis period, and (d) develop adaptive coping strategies.

Crisis intervention focuses on the here-and-now, is time limited (most crises last from 4 to 6 weeks), is directive, and requires high levels of activity and involvement from a social worker. A social worker sets specific goals and tasks in order to increase a client's sense of mastery and control.

TASK-CENTERED PRACTICE

A task-centered approach aims to quickly engage clients in the problem-solving process and to maximize their responsibility for treatment outcomes. In this modality, the duration of treatment is usually limited due to setting constraints, limitations imposed by third-party payers, or other reasons. Thus, at the outset, the expectation is that interventions from learning theory and

---

* A social worker should remember that a client's strengths should be included in the assessment. It is not just about weaknesses.

behavior modification will be used to promote completion of a well defined task to produce measurable outcomes. The focus is on the "here and now." This type of practice is often preferred by clients, as they are able to see more immediate results.

The problem is partialized into clearly delineated tasks to be addressed consecutively (assessment leads to goals, which lead to tasks). A client must be able to identify a precise psychosocial problem and a solution confined to a specific change in behavior or a change of circumstances. A client must also be willing to work on the problem. It is essential that a social worker and client establish a strong working relationship quickly. A social worker's therapeutic style must be highly active, empathic, and sometimes directive in this approach.

Assessment focuses on helping a client identify the primary problem and explore the circumstances surrounding the problem. Specific tasks are expected to evolve from this process. Consideration is given to how a client would ideally like to see the problem resolved. Termination, in this modality, begins almost immediately upon the onset of treatment.

SHORT-TERM INTERVENTIONS

The growing need for time limited treatment, fueled by the widening influence of managed care in the behavioral health field, has produced a renewed focus on short-term therapy. Short-term interventions vary greatly in their duration.

Research has suggested that a social worker's and client's views on the time of treatment are more important than the duration of treatment itself. Sometimes these approaches are used because of organizational or financial constraints. In other instances, clients are choosing them over open-ended approaches. Although some have been wary of the effectiveness of these techniques to instill long-lasting change, they are being used more broadly than ever before. Some short-term interventions include a psychodynamic model, a crisis intervention model, and a cognitive-behavioral model.

Although psychoanalysis is often thought of as long-term, this was not the case with Freud's early work, and psychoanalysis did not start out this way. A number of short-term psychodynamic approaches focus on the belief that childhood experiences are the root of adult dysfunction.

METHODS USED TO PROVIDE EDUCATIONAL SERVICES TO CLIENTS

One of the ways that social workers provide information to clients is through psychoeducation. This model allows a social worker to provide clients with information necessary to make informed decisions that will allow them to reach their respective goals. In addition to focusing on clients' education, it also provides support and coping skills development.

Psychoeducation is delivered in many service settings and with many types of client populations. It is provided to those who are experiencing some sort of issue or problem with the rationale that, with a clear understanding of the problem, as well as self-knowledge of strengths, community resources, and coping skills, clients are better equipped to deal with problems and to contribute to their emotional well-being.

The core psychoeducational principle is that education has a role in emotional and behavioral change. With an improved understanding of the causes and effects of problems, psychoeducation broadens clients' perception and interpretation of them, positively influencing clients' emotions and behavior. In other words, clients feel less helpless about the situation and more in control of themselves.

METHODS OF CONFLICT RESOLUTION

Management of conflict entails four steps:

1. The recognition of an existing or potential conflict
2. An assessment of the conflict situation
3. The selection of an appropriate strategy
4. Intervention

When previous attempts to resolve a conflict have only escalated the conflict, a useful technique is to structure the interactions between the parties. Structuring techniques include:

1. Decreasing the amount of contact between the parties in the early stages of conflict resolution
2. Decreasing the amount of time between problem-solving sessions
3. Decreasing the formality of problem-solving sessions
4. Limiting the scope of the issues that can be discussed
5. Using a third-party mediator

USE OF CASE MANAGEMENT

Case management has been defined in many ways. However, all models are based on the belief that clients often need assistance in accessing services in today's complex systems, as well as the need to monitor duplication and gaps in treatment and care.

Although there may be many federal, state, and local programs available, there are often serious service gaps. A client might have a specific need met in one program and many related needs ignored because of the lack of coordination. Systems are highly complex, fragmented, duplicative, and uncoordinated.

Social workers provide case management services to different client populations in both nonprofit and for-profit settings.

The primary goal of social work case management is to optimize client functioning and well-being by providing and coordinating high-quality services, in the most effective and efficient manner possible, to individuals with multiple complex needs (*NASW Standards for Social Work Case Management*, 2013).

Five case management activities are (a) assessment, (b) planning, (c) linking, (d) monitoring, and (e) advocacy.

TECHNIQUES USED TO EVALUATE A CLIENT'S PROGRESS

Evaluating progress is a critical part of the problem-solving process. Examining with a client what has occurred and what still needs to occur involves him or her in treatment decisions.

Evaluation methods can be simple or complex. They can rely on quantitative information that shows data on reductions in target behaviors, health care improvements, or psychiatric symptom increases, and/or qualitative information in which a client and/or social worker subjectively report on progress made in various areas.

When evaluating progress, a social worker and client should gather all needed information and identify factors that helped or hindered progress. Goals outlined in the contract/service plan should be modified, if needed, based upon the outcome of the evaluation.

Social workers should assist clients to understand the progress they have made so they can clearly understand and celebrate their accomplishments, as well as identify areas that need attention. This process should ensure that clients understand why progress has happened, as well as include a dialogue about any changes that need to occur in the problem-solving process to facilitate continued growth.

USE OF CONTRACTING AND GOAL-SETTING WITH CLIENTS

A social worker and client work together to develop a contract (intervention or service plan), including an agreement on its implementation or the activities used to help a client attain his or her goals. Modification of the contract may be required as new information about a client's situation emerges and/or as the situation changes.

When clients seek to attain their goals, changes may need to be made to themselves, groups, families, and/or systems in the larger environment. This choice of targets is an even more complex issue than it first appears because the process of changing one system may bring about changes in others.

Change Strategies

- *Modify systems*: The decision to help a client on a one-to-one basis or in the context of a larger system must take into consideration a client's preferences and previous experiences, as well as the degree to which a client's problem is a response to forces within the larger system and whether change can be readily attained by a change in the larger system.

- *Modify individual thoughts*: A social worker may teach how to problem solve, alter his or her self-concepts by modifying self-defeating statements, and/or make interpretations to increase a client's understanding about the relationship between events in his or her life.

- *Modify individual actions*: A social worker may use behavior modification techniques, such as reinforcement, punishment, modeling, role-playing, and/or task assignments. *Modeling and role modeling are very effective methods for teaching. They should be used whenever possible.*

- Thoughts can be modified by feedback from others and behaviors can be modified through the actions of others in a system (by altering reinforcements).

- A social worker can also *advocate* for a client and seek to secure a change in a system on his or her behalf.

- A social worker can be a *mediator* by helping a client and another individual or system to negotiate with each other so that each may attain their respective goals.

USE OF TIMING IN INTERVENTION

The use of timing in social work interventions is critical. Both verbal expressions and nonverbal communication by a social worker, if timed appropriately, can cause a client to feel joined with a social worker, resulting in a stronger therapeutic alliance; this can lead to enhanced outcomes. However, the same expressions or communication at the wrong time can result in a client thinking that a social worker is not aligned or relating to a client's experiences.

Social workers must examine cues provided by clients to determine the appropriateness of communication styles and strategies, as well as when clients are ready to move forward in the problem-solving process. In addition, sometimes a social worker must reassess, with a client, the continued appropriateness of an agreed-upon intervention, because factors have made it no longer feasible or desirable.

PHASES OF INTERVENTION

Social work aims to assist with making change on the micro, meso, or macro levels to enhance well-being. Despite the level of intervention, the steps that a social worker takes are similar.

Step 1	Engagement with client, group, or community
Step 2	Assessment of strengths and needs to be used in the intervention process
Step 3	Planning or design of intervention to address problem
Step 4	Intervention aimed at making change
Step 5	Evaluation of efforts
Step 6	Termination and anticipation of future needs

Usually change does not occur easily and there are stages of change that occur. Understanding these stages can help achieve goals.

Precontemplation	Denial, ignorance of the problem
Contemplation	Ambivalence, conflicted emotion
Preparation	Experimenting with small changes, collecting information about change
Action	Taking direct action toward achieving a goal
Maintenance	Maintaining a new behavior, avoiding temptation
Relapse	Feelings of frustration and failure

In order for real change to occur, all intervention steps must occur and change must be understood in these sequential stages.

INDICATORS OF CLIENT READINESS FOR TERMINATION

Readiness for termination may be marked when meetings between a social worker and client seem uneventful and the tone becomes one closer to cordiality rather than challenge, as well as when no new ground has been discovered for several sessions in a row.

In termination, a social worker and client (a) evaluate the degree to which a client's goals have been attained, (b) acknowledge and address issues related to the ending of the relationship, and (c) plan for subsequent steps a client may take relevant to the problem that do not involve a social worker (such as seeking out new services, if necessary).

The process of evaluation helps a client determine if his or her goals have been met and if the helping relationship was beneficial. As a result of the evaluation process, a social worker can become a more effective practitioner and provide better services. *There must always be a method to evaluate the effectiveness of the services received. Evaluation measures, when compared with those taken at baseline, assist in determining the extent of progress and a client's readiness for termination.*

A social worker helps a client cope with the feelings associated with termination. This process may help a client cope with future terminations.

By identifying the changes accomplished and planning how a client is going to cope with challenges in the future, a social worker helps a client maintain these changes.

TECHNIQUES USED FOR FOLLOW-UP IN SOCIAL WORK PRACTICE

The standard of practice is that social workers must involve clients and their families (when appropriate) in making their own decisions about follow-up services or aftercare. Involvement must include, at a minimum, discussion of client and family preferences (when appropriate).

Social workers are often responsible for coordination of clients' follow-up services, when needed.

A return of clients to services quickly may suggest either that they did not receive needed follow-up services or that these services were inadequate. Termination may have occurred prematurely.

Clients who are at high risk for developing problems after services have ended should receive regular assessments after discharge to determine whether services are needed or discharge plans are being implemented as planned.

USE OF ACTIVE LISTENING SKILLS

Active listening skills are an essential part of building relationships and trust. The active part in the listening process can be achieved by showing interest in clients' words. Once clients notice that social workers are understanding what is said and really taking an interest, communication will be more open.

Active listening establishes trust and respect, so clients will feel comfortable confiding in social workers. Thus, it helps build a therapeutic alliance.

Active listening can also include speaking by using mirroring techniques to paraphrase and reflect back to clients what they have just said. For example, a client may say, "I hate my job and my boss yells at me all the time." An active listening response might involve saying something such as, "So you feel like your boss doesn't appreciate you or treat you with respect." Responses need to be tailored to what clients are saying to demonstrate listening and engagement in what is being said.

TECHNIQUES USED TO MOTIVATE CLIENTS

A motivational approach aims to help clients realize what needs to change and to get them to talk about their daily lives, as well as their satisfaction with current situations. Social workers want to create doubt that everything is "OK" and help clients recognize consequences of current behaviors or conditions that contribute to dissatisfaction.

It is much easier if clients believe goals can be achieved and life can be different. Sometimes clients are incapacitated by conditions that need to be addressed first (i.e., depression). Social workers can help clients think of a time when things were better or create a picture of what their lives could look like with fewer stresses.

The role of a social worker is to create an atmosphere that is conducive to change and to increase a client's intrinsic motivation, so that change arises from within rather than being imposed from without.

Motivation is a state of readiness or eagerness to change, which may fluctuate from one time or situation to another.

Some additional techniques include:

- Clearly identifying the problem or risk area
- Explaining why change is important
- Advocating for specific change
- Identifying barriers and working to remove them
- Finding the best course of action
- Setting goals
- Taking steps toward change
- Preventing relapse

Empathy is a factor that increases motivation, lowers resistance, and fosters greater long-term behavioral change.

TECHNIQUES USED TO TEACH SKILLS TO CLIENTS

Social workers assist clients in realizing how their lives can improve and/or how they can learn from mistakes that they have made. The techniques that social workers employ are a form of informal or didactic teaching.

For example, social workers may help clients see:

- How their histories have shaped them
- Needs associated with medical and/or behavioral health conditions
- Developmental issues related to various phases across the life span
- The workings of systems in which they operate
- Ways of coping in various situations

A social worker must use the problem-solving process to teach clients skills needed to make changes in their lives.

In addition, social workers may collaborate with or inform clients of colleagues who may also assist with more formal teaching, such as learning to read, obtaining a driver's license, and so on.

USE AND EFFECTS OF OUT-OF-HOME PLACEMENT

The use of out-of-home placement is generally viewed as an intervention that only occurs when there is a health or safety risk in the home. This risk can be due to the individual who is being removed (caused by a medical or behavioral health issue of the individual being removed) or his or her family members (caused by child abuse or neglect, medical or behavioral health issues of a family member, etc.). Often, out-of-home placement occurs after in-home interventions have been tried and failed.

Individuals who are placed outside of their homes often experience significant life problems. Determining whether these issues are directly caused by the removal is difficult as these individuals are likely to be at-risk for such problems prior to the placements.

For example, children who are removed from their homes due to abuse and/or neglect typically are higher users of mental health or other social services than before they were placed away from their parents. These children often report a high level of stress, which may manifest in substance abuse, chronic aggressive or destructive behavior, suicidal ideation or acting out, and/or patterns of runaway behavior. Academic problems are also common among these children.

For all those leaving their homes, regardless of age, there is a disruption of emotional bonds with other family members, which is often accompanied by rage, grief, sadness, and/or despair.

METHODS USED TO DEVELOP BEHAVIORAL OBJECTIVES

When outlining the goals for treatment, it is important that the broad overarching aims of treatment are broken down by a social worker and client into smaller, more tangible items that must be achieved in order to reach the overall goal. Behavioral objectives are the smaller, observable, and measurable intermediate steps that lead to broader long-term goals. Behavioral objectives help a social worker and client understand whether the strategies they are using to achieve the goal are resulting in change or whether they need to modify their efforts to improve the likelihood of accomplishing the desired outcome.

There are several important elements of behavioral objectives.

1. Good behavioral objectives are client-oriented and place the emphasis upon what a client will need to do in order for change to occur.

2. Good behavioral objectives are clear and understandable and contain a clearly stated verb that describes a definite action or behavior.

3. Good behavioral objectives are observable and describe an action that results in observable products.

4. Good behavioral objectives contain the behavior targeted for change, conditions under which a behavior will be performed, and the criteria for determining when the acceptable performance of the behavior occurs.

CLIENT SELF-MOTIVATING TECHNIQUES

There are many techniques that a client can use to assist in motivating him or her to reach a goal. A social worker can assist a client in identifying which of these techniques may be useful, as well as creating others that may be helpful. Some common self-motivating techniques include a client:

- Visualizing his or her goals, including using visual images on the refrigerator or in a place that will remind a client of the desired aim
- Reminding himself or herself of why change is needed
- Making up a contract with himself or herself of steps that will be taken toward reaching the desired end result
- Rewarding himself or herself when progress is made on the goals
- Taking a break to do something that is liked or be with a friend to stay encouraged
- Being around positive people who will encourage and not create barriers to change

- Educating himself or herself about steps that will assist in the change effort
- Breaking down goals into achievable steps
- Forgiving himself or herself when setbacks in progress occur
- Conceptualizing a new reality or what life will be like when change happens

TECHNIQUES OF ROLE-PLAY

Role-playing is a teaching strategy that offers several advantages. Role-playing in social work practice may be seen between supervisor and supervisee or social worker and client.

In all instances, role-playing usually raises interest in a topic as clients are not passive recipients in the learning process. In addition, role-playing teaches empathy and understanding of different perspectives as clients take on the role of another, learning and acting as that individual would in the specified setting. In role-playing, participation helps embed concepts. Role-playing gives clarity to information that may be abstract or difficult to understand.

The use of role-playing emphasizes personal concerns, problems, behavior, and active participation. It improves interpersonal skills, improves communication skills, and enhances communication.

Role-playing activities can be divided into four stages:

1. Preparation and explanation of the activity
2. Preparation of the activity
3. Role-playing
4. Discussion or debriefing after the role-play activity

ASSERTIVENESS TRAINING

Assertiveness training is when procedures are used to teach clients how to express their positive and negative feelings and to stand up for their rights in ways that will not alienate others.

Assertiveness training typically begins with clients thinking about areas in their life in which they have difficulty asserting themselves. The next stage usually involves role-plays designed to help clients practice clearer and more direct forms of communicating with others. Feedback is provided to improve responses, and the role-play is repeated. Clients are asked to practice assertive techniques in everyday life.

Assertiveness training promotes the use of "I" statements as a way to help clients express their feelings. "I" statements tell others how their actions may cause clients to be upset, but are in contrast with "you" statements, which are often seen as blaming or aggressive.

Learning specific techniques and perspectives, such as self-observation skills, awareness of personal preferences, and assuming personal responsibility, are important components of the assertiveness training process.

ROLE-MODELING TECHNIQUES

Role modeling emphasizes the importance of learning from observing and imitating and has been used successfully in helping clients acquire new skills, including those associated with assertiveness.

Role modeling works well when it is combined with role-play and reinforcement to produce lasting change.

There are different types of modeling, including live modeling, symbolic modeling, participant modeling, or covert modeling.

Live modeling refers to watching a real person perform the desired behavior.

Symbolic modeling includes filmed or videotaped models demonstrating the desired behavior. Self-modeling is another form of symbolic modeling in which clients are videotaped performing the target behavior.

In participant modeling, an individual models anxiety-evoking behaviors for a client and then prompts the client to engage in the behavior.

In covert modeling, clients are asked to use their imagination, visualizing a particular behavior as another describes the imaginary situation in detail.

Models in any of these forms may be presented as either a coping or a mastery model. The coping model is shown as initially fearful or incompetent, and then is shown as gradually becoming comfortable and competent performing the feared behavior. The mastery model shows no fear and is competent from the beginning of the demonstration.

LIMIT SETTING

Clients of all ages are frequently desperate for an environment with consistent boundaries. For this reason, it is helpful if social workers can learn limit-setting skills. Limit setting is facilitative as clients do not feel safe or accepted in a completely permissive environment.

In addition, although compassion is important for a social worker, it is important to maintain a client–social worker relationship. Understanding boundaries and being able to maintain those boundaries with clients are essential.

METHODS USED TO DEVELOP LEARNING OBJECTIVES WITH CLIENTS

There are six levels of cognition:

1. Knowledge: rote memorization, recognition, or recall of facts
2. Comprehension: understanding what the facts mean
3. Application: correct use of the facts, rules, or ideas
4. Analysis: breaking down information into component parts
5. Synthesis: combination of facts, ideas, or information to make a new whole
6. Evaluation: judging or forming an opinion about the information or situation

Ideally, in order for a client to learn, there should be objectives at each of these levels.

Clients may have goals to learn in any of three domains of development:

1. *Cognitive:* mental skills (knowledge)
2. *Affective:* growth in feelings or emotional areas (attitude or self)
3. *Psychomotor:* manual or physical skills (skills)

MODELS OF INTERVENTION WITH FAMILIES

Working with families has always been central to social work practice. Family interventions require treating not just an individual but all those within a family unit, with the focus of assessment and intervention directed at the interaction of family members.

In order to work effectively with families, social workers must:

1. Understand the development of, as well as the historical, conceptual and contextual issues influencing, family functioning
2. Have awareness of the impact of diversity in working with families, particularly race, class, culture, ethnicity, gender, sexual preference, aging, and disabilities
3. Understand the impact of a social worker's family of origin, current family structure, and its influence on a social worker's interventions with families
4. Be aware of the needs of families experiencing unique family problems (domestic violence, blended families, trauma and loss, adoptive families, etc.)

COUPLES INTERVENTION/TREATMENT APPROACHES

There are often reasons that couples experience problems including, but not limited to:

- Re-triggering emotional trauma and not repairing it
- An inability to bond or reconnect after hurting or doing damage to one another
- Lack of skills or knowledge

Many treatment techniques are used with individuals that can be adapted in work with couples, including:

Behavior modification—Successful couples counseling methods will address and attempt to modify any dysfunctional behavior so that couples can change the way each individual behaves with the other.

Insight-oriented psychotherapy—A good deal of time is spent studying interactions between individuals in order to develop a hypothesis concerning what caused individuals to react to each other in the way they do.

There are also specific couples therapy approaches, including the *Gottman Method,* which is based on the notion that healthy relationships are ones in which individuals know each other's stresses and worries, share fondness and admiration, maintain a sense of positiveness, manage conflicts, trust one another, and are committed to one another.

The Gottman Method focuses on conflicting verbal communication in order to increase intimacy, respect, and affection; removes barriers that create a feeling of stagnancy in conflicting situations; and creates a heightened sense of empathy and understanding within relationships.

With all approaches, there are actions that a social worker can take to facilitate effective couples' treatment.

For example, when developing a collaborative alliance with each person, a social worker should validate the experience of each and explore each person's reservations about engaging in couples therapy. In addition, when developing an alliance with the couple as a unit, a social worker can reframe individual problems in relationship terms and support each person's sense of himself or herself as being part of a unit, as well as a separate individual.

INTERVENTIONS WITH GROUPS

Group work is a method of working with two or more people for personal growth, the enhancement of social functioning, and/or for the achievement of socially desirable goals.

Social workers use their knowledge of group organization and functioning to affect the performance and adjustment of individuals.

Individuals remain the focus of concern and the group is the vehicle of growth and change.

There are different kinds of groups. For example:

Open Versus Closed

Open groups are those in which new members can join at any time. Closed groups are those in which all members begin the group at the same time.

Short-Term Versus Long-Term

Some groups have a very short duration, whereas others meet for a longer duration.

A social worker takes on different roles throughout the group process, which has a beginning, middle, and end.

Beginning

A social worker identifies the purpose of the group and his or her role. This stage is characterized as a time to convene, to organize, and to set a plan. Members are likely to remain distant or removed until they have had time to develop relationships.

Middle

Almost all of the group's work will occur during this stage. Relationships are strengthened as a group so that the tasks can be worked on. Group leaders are usually less involved.

End

The group reviews its accomplishments. Feelings associated with the termination of the group are addressed.

TECHNIQUES FOR WORKING WITH INDIVIDUALS WITHIN THE GROUP CONTEXT

People clearly behave differently when they are part of a group. For example, when presented with danger alone, individuals will act, but they often do not act in a group, because they think others will take the responsibility (known as "diffusion of responsibility").

When in groups, individuals also take on various roles, including the "energizer" who prods the group to action or decision and the "encourager" who praises, agrees with, and accepts the contribution of the others.

When leading groups, a social worker should understand the ways in which the group context influences individual actions and determine the roles that individuals have taken within groups. This knowledge is critical so that a social worker can determine the techniques that are needed to make change and where the locus of the change effort should lie (i.e., by focusing primarily on the individual, the larger group, or both).

In addition, when facilitating a task or psychotherapeutic group, a social worker may be called upon to remind the group of its goals and rules and confront relationships that may be interfering with the overall purpose of the group.

USE OF EXPERTISE FROM OTHER DISCIPLINES

The *NASW Standards for the Practice of Clinical Social Work (1989)* specify that social workers should maintain access to professional case consultation. Often, this consultation may be from qualified professionals in other disciplines. Each discipline has its own set of assumptions, values, and priorities; in order to ensure that the assessment of a client's problems consider all possible root causes (including medical) and all needs of a client are met, the social worker should consult with experts in other fields, as well as refer a client to them when needed.

Social workers often work together with others from various professions. This is known as an interdisciplinary approach. Some interdisciplinary teams interface daily, whereas others may only meet periodically.

Sometimes social workers form interdisciplinary relationships that do not constitute team practice, but are nevertheless necessary for effective service. These relationships may be with legal or educational professionals. To practice effectively, social workers must be prepared to work with professionals from all other disciplines that may be needed by a client.

In turn, social work knowledge is influenced by, and in turn influences, other disciplines, including family studies, medicine, psychiatry, sociology, education, and psychology.

APPROACHES USED IN CONSULTATION

Social workers are often called upon to seek consultation for a problem related to a client, service, organization, and/or policy. Consultation is the utilization of an "expert" in a specific area to assist with developing a solution to the issue. Consultation is usually time limited and the advice of the consultant can be used by a social worker in the problem-solving process. Although a consultant does not have any formal authority over a social worker, he or she has informal authority as an "expert." However, a social worker is not required to follow the recommendations of a consultant.

Four things are critical in consultation:

1. Defining the purpose of the consultation
2. Specifying the consultant's role
3. Clarifying the nature of problem
4. Outlining the consultation process

Social workers should seek the advice and counsel of colleagues whenever such consultation is in the best interests of clients, but should only do so from colleagues who have demonstrated knowledge, expertise, and competence related to the subject of the consultation (*NASW Code of Ethics, 1999—2.05 Consultation*).

When seeking consultation, social workers need to get the permission of clients if any identifying or specific information will be shared. In addition, social workers should only disclose information that is absolutely necessary when interacting with consultants.

Social workers may also provide consultation. They should have the appropriate knowledge and skill to do so and should follow all ethical standards, including avoiding conflicts of interest and maintaining boundaries (*NASW Code of Ethics, 1999—3.01 Supervision and Consultation*).

PROCESSES OF INTERDISCIPLINARY COLLABORATION

Interdisciplinary collaboration is a rewarding, yet challenging, social work activity. Collaboration, a learned skill that can be improved through practice, is a vehicle for improving services for all clients. It means working with others for the betterment of a client. Collaborative teams are more likely to develop important new and innovative approaches to dealing with problems.

Collaboration goes beyond people sitting around a table. It includes premeeting work (i.e., making telephone calls), how members typically conduct themselves (i.e., being friendly), and how meetings proceed (i.e., choosing to ignore minor irritations in order to get on with the agenda).

Social workers must understand their own styles and focus on their behavior as part of a group, rather than on how others should change.

Collaboration involves strong interpersonal communication and group process skills, as well as being able to have empathy to identify and understand the perspectives of others. It can be discrete (distinct or separate; limited to single occurrence or action) or continuous (ongoing or repetitive).

The following list provides some guidelines that can be helpful when social workers participate in such collaboration.

1. Social workers should clearly articulate their roles on interdisciplinary teams.

2. Social workers should understand the roles of professionals from other disciplines on these teams.

3. Social workers should seek and establish common ground with these professionals, including commonalities in professional goals.

4. Social workers should acknowledge the differences within the field and across other disciplines.

5. Social workers should address conflict within teams so that it does not interfere with the collaborative process and the teams' outcomes.

6. Social workers should establish and maintain collegial relationships.

There are also ethical guidelines that must be followed when social workers are part of interdisciplinary collaboration (*NASW Code of Ethics, 1999—2.03 Interdisciplinary Collaboration*).

1. Social workers who are members of an interdisciplinary team should participate in and contribute to decisions that affect the well-being of clients by drawing on the perspectives, values, and experiences of the social work profession. Professional and ethical obligations of the interdisciplinary team as a whole and of its individual members should be clearly established.

2. Social workers for whom a team decision raises ethical concerns should attempt to resolve the disagreement through appropriate channels. If the disagreement cannot be resolved, social workers should pursue other avenues to address their concerns consistent with client well-being.

METHODS USED TO COORDINATE SERVICES AMONG SERVICE PROVIDERS

Fragmentation presents one of the biggest service delivery challenges for clients and those who are assisting them, such as social workers. Clients can fall through the cracks because the connections between services are either absent or problematic, or needed services are missing altogether.

The purpose of coordinating services for clients is to improve outcomes. The assumption is that collaborative activity can facilitate access to services, reduce unnecessary duplication of effort, and produce a more effective and efficient social service system.

Social workers are uniquely positioned to coordinate services.

One method of coordination is the *integration of services* in which services are combined and provided simultaneously. Such an approach is often used with mental health and substance use interventions in which they are combined within a primary treatment relationship or service setting.

Another method of coordination is *wrap-around services* in which multiple providers and services may overlap in some ways, but are not combined to the same degree as integrated services.

A third method of coordination is *case management* or care coordination. Although there are many models of these two concepts, the aim of most is linking a client to needed services.

In addition, "roundtables" or interdisciplinary team approaches also are useful in ensuring that all professionals are brought together to stay informed of total client care and work together to avoid fragmentation and/or duplication.

MULTIDISCIPLINARY TEAM APPROACH

A multidisciplinary team is a group of individuals from different disciplines, each with unique skills and perspectives, who work together toward a common purpose or goal.

The benefits of this approach are well documented. Multidisciplinary teams are often seen as advantageous to clients because they do not have the burden of navigating multiple service systems and communicating to multiple professionals involved in their care. Multidisciplinary teams also can have increased positive outcomes and be cost effective.

A multidisciplinary approach can also have benefits for social workers as they:

1. Provide peer support, especially when working with stressful problems associated with involuntary service delivery, violence, suicide, and so on

2. Allow for work to be assigned across multiple professionals

3. Fulfill professional goals by ensuring all aspects of a client's biopsychosocial-spiritual-cultural care are delivered

4. Create cross-fertilization of skills between professionals

5. Facilitate decision making related to all aspects of client care, which can lead to increased job satisfaction

6. Streamline work practices by sharing of information

CASE RECORDING AND RECORD-KEEPING

The proper documentation of client services is paramount to competent practice. Without proper case recording or record-keeping, the quality of service may be compromised, the continuity of service may be disrupted, there may be misinterpretation that can cause harm, client confidentiality may be breached, and a client's confidence in the integrity of a social worker may be impacted.

In addition to client harm, a social worker, as well as his or her agency, if applicable, may be at risk of liability due to malpractice, negligence, and/or breach of confidentiality.

Some important "rules" about case recording include that it is:

- A clear, accurate, and unbiased representation of the facts
- A written record of all decisions
- Free of value judgments and subjective comments
- Timely

It should also include only information that is directly relevant to the delivery of services.

The release and storage of case recordings is also critical. Social workers must make sure that records are not released without proper client consent and records are properly stored during and following the termination of services. Records should be maintained for the number of years required by state statutes and regulations and relevant contracts.

METHODS USED TO FACILITATE COMMUNICATION

There are many methods that social workers use to facilitate communication with clients. Central to the formation of a therapeutic alliance is displaying *empathy*. Empathy is distinguished from sympathy as the latter denotes pity or feeling bad for a client, whereas the former means that a social worker understands the ideas expressed, as well as the feelings of a client. To be empathetic, a social worker must accurately perceive a client's situation, perspective, and feelings, as well as communicate this understanding in a helpful (therapeutic) way.

A social worker should also display *genuineness* in order to build trust. Genuineness is needed in order to establish a therapeutic relationship. It involves listening to and communicating with clients without distorting their messages, as well as being clear and concrete in communications.

Another method is the use of *positive regard*, which is the ability to view a client as being worthy of caring about and as someone who has strengths and achievement potential. It is built on respect and is usually communicated nonverbally.

Communication is also facilitated by *listening, attending, suspending value judgments,* and helping clients develop their own resources. A social worker should always use *culturally appropriate communication*.

It is also essential to clearly establish *boundaries* with clients to facilitate a safe environment for change.

VERBAL AND NONVERBAL COMMUNICATION TECHNIQUES

In order to facilitate change through the problem-solving process, a social worker must use various verbal and nonverbal communication techniques to assist clients to understand their behavior and feelings. In addition, to ensure clients are honest and forthcoming during this process, social workers must build trusting relationships with clients. These relationships develop through effective verbal and nonverbal communication. Social workers must be adept at using both forms of communication successfully, as well as understanding them, because verbal and nonverbal cues will be used by clients throughout the problem-solving process. Insight into their meaning will produce a higher degree of sensitivity to clients' experiences and a deeper understanding of their problems.

There are many verbal and nonverbal communication methods, including:

- *Active listening*, in which social workers are sitting up straight and leaning toward clients in a relaxed and open manner. Attentive listening can involve commenting on clients' statements, asking open-ended questions, and making statements that show listening is occurring.

- *Silence* by social workers, which can show acceptance of clients' feelings and promotes introspection or time to think about what has been learned.

- *Questioning* using open- and closed-ended formats to get relevant information in a nonjudgmental manner.

- *Reflecting or validating* to show empathetic understanding of clients' problems. These techniques can also assist clients in understanding negative thought patterns.

- *Paraphrasing and clarifying* by social workers to rephrase what clients are saying in order to join together information. Clarification uses questioning, paraphrasing, and restating to ensure full understanding of clients' ideas and thoughts.

- *Reframing* by social workers shows clients that there are different perspectives and ideas that can help to change negative thinking patterns and promote change.

- Exhibiting *desirable facial expressions*, which include direct eye contact if culturally appropriate, warmth and concern reflected, and varied facial expressions.

- Using *desirable postures or gestures*, which include appropriate arm movements and attentive gestures.

TECHNIQUES THAT EXPLORE THE UNDERLYING MEANING OF COMMUNICATION

In communication, there are two types of content, manifest and latent. *Manifest content* is the concrete words or terms contained in a communication, whereas *latent content* is that which is not visible, the underlying meaning of words or terms.

Relying just on the manifest content to understand client experiences or problems may result in *not* really understanding their meaning to individuals.

There are social work techniques such as *clarifying*, *paraphrasing*, *confronting*, and *interpreting* that can assist social workers in developing a better understanding of the meaning of clients' communication.

In addition, therapeutic techniques, such as psychoanalysis, focus on the hidden meaning of fantasies or dreams.

METHODS USED TO OBTAIN/PROVIDE FEEDBACK

Social workers interface with professionals and others in order to achieve the best possible outcomes for clients. Feedback is essential in order to learn what works and what can be done better.

There is no single method for social workers to seek feedback. Many factors may impact on how such feedback is solicited and incorporated into practice. However, there are some important principles that social workers should adhere to when obtaining or providing feedback.

1. Feedback may be either verbal or nonverbal, so social workers must make efforts to see what clients are trying to convey verbally or via their behavior and nonverbal cues in order to see whether interventions should be altered.

2. When social workers involve consultants or others in the feedback process related to client care, clients should provide consent.

3. Social workers should ask for feedback in difficult circumstances— not just when circumstances appear neutral or positive. It can be tempting only to ask for feedback from people who will say something positive. Sometimes the best learning can be from those who will be critical. Talking through difficult feedback in supervision is important.

4. Feedback is especially critical at key decision points (such as when transferring or closing cases).

5. It is important to guard against influencing people to respond in a particular way; this influence may be unintentional, because a social worker may have more influence or power than the individual from whom feedback is sought.

6. Confidentiality should be respected if the informant wants it.

7. Always be clear about why feedback is needed and what will be done with the information.

8. Documentation of feedback is essential.

9. Be aware that the feedback may be very different depending upon when it is solicited. It is critical to realize how recent events may have influenced information received. Getting feedback repeatedly at several different times may be needed to see if responses differ.

10. A social worker must make sure that the communication method is appropriate. For a younger person, texting, e-mail, or an online questionnaire may work, whereas a face-to-face conversation may be needed for others. The language should be jargon-free and issues such as language, culture, and disability may affect the ways in which people both understand and react to requests for feedback. A social worker may want to use close-ended questions and/or open ones to capture needed data.

METHODS USED TO INTERPRET AND COMMUNICATE POLICIES AND PROCEDURES

Social workers are often called upon to develop and/or communicate policies and procedures. There is no one method for doing so, but there are elements that need to be remembered in order to ensure that these tasks are done in a manner that is consistent with the values and principles of the profession, as well as maximizes client benefit.

1. Policies and procedures are essential to ensure that individuals have a clear understanding of expectations and proper ways of conducting activities. However, there are always instances in which exceptions may need to be made. A social worker must recognize that "one size does not fit all" and have ways to evaluate alternatives when needed.

2. Policies and procedures should be clear and concise, and communicated in a manner that facilitates understanding. They should be broadly communicated so all are clear about the expectation. Copies of the policies and procedures should be available for reference, if needed.

3. Policies and procedures should always support actions that are in the best interest of clients. Social workers have the mandate to challenge those that are not. They should be tailored to the service setting, as well as client needs, and not be "packaged procedures" that do not take into account cultural and other differences.

4. Training on policies and procedures should be available and continually done as part of a process of self-development.

5. Policies and procedures need to be reviewed periodically—not just when there is a problem. Regular review will ensure that changes within and outside an agency are considered and modifications to the policies and procedures are made accordingly.

6. Effective policies and procedures are "owned" by all those asked to follow them. Feedback on what is working and not working is essential. Their development must be based on the experiences of social workers and clients who are expected to adhere to them.

METHODS USED TO CLARIFY THE BENEFITS AND LIMITATIONS OF RESOURCES WITH CLIENTS

Social workers must respect the rights to self-determination of clients. In order for clients to make informed decisions, it is critical that they understand the range of services available and be informed about any opportunities they have to obtain services from other service providers. Clients should also understand their right to be referred to other professionals for assistance, as well as their right to refuse services and possible consequences of such refusals.

Throughout the problem-solving process, social workers should be assisting clients to access available resources, as well as create new ones if they do not exist or are not appropriate. In order for clients to choose between alternative resources, social workers must review the advantages and disadvantages of using each.

USE OF CASE RECORDING FOR PRACTICE EVALUATION OR SUPERVISION

Case records are often an excellent source of information for evaluating the impacts of services. They are existing sources of data, so there is no additional cost or time associated with their collection. However, there are a few limitations. If looking at records completed by multiple workers, there may be inconsistencies in recording styles or detail that may impact on the evaluation. Also, information of interest may not be contained in the records; evaluations would need to be limited to only information that is explicitly stated, which may not reflect all progress that has been made.

In addition, the opinions about how a client views both the process and outcome of service delivery are also critical and may not be fully captured in the record. Ensuring that a client's views are the center of any practice evaluation is critical. Thus, a social worker may want to use the case record as one source of information, but include others as well, to ensure all aspects of a client's care, including satisfaction with services, are included.

Social workers engaged in formal evaluation beyond that used to determine individual client progress should obtain voluntary and written informed consent from clients regarding the use of their records without any penalty for refusal to participate or undue inducement to participate (*NASW Code of Ethics, 1999—5.02 Evaluation and Research*).

Review of case records by supervisors is also essential. This review will ensure that a social worker is documenting properly and recording information in an unbiased manner. Clients must understand and consent to supervisory review of records.

When reviewing information, supervisors should adhere to the same standards of confidentiality as a social worker. The supervisor should not review the records unless it is for the betterment of a client and only within the supervisory context to ensure the quality of services. If the supervisor is a consultant, a client must consent unless there is a compelling need for such disclosure.

USE OF SINGLE-SUBJECT DESIGN IN PRACTICE

Single-subject designs aim to determine whether an intervention has the intended impact on an individual, or on many individuals who form a group. The most common single-subject research design is *pre–post design or single-case study* (AB) in which there is a comparison of behavior before treatment (baseline denoted by an "A") and behavior after the start of treatment (intervention denoted by a "B"). The *reversal or multiple baseline design* (ABA or ABAB) is also commonly used.

In each design, a client is used as his or her own control. The focus of single-subject designs differs from experimental research, which looks at the average effect of an intervention between groups of people.

Single-subject designs are ideal for studying the behavioral change a client exhibits as a result of some treatment. When done correctly and carefully, single-subject research can show a causal effect between the intervention and the outcome.

The flexibility, simplicity, and low cost of these designs are also beneficial. Single-subject research can be more flexible and easier to plan, since it is usually smaller in scale than experimental research.

All designs attempt to maximize both internal and external validity. Internal validity addresses the extent to which causal inferences can be made about the intervention and the targeted behavior. External validity addresses how generalizable those inferences are to the general population. Due to the small number of study participants, single-subject research tends to have poor external validity, limiting the ability to generalize the findings to a wider audience.

It is important to remember that, in some cases, it would be unethical to withdraw treatment if clients were at risk for harm. Also, in a crisis, treatment would not be delayed in order to obtain baseline data.

EVALUATION OF PRACTICE

Social workers have an ethical mandate to ensure that they are providing the most efficient and effective services possible. They also must do no harm and ensure that the intervention provided enhances the well-being of clients.

These goals require the evaluation of practice. Routine practice evaluation by social workers can enhance treatment outcomes and agency decision making, planning, and accountability.

There are two main types of evaluations—*formative* and *summative*. Formative evaluations examine the process of delivering services, whereas summative evaluations examine the outcomes.

Formative evaluations are ongoing processes that allow for feedback to be implemented during service delivery. These types of evaluations allow social workers to make changes as needed to help achieve program goals. Needs assessments can be viewed as one type of formative evaluation.

Summative evaluations occur at the end of services and provide an overall description of their effectiveness. Summative evaluation examines outcomes to determine whether objectives were met. Summative evaluations enable decisions to be made regarding future service directions that cannot be made during implementation. Impact evaluations and cost-benefit analyses are types of summative evaluations.

There are also ethical standards that must be followed when evaluating practice (*NASW Code of Ethics, 1999—5.02 Evaluation and Research*). Some of these guidelines include:

1. Obtaining voluntary and written informed consent from clients, when appropriate, without any implied or actual deprivation or penalty for refusal to participate; without undue inducement to participate; and with due regard for participants' well-being, privacy, and dignity

2. Informing clients of their right to withdraw from evaluation and research at any time without penalty

3. Ensuring clients in evaluations have access to appropriate supportive services

4. Avoiding conflicts of interest and dual relationships with those being evaluated

INTERPRETING AND APPLYING RESEARCH FINDINGS TO PRACTICE

The promotion of evidence-based research within social work is widespread. Evidence-based research gathers evidence that may be informative for clinical practice or clinical decision making. It also involves the process of gathering and synthesizing scientific evidence from various sources and translating it to be applied to practice.

The use of evidence-based practice places the well-being of clients at the forefront, desiring to discover and use the best practices available. The use of evidence-based practice requires social workers to only use services and techniques that were found effective by rigorous, scientific, empirical studies—that is, outcome research.

Social workers must be willing and able to locate and use evidence-based interventions. In areas in which evidence-based interventions are not available, social workers must still use research to guide practice. Applying knowledge gleaned from research findings will assist social workers in providing services informed by scientific investigation and lead to new interventions that can be evaluated as evidence-based practices.

When reading and interpreting experimental research findings, social workers must be able to identify independent variables (or those that are believed to be causes) and dependent variables (which are the impacts or results). In many studies, the independent variable is the treatment provided and the dependent variable is the target behavior that is trying to be changed.

The reliability and validity of research findings should also be assessed.

Reliability (dependability, stability, consistency, predictability): Can you get the same answer repeatedly?

Validity (accuracy): Is what is believed to be measured actually being measured or is it something else?

External validity: Can the results be generalized?

Internal validity: Is there confidence in cause and effect?

PROCESS USED TO REFER CLIENTS FOR SERVICES

There are important steps, as well as ethical concerns, that must be taken when referring clients for services.

Step 1: Clarifying the Need or Purpose for the Referral

Social workers should refer clients to other professionals when the other professionals' specialized knowledge or expertise is needed to serve clients fully or when social workers believe that they are not being effective or making reasonable progress with clients and additional service is required (*NASW Code of Ethics, 1999—2.06 Referral for Services*).

Step 2: Researching Resources

When making a referral, it is critical that a social worker refers to a competent provider, someone with expertise in the problem that a client is experiencing. When researching resources, a client's right to self-determination should be paramount. In addition, if a client is already receiving services from an agency, it may be advisable to see if there are available services provided by this agency in order to avoid additional coordination and fragmentation for a client.

Step 3: Discussing and Selecting Options

Social workers are prohibited from giving or receiving payment for a referral when no professional service is provided by the referring social worker (*NASW Code of Ethics, 1999—2.06 Referral for Services*).

Step 4: Planning for Initial Contact

Social workers may want to work with a client to prepare for the initial meeting. Preparation may include helping a client to understand what to expect or reviewing needs and progress made so that it can be discussed with the new provider.

Step 5: Initial Contact

Social workers who refer clients to other professionals should take appropriate steps to facilitate an orderly transfer of responsibility. Social workers who refer clients to other professionals should disclose, with clients' consent, all pertinent information to the new service providers (*NASW Code of Ethics, 1999—2.06 Referral for Services*).

Step 6: Follow-Up to See If Need Was Met

Social workers should always follow-up to ensure that there was not a break in service and that the new provider is meeting a client's needs.

USE OF COGNITIVE BEHAVIORAL TECHNIQUES

Cognitive behavioral therapy (CBT) is a hands-on, practical approach to problem-solving. Its goal is to change patterns of thinking or behavior that are responsible for clients' difficulties, and so change the way they feel. CBT works by changing clients' attitudes and their behavior by focusing on the thoughts, images, beliefs, and attitudes that are held (cognitive processes) and how this relates to behavior, as a way of dealing with emotional problems.

CBT can be thought of as a combination of psychotherapy and behavioral therapy. Psychotherapy emphasizes the importance of the personal meaning placed on things and how thinking patterns begin in childhood. Behavioral therapy pays close attention to the relationship between problems, behaviors, and thoughts.

This approach is active, collaborative, structured, time limited, goal-oriented, and problem-focused. This approach lends itself to the requirements posed by managed care companies, including brief treatment, well-delineated techniques, goal and problem-oriented, and empirically supported evidence of its effectiveness.

Steps in Cognitive Restructuring

Assist clients in:

1. Accepting that their self-statements, assumptions, and beliefs determine or govern their emotional reaction to life's events
2. Identifying dysfunctional beliefs and patterns of thoughts that underlie their problems
3. Identifying situations that evoke dysfunctional cognitions
4. Substituting functional self-statements in place of self-defeating thoughts
5. Rewarding themselves for successful coping efforts

Foundational to this treatment is *client self-monitoring*. Clients are encouraged to pay attention to any subtle shift in feelings. Clients frequently keep thought or emotion logs that include three components: (a) disturbing emotional states; (b) the exact behaviors engaged in at the time of the emotional states; and (c) thoughts that occurred when the emotions emerged. Homework is often done between sessions to record these encounters.

CULTURALLY COMPETENT SOCIAL WORK PRACTICE

Cultural competence involves working in conjunction with natural, informal support and helping networks within the minority community (neighborhoods, churches, spiritual leaders, healers, etc.). It extends the concept of self-determination to the community. Only when a community recognizes and owns a problem does it take responsibility for creating solutions that fit the context of the culture.

Social workers should promote conditions that encourage respect for cultural and social diversity and promote policies and practices that demonstrate respect for difference, support the expansion of cultural knowledge and resources, advocate for programs and institutions that demonstrate cultural competence, and promote policies that safeguard the rights of all people.

Social workers should act to prevent and eliminate domination of, exploitation of, and discrimination against any person, group, or class on the basis of race, ethnicity, national origin, color, sex, sexual orientation, gender identity or expression, age, marital status, political belief, religion, immigration status, and mental or physical disability.

Since every client's cultural experiences are different, services must be delivered using a flexible and individualized approach. Social workers should be aware of the standards on cultural competence and social diversity (*NASW Code of Ethics, 1999*).

1. Social workers should understand culture and its function in human behavior and society, recognizing the strengths that exist in all cultures.
2. Social workers should have a knowledge base of their clients' cultures and be able to demonstrate competence in the provision of services that are sensitive to clients' cultures and to differences among people and cultural groups.
3. Social workers should obtain education about and seek to understand the nature of social diversity and oppression with respect to race, ethnicity, national origin, color, sex, sexual orientation, gender identity or expression, age, marital status, political belief, religion, immigration status, and mental or physical disability.
4. Social workers should also not use derogatory language in their written or verbal communications to or about clients. Social workers should use accurate and respectful language in all communications to and about clients (*NASW Code of Ethics, 1999—1.12 Derogatory Language*).

Social workers should be aware of terminology related to cultural barriers and goals.

Ethnocentrism: an orientation that holds one's own culture, ethnic, or racial group as superior to others

Stratification: structured inequality of entire categories of people who have unequal access to social rewards (e.g., ethnic stratification, social stratification)

Pluralism: a society in which diverse members maintain their own traditions while cooperatively working together and seeing others' traits as valuable (cultural pluralism—respecting and encouraging cultural difference)

Social workers must possess specific knowledge about the cultural groups with whom they work, including diverse historical experiences, adjustment styles, socioeconomic backgrounds, learning styles, cognitive skills, and/or specific cultural customs. This knowledge must include theories and principles concerning human behavior development, psychopathology, therapy, rehabilitation, and community functioning because they relate to cultural group members. Institutions, class, culture, and language barriers that prevent ethnic group members from accessing or using services must be identified and addressed.

8

Indirect (Macro)

APPLYING CONCEPTS OF ORGANIZATIONAL THEORIES

Organizational theory attempts to explain the workings of organizations. Many theories have emerged from varying bodies of knowledge and disciplines. These theories can be useful to social workers in understanding the environments in which they deliver services and the workings of organizations with which clients interact.

Classical Organizational Theories

The *scientific management theory* (Theory X) is based on (a) finding the one "best way" to perform each task; (b) carefully matching each worker to each task; (c) closely supervising workers, using reward and punishment as motivators; and (d) managing and controlling behavior.

Weber's bureaucratic theory emphasized the need for a hierarchical structure of power to ensure stability and uniformity. Weber also put forth the notion that organizational behavior is a network of human interactions, where all behavior could be understood by looking at cause and effect.

Administrative theory emphasized establishing a universal set of management principles that could be applied to all organizations.

The major deficiency with classical organizational theories was that they attempted to explain people's motivation to work strictly as a function of economic reward.

Neoclassical Theories

These theories were based upon the Hawthorne experiments and focused on workers.

The Hawthorne experiments took place at Western Electric's factory at Hawthorne, a suburb of Chicago, in the late 1920s and early 1930s. The original purpose of the experiments was to study the impacts of physical conditions on productivity. The experimenters concluded that it was not the changes in physical conditions that were affecting the workers' productivity. Rather, it was the fact that someone was actually concerned about their workplace, and the opportunities this gave them to discuss changes before they took place.

Human relations theory (Theory Y) evolved as a reaction to the tough, authoritarian structure of classical theory. It displayed genuine concern for human needs in order to produce creativity and emphasized the importance of cohesive work groups, participatory leadership, and open communication.

Modern Organizational Approaches

Systems approach considers the organization as a system composed of a set of interrelated—and thus mutually dependent—subsystems. Thus, the organization consists of components, linking processes and goals.

Sociotechnical approach considers the organization as composed of a social system, technical system, and its environment. These interact with each other, so it is necessary to balance them appropriately for effective functioning of the organization.

Contingency or situational approach recognizes that organizational systems are interrelated with their environment and that different environments require different organizational systems for effectiveness.

IMPACT OF SOCIAL WELFARE LEGISLATION ON SOCIAL WORK PRACTICE

Social workers should be fully informed of existing laws, policies, practices, and procedures that impact or govern service delivery.

Social workers are also expected to keep up-to-date with new public laws and policies.

Many laws affect social work practice. Although social workers may not be responsible for implementing these pieces of legislation, they provide protections or programs that are critical to those served.

Some relevant federal legislation is listed in chronological order in the following list.

1. *Title VI of the Civil Rights Act of 1964* states that no person shall "on the grounds of race, color, or national origin, be excluded from participation in, denied the benefits of, or be subjected to discrimination under any program or activity receiving federal financial assistance." It desegregated all schools and public buildings and required all agencies that receive federal funds to terminate discriminatory hiring practices. Social workers are charged with challenging discriminatory practices and upholding the belief of equal rights for all.

2. The *Older Americans Act (OAA) of 1965* offers services to older Americans. It established the Administration on Aging, which empowers the federal government to distribute funds to the states for supportive services for individuals over the age of 60. The Administration achieves its aim by awarding grants to states, which pass them along to local Area Agencies on Aging (AAA). Some programs target vulnerable older adults who need help staying in their homes. Other programs provide access services, in-home services, community services, caregiver services, and opportunities for volunteer work.

3. The *Child Abuse Prevention and Treatment Act of 1974* is key legislation for addressing child abuse and neglect. It has been amended several times and provides federal funding to states in support of prevention, assessment, investigation, prosecution, and treatment activities; it also provides grants to public agencies and nonprofit organizations for demonstration programs and projects.

4. The *Family Educational Rights and Privacy Act (FERPA) of 1974* protects the privacy of educational records. The law applies to all schools that receive funds under an applicable program of the United States Department of Education. FERPA gives parents certain rights with respect to their children's education records. These rights transfer to the student when he or she reaches the age of 18 or attends a school beyond the high school level. Prior to 18, parents have the right to inspect and review a student's education records maintained by the school. Schools are not required to provide copies of records unless, for reasons such as great distance, it is impossible for parents to review the records. Schools may charge a fee for copies. Parents also have the right to request that a school correct records that they believe to be inaccurate or misleading. If the school decides not to amend the record, the parent or eligible student then has the right to a formal hearing. After the hearing, if the school still decides not to amend the record, the parent has the right to place a statement with the

record setting forth his or her view about the contested information. Generally, schools must have written permission from the parent in order to release any information from a student's education record, though there are some exceptions related to the student's care.

5. The *Education for Handicapped Children Act of 1975* guarantees a free, appropriate public education to all children with disabilities between the ages of 3 and 21. Children receiving such services should be provided with Individual Educational Plans (IEPs) that are revised annually. A team composed of a social worker, teacher, administrator, and other relevant school personnel typically create the IEP. The parents, and often the child, also participate. The IEP includes goals, means of attaining goals, and ways of evaluating goal attainment. A child who has an IEP must also be educated in the "least restrictive environment." Thus, the child should either spend part or all of his or her time in a regular classroom or in an environment that is as close to this as possible while still leading to the attainment of the educational goals. Services that are needed, such as speech therapy and others related to educational goals, are provided at no extra cost to the family.

6. *Indian Child Welfare Act of 1978* gives American Indian/Native American/Indigenous nations or organizations jurisdiction over child welfare cases that involve an American Indian/Native American/Indigenous child in order to protect the integrity of American Indian/Native American/Indigenous families. The law specifies a hierarchical procedure for placement of an American Indian/Native American/Indigenous child: (a) verify the ethnic and tribal identity of the child; (b) allow tribal jurisdiction over case; (c) if tribe rejects jurisdiction, placement with family member or; (d) if that is impossible, placement with family of the same tribe. The last resort is placing the child in a home with a family that is not American Indian/Native American/Indigenous.

7. The *Adoption Assistance and Child Welfare Act of 1980* focuses on family preservation efforts to help keep families together and children out of foster care or other out-of-home placements. This law also focuses on family reunification or adoption if a child is removed from a home. The act requires courts to review child welfare cases more regularly and mandates that states make "reasonable efforts" to keep families together via prevention and family reunification services. States are also required to develop reunification and preventive programs for foster care and assure that children in nonpermanent settings are seen at least every 6 months. An adoption subsidy reimbursed by the federal government is also provided through this law for children with complex needs or disabilities.

8. The *Americans with Disabilities Act (ADA) of 1990* is civil-rights legislation that prohibits discrimination on the basis of disability.

It has been amended and affords similar protections as the Civil Rights Act of 1964 for discrimination based on race, religion, sex, national origin, and other characteristics. Unlike the Civil Rights Act of 1964, the ADA also requires covered employers to provide reasonable accommodations to employees with disabilities and imposes accessibility requirements on public accommodations. ADA disabilities include both mental and physical conditions. A condition does not need to be severe or permanent to be a disability.

9. The *Patient Self-Determination Act (PSDA) of 1991* introduced a new set of federal requirements intended to implement advance directive policies at all health care facilities that receive federal funding through Medicaid and Medicare programs. The Act specified that these facilities must inform clients of their rights to make decisions concerning their own health care, ask and document whether a client has an advance directive, and provide education for staff and the community.

   Advance directives are a legal way of indicating that a person has given the legal rights to a designated person to make decisions on his or her behalf about continuation of support measures should the individual be incapable physically or mentally of making wants known.

   The purpose of advance directives is to respond to judicial decisions that have been made indicating that if a person has not told someone of his or her wishes, in case of severe physical injury, the decision to remove a person from life supports or to place the person on life supports cannot be made. Therefore, it has become increasingly imperative that people indicate their wishes and identify individuals that they designate to make these decisions if needed.

   Advance directives have been paired with *living wills* to give people control over what happens to them in a severe illness or injury. A living will allows individuals to retain some control over what happens at the end of their lives, even if the individuals are then no longer competent to make personal choices for terminal care, while they are still healthy and at a time when there is no doubt of their mental competence.

10. The *Family and Medical Leave Act (FMLA) of 1993* requires covered employers to provide up to 12 weeks of unpaid, job-protected leave to "eligible" employees for certain family and medical reasons with continuation of group health insurance coverage under the same terms and conditions as if the employee had not taken leave.

11. The *Multiethnic Placement Act of 1994 (MEPA)* and its subsequent amendments, prohibits agencies from refusing or delaying foster or adoptive placements because of a child's or foster/adoptive parent's race, color, or national origin and prohibits agencies from considering race, color, or national origin as a basis for denying approval as a foster and/or adoptive parent. It also requires

agencies to diligently recruit a diverse base of foster and adoptive parents to better reflect the racial and ethnic makeup of children in out-of-home care.

12. The *Violence Against Women Act (VAWA) of 1994* has improved the criminal justice response to violence against women by strengthening federal penalties for repeat sex offenders and creating a federal "rape shield law," which is intended to prevent offenders from using victims' past sexual conduct against them during a rape trial; keeping victims safe by requiring that a victim's protection order will be recognized and enforced in all state, tribal, and territorial jurisdictions; increasing rates of prosecution, conviction, and sentencing of offenders by helping communities develop dedicated law enforcement and prosecution units and domestic violence dockets; training law enforcement officers, prosecutors, victim advocates, and judges; and ensuring access to the services needed by victims to achieve safety and rebuild their lives.

13. The *Personal Responsibility and Work Opportunity Reconciliation Act of 1996 (PRWORA)* was considered to be a fundamental shift in both the method and goal of federal cash assistance to the poor. It added a workforce development component to welfare legislation, encouraging employment among the poor. PRWORA instituted Temporary Assistance for Needy Families (TANF), which became effective July 1, 1997. TANF replaced the Aid to Families With Dependent Children (AFDC) program, which had been in effect since 1935, and also supplanted the Job Opportunities and Basic Skills (JOBS) Training Program of 1988. It also imposed a lifetime 5-year limit on the receipt of benefits.

14. The *Health Insurance Portability and Accountability Act (HIPAA) of 1996* (HIPAA) provides individuals with access to their medical records and more control over how their personal health information is used and disclosed. It represents a uniform, federal floor of privacy protections for individuals across the country. State laws providing additional protections are not affected by HIPAA, which took effect on April 14, 2003.

15. The *Patient Protection and Affordable Care Act of 2010 (ACA)* expands access to insurance, increases protections, emphasizes prevention and wellness, improves quality and system performance, expands the health workforce, and curbs rising health care costs. Key provisions of the ACA that intend to address rising health costs include providing more oversight of health insurance premiums and practices; emphasizing prevention, primary care, and effective treatments; reducing health care fraud and abuse; reducing uncompensated care to prevent a shift onto insurance premium

costs; fostering comparison shopping in insurance exchanges to increase competition and price transparency; implementing Medicare payment reforms; and testing new delivery and payment system models in Medicaid and Medicare.

16. The *Workforce Innovation and Opportunity Act of 2014 (WIOA)* reauthorizes the Workforce Investment Act (WIA) of 1998 with several key changes in areas such as Workforce Development Boards structure; One-Stop Operations; Job-Driven Training for Adults and Dislocated Workers; and Integrated Performance and Youth Services.

METHODS USED TO ESTABLISH SERVICE NETWORKS OR COMMUNITY RESOURCES

The need for services to not be duplicative and complement one another is central to meeting client needs. Social workers are often called upon to assist with developing or navigating service networks, as well as creating community resources where they are lacking. Integrating services takes sustained effort and hard work. Though the concept of service integration may seem simple, it is not and usually takes several administrative and operational strategies. Strong leadership and sound management are critical.

In order to effectively meet client needs, organizations are increasingly recognizing collaborations, networks, alliances, and/or partnerships. There are two distinct network forms—*mandated network arrangements* and *self-organizing networks*.

Within each of these forms, there may be a lead organization or a model in which all organizations share decision-making power. The former is often associated with a centralized structure, whereas the latter is more indicative of a decentralized one. Networks can also have strong and weak arrangements in which the parameters of integration are highly regulated or not.

The willingness and ability of social service organizations to form networks often depends on organizational size, resource dependency, and collaborative experience.

TECHNIQUES FOR MOBILIZING COMMUNITY PARTICIPATION

Community participation is critical in social work practice. Community participation informs others about needed changes that must occur. Policies, programs, and services that were effective or appropriate previously may not be so currently.

Community participation also creates relationships and partnerships among diverse groups who can then work together, but may not usually do so.

Community participation puts decision-making power partly or wholly with the community, ensuring that individuals will remain interested and involved over time.

When engaging in community-based decision making, individuals will typically go through various stages.

Orientation stage—This phase is where community members may meet for the first time and start to get to know each other.

Conflict stage—Disputes, little fights, and arguments may occur. These conflicts are eventually worked out.

Emergence stage—Community members begin to see and agree on a course of action.

Reinforcement stage—Community members finally make a decision and justify why it was correct.

Community members are far more likely to buy into policy that has been created with their participation. Their support over time will lead to permanent change.

Community participation energizes the community to continue to change in positive directions. Once involved in a successful change effort, community members see what they can accomplish collectively and take on new challenges.

Lastly, community members must inform policy makers and planners of the real needs of the community, so that the most important problems and issues can be addressed. They must also provide information about what has been tried before and worked or not worked.

TECHNIQUES OF SOCIAL PLANNING METHODS

Social planning is defined as the process by which a group or community decides its goals and strategies relating to societal issues. It is not an activity limited to government, but includes activities of the private sector, social movements, professions and other organizations focused specifically on social objectives.

Models of social planning in social work practice include those that are based on community participation. Rather than planning "for" communities, social workers as planners engage "with" community members. Social planning does not merely examine sociological problems that exist, but also includes the physical and economic factors that relate to societal issues.

All issues confronting those who are served by social workers are really human or social issues. Social workers can help facilitate the process of planning through all stages: organizing community members; data gathering related to the issue—including identifying economic, political, and social causes; problem identification; weighing of alternatives; policy/program implementation; and evaluation of effectiveness.

TECHNIQUES OF SOCIAL POLICY ANALYSIS

Policy analysis is a systematic approach to solving problems through policies. It involves identifying the problem, developing alternatives, assessing the impacts of the alternatives (such as conducting a cost/benefit analysis), selecting the desired option, designing and implementing the policy, and evaluating the outcomes.

Critical to social policy analysis is the identification of alternative policy options and the evaluation of these alternatives. Analyses include developing an understanding of who "wins" and who "loses." Some of the values upon which alternatives are weighed include equity, efficiency, and liberty.

The policy analysis field has become more diversified; thus, it is highly influenced by theories from other fields. Often there are many stakeholders involved, such as federal, state, and local government agencies, stakeholders, community leaders, and clients, all of which will bring in their own set of values. Thus, the chosen approach will be influenced by who participates.

TECHNIQUES TO INFLUENCE SOCIAL POLICY

Social policy is influenced by many factors, such as the following.

Knowledge/Innovation
Knowledge and innovation create new opportunities to change, as well as information that current practices may need to be reformed. Technological advances are often drivers of changes in policy.

Social, Political, and Economic Conditions/Resources
Good policies are often not adopted because they are proposed without the social, political, or economic resources to move them through the policy process and/or implement them.

Social norms change over time and foster or impede social policy development or revision.

Political and/or economic conditions can also promote or hinder the creation and/or revision of policy, as well as whether policy alternatives are suggested or considered for adoption.

Legal Issues/Laws

Understanding how new policies will influence or interact with existing laws is essential. Policies may not be supported if they are believed to negatively impact on existing policies that are seen as beneficial.

Institutional Influences

The structure of institutions, such as government agencies, private sector organizations, and so on, can also impact the ability to influence and efficiently or effectively implement social policies. Sometimes policies are so complex or integrated into the practices of complex institutional systems that it is difficult to understand them; therefore, change is less likely.

External Influences

The media and other external influences can be very influential. Media can be used to call attention to a problem. More media coverage of one policy alternative may influence its support as it is more familiar. Public opinion is a very salient influence as to whether policies will be proposed and/or adopted.

Social workers who want to promote certain social policies must be aware of these influences and use methods to support policies as they relate to these areas. Contrarily, social workers can decrease the desirability of policies by creating barriers or removing positive influences in these areas.

Problems are also often associated with policy implementation. Policies may not be clearly communicated, leaving implementers and others at a loss as to how to follow them in order to achieve the intended goals. Negative attitudes of service personnel, lack of resources to carry out policies, and/or the conflict with previously established procedures or structures can also be obstacles to implementation.

TECHNIQUES OF WORKING WITH LARGE GROUPS

Working with large groups takes special planning and skills by a social worker. Some critical factors in working with large groups are as follows.

Establishing a common goal—Everyone in the group should have some common ground—whether it is the desire to take action or sharing views on an issue. Finding the common goal and bringing the group back to it when differences arise is essential.

Committing to consensus building—Consensus requires commitment, patience, tolerance, and a willingness to put the group first. In a large group, there may be more disagreement and conflict. Using a consensus model, disagreement can be used as a tool for helping to build cohesiveness.

Sufficient time—All decision-making techniques need enough time if the quality of decision is going to be good. Work with large groups will take longer so that all viewpoints can be heard and consensus can be reached.

Clear process—It is essential that the group has a shared understanding of the process and what to expect. Ground rules should be agreed upon by the group as its first consensus-building task.

Good facilitation and active participation—There may be a need to have more than one facilitator help with managing a large group. In addition, using techniques so that all can be heard, but are not fighting for attention, will be essential. Activities that keep group members engaged will need to be incorporated into group sessions.

There are a number of large scale intervention methods, such as a *World Café* where people with an interest in a topic or issues are brought together for a meeting. The host explains the purpose and logistics. There are then progressive rounds of conversations by smaller subgroups that move between small tables, exploring questions that matter and connecting diverse perspectives. A facilitator listens for patterns and insights that are shared with the larger group for validation.

USE OF NETWORKING

The importance of networking has been stressed heavily in business, but it has received far less attention in social work practice. This void is interesting, because it is critical to the effective delivery of services. Networking involves building relationships with other professionals who share areas of interest. It is about creating a community around common interests and building alliances. It is also about creating opportunities to work with others toward the achievement of mutual goals.

Although networking in business is a way to attract patrons/customers or to get jobs, it has a broader, and more altruistic, focus in social work.

For example, learning about others who do similar or complementary work can result in a sharing of resources and expertise, which could be beneficial to clients by keeping the cost of services contained and/or increasing the skills of practitioners. Learning about the skills of others and establishing professional relationships through networking can also provide resources for clients who may need referrals to other professionals.

Networking helps improve social skills and the ability to relate to others in a variety of settings. It puts social workers "out there" so that others can be aware of the important work that they do. Educating others about social problems is an important part of making systematic changes. Lastly, networking can identify individuals who would be good candidates for jobs. Recruiting qualified individuals into the agencies where social workers are employed results in clients receiving quality care.

APPROACHES TO CULTURALLY COMPETENT PRACTICE WITH ORGANIZATIONS AND COMMUNITIES

The *NASW Standards for Cultural Competence (2001)* provide essential elements that contribute to the ability to become more culturally competent. Organizations and communities should (a) value diversity, (b) engage in cultural self-assessment, (c) be aware of the dynamics when cultures interact, and (d) develop services that reflect an understanding of diversity between and within cultures.

Social workers should assist organizations and communities to expand choice and opportunity for all people, especially for those who are vulnerable, disadvantaged, oppressed, and exploited (*NASW Code of Ethics, 1999—6.04 Social and Political Action*).

Social workers should promote conditions that encourage respect for cultural and social diversity and promote policies that ensure the rights of people based on a respect for difference. Social workers should also support the expansion of cultural knowledge and resources within organizations and communities (*NASW Code of Ethics, 1999—6.04 Social and Political Action*).

Some approaches within organizations to promote cultural competency include recruiting multiethnic staff, including cultural competence requirements in job descriptions and performance/promotion measures, reviewing demographic trends for the geographic area served to determine service needs, creating service delivery systems that are more appropriate to the diversity of the target population, and advocating for clients as major stakeholders in the development of service delivery systems to ensure they are reflective of their cultural heritage.

ADVOCACY WITH COMMUNITIES AND ORGANIZATIONS

Advocacy is one of a social worker's most important tasks. Social workers may advocate when working with an individual client to ensure that his or her needs are met. However, social workers have an ethical mandate to make systematic changes to address the problems experienced by groups of individuals who are vulnerable and/or who are unable to speak for themselves.

A social worker may engage in advocacy by convincing others of the legitimate needs and rights of members of society. Such work can occur on the local, county, state, or national levels. Some social workers are even involved in international human rights and advocacy for those in need in other countries.

Fundamental to social work is advocating to change the factors that create and contribute to problems.

Sometimes advocacy can be achieved by working through the problem-solving process as it relates to a problem, including acknowledging the problem, analyzing and defining the problem, generating possible solutions, evaluating each option, implementing the option of choice, and evaluating the outcomes.

In other instances, social workers may engage in obtaining legislative support or using the media to draw attention to a concern.

In all instances, social workers should be working with clients to have their voices heard and should not be speaking for them. The goal of social work advocacy is to assist clients to strengthen their own skills in this area. Social workers may assist by locating sources of power that can be shared with clients to make changes.

IMPACT OF AGENCY POLICY AND FUNCTION ON SERVICE DELIVERY

The context of social work practice clearly has a profound influence on the quality and standards of professional activities and the ability of social workers to practice ethically and effectively. Social work takes place in a wide variety of settings, including, but not limited to, private practices, public sector organizations (government), schools, hospitals, correctional facilities, and private nonprofit agencies.

To meet the needs of clients, social workers must have work environments that support ethical practice and are committed to standards and good quality services. A positive working environment is created where the values and principles of social workers are reinforced in agency policies and procedures.

To achieve this aim, employers must understand social work practice and provide supervision, workload management, and continuing professional development consistent with best practices.

Policies setting out standards of ethical practice should be written and clear. Social workers should never be required to do anything that would put at risk their ability to uphold ethical standards, including those in the areas of confidentiality, informed consent, and safety/risk management.

The public, including clients, should be regularly informed of agency policies and procedures and provided with information about how to raise concerns or make complaints about them.

Policies that do not tolerate dangerous, discriminatory, and/or exploitative behavior must be in place so that social workers and their clients are safe from harm.

The adoption and implementation of policies and procedures on workload and caseload management contribute greatly to the provision of quality services to clients. In addition, policies and procedures for confidential treatment and storage of records should be established.

Continuing professional development and further training enable social workers to strengthen and develop their skills. Orientation and other relevant training provided to social workers upon hire and when assuming other jobs within the setting are essential.

Good quality, regular social work supervision by professionals who have the necessary experience and qualifications in social work practice is a critical tool to ensure service quality.

Rates of pay for social workers need to be comparable with similar professionals, and the skill and qualifications of social workers must be recognized, while ensuring services are affordable to clients.

Professional Relationships, Values, and Ethics (27%)

Professional Values and Ethical Issues

9

PROFESSIONAL VALUES AND ETHICS

The mission of the social work profession is rooted in a set of core values. These core values are the foundation of social work practice:

- Service
- Social justice
- Dignity and worth of the person
- Importance of human relationships
- Integrity
- Competence

Professional ethics are based on these basic values and guide social workers' conduct. These standards are relevant to all social workers, regardless of their professional functions, the settings in which they work, or the populations they serve.

Professional ethics are "rules" based on the core values of the profession that should be adhered to by social workers. They are statements to the general public about what they can expect from a social worker. These standards tell new social workers what is essential for practice based on the profession's core values. Social workers are judged with regard to competency based on these standards.

Professional standards are also helpful in guiding social workers when they are unsure about a course of action or conflicts arise.

CLIENT SELF-DETERMINATION

Social workers respect and promote the right of clients to self-determination and assist clients in their efforts to identify and clarify their goals. Social workers may limit clients' right to self-determination when, in a social workers' professional judgment, clients' actions or potential actions pose a serious, foreseeable, and imminent risk to themselves or others (*NASW Code of Ethics, 1999–1.02 Self-Determination*).

INTRINSIC WORTH AND VALUE OF THE INDIVIDUAL

The social work profession is based on the belief that every person has dignity and worth. It is essential that social workers respect this value and treat everyone in a caring and respectful fashion. Social workers should also be mindful of individual differences, as well as cultural and ethnic diversity.

Social workers should promote clients' right to self-determination and act as a resource to assist clients to address their own needs. Social workers have a dual responsibility to clients and to the broader society and must resolve any conflicts, in a socially responsible and ethical manner, that arise due to this dual mandate.

CLIENT'S RIGHT TO REFUSE SERVICES

Social workers should provide services to clients only in the context of a professional relationship based, when appropriate, on valid informed consent. Social workers should use clear and understandable language to inform clients of the purpose of the services, risks related to the services, limits to services because of the requirements of a third-party payer, relevant costs, reasonable alternatives, clients' right to refuse or withdraw consent, and the time frame covered by the consent. Social workers should provide clients with an opportunity to ask questions (*NASW Code of Ethics, 1999–1.03 Informed Consent*).

In instances when clients are receiving services involuntarily, social workers should provide information about the nature and extent of services and about the extent of clients' right to refuse service (*NASW Code of Ethics, 1999–1.03 Informed Consent*).

ETHICAL ISSUES REGARDING TERMINATION

Social workers should terminate services to clients and professional relationships with them when such services and relationships are no longer required or no longer serve client needs or interests *(NASW Code of Ethics, 1999–1.16 Termination of Services).*

Social workers should take reasonable steps to avoid abandoning clients who are still in need of services. Social workers should withdraw services precipitously only under unusual circumstances, giving careful consideration to all factors in the situation and taking care to minimize possible adverse effects. Social workers should assist in making appropriate arrangements for continuation of services when necessary *(NASW Code of Ethics, 1999–1.16 Termination of Services).*

Social workers in fee-for-service settings may terminate services to clients who are not paying an overdue balance if the financial contractual arrangements have been made clear to a client, if a client does not pose an imminent danger to self or others, and if the clinical and other consequences of the current nonpayment have been addressed and discussed with a client *(NASW Code of Ethics, 1999–1.16 Termination of Services).*

Social workers should not terminate services to pursue a social, financial, or sexual relationship with a client *(NASW Code of Ethics, 1999–1.16 Termination of Services).*

Social workers who anticipate the termination or interruption of services to clients should notify clients promptly and seek the transfer, referral, or continuation of services in relation to client needs and preferences *(NASW Code of Ethics, 1999–1.16 Termination of Services).*

Social workers who are leaving an employment setting should inform clients of appropriate options for the continuation of services and of the benefits and risks of the options *(NASW Code of Ethics, 1999–1.16 Termination of Services).*

It is *unethical to continue to treat clients when services are no longer needed or in their best interests.*

A social worker may terminate services to clients who are not paying an overdue balance if the financial contractual arrangements have been made clear to clients and they are not in imminent danger to self or others. Nonpayment consequences should also be discussed with clients prior to termination.

Another standard also relevant to termination of services mandates that social workers should make reasonable efforts to ensure continuity of services in the event that services are interrupted by factors such as unavailability, relocation, illness, disability, or death *(NASW Code of Ethics, 1999–1.15 Interruption of Services).*

BIOETHICAL ISSUES

Social workers are challenged in today's society by technology and medical advances.

Bioethics is the study of the ethical and moral implications of new biological discoveries and biomedical advances, as in the fields of genetic engineering and drug research. The National Commission for the Protection of Human Subjects of Biomedical and Behavioral Research was initially established in 1974 to identify the ethical principles that should be implemented during the conduct of biomedical and behavioral research involving human subjects. However, the fundamental principles announced in the Belmont Report (1979)—namely, autonomy, beneficence, and justice—have influenced the thinking of bioethicists. Nonmaleficence, human dignity, and the sanctity of life can also be added to this list of cardinal values.

Some areas of health sciences that are the subject of bioethical analysis include abortion, artificial insemination, assisted suicide, cloning, contraception, life support, organ donation, sex reassignment surgery, stem cell research, surrogacy, and transplants.

IDENTIFICATION AND RESOLUTION OF ETHICAL DILEMMAS

An ethical dilemma is a predicament when a social worker must decide between two viable solutions that seem to have similar ethical value. Sometimes two viable ethical solutions can conflict with each other. Social workers should be aware of any conflicts between personal and professional values and deal with them responsibly.

In instances where social workers' ethical obligations conflict with agency policies or relevant laws or regulations, they should make a responsible effort to resolve the conflict in a manner that is consistent with the values, principles, and standards expressed in the *Code of Ethics*.

In order to resolve this conflict, ethical problem-solving is needed.

Essential Steps in Ethical Problem-Solving

1. Identify ethical standards, as defined by the professional *Code of Ethics*, that are being compromised (always go to the *Code of Ethics* first—do not rely on supervisor or coworkers)

2. Determine whether there is an ethical issue or dilemma

3. Weigh ethical issues in light of key social work values and principles as defined by the *Code of Ethics*

4. Suggest modifications in light of the prioritized ethical values and principles that are central to the dilemma

5. Implement modifications in light of prioritized ethical values and principles

6. Monitor for new ethical issues or dilemmas

APPLYING ETHICS TO PRACTICE SITUATIONS

Social workers' primary responsibility is to promote the well-being of clients. In general, clients' interests are primary. However, social workers' responsibility to the larger society or specific legal obligations may, on limited occasions, supersede the loyalty owed clients, and clients should be so advised *(NASW Code of Ethics, 1999–1.01 Commitment to Clients)*. Examples include when a social worker is required by law to report that a client has abused a child or has threatened to harm self or others.

Sometimes in practice, ethical issues can arise related to the payment of services. These standards indicate what rules social workers should follow in these situations.

When setting fees, social workers should ensure that the fees are fair, reasonable, and commensurate with the services performed. Consideration should be given to clients' ability to pay *(NASW Code of Ethics, 1999–1.13 Payment for Services)*.

Social workers should avoid accepting goods or services from clients as payment for professional services. Bartering arrangements, particularly involving services, create the potential for conflicts of interest, exploitation, and inappropriate boundaries in social workers' relationships with clients. Social workers should explore and may participate in bartering only *in very limited circumstances* when it can be demonstrated that such arrangements are an accepted practice among professionals in the local community, considered to be essential for the provision of services, negotiated without coercion, and entered into at a client's initiative and with a client's informed consent. Social workers who accept goods or services from clients as payment for professional services assume the full burden of demonstrating that this arrangement will not be detrimental to a client or the professional relationship *(NASW Code of Ethics, 1999–1.13 Payment for Services)*.

Social workers should not solicit a private fee or other remuneration for providing services to clients who are entitled to such available services through social workers' employers or agencies *(NASW Code of Ethics, 1999–1.13 Payment for Services)*.

Social workers *should obtain information on procedures for using insurance coverage* when a client wants to use an employee benefit package for behavioral health services.

RESPONSIBILITY TO SEEK SUPERVISION

The short-term objectives of supervision are to increase a social worker's capacity to work more effectively, to provide a work context conducive to productivity, and to help a social worker take satisfaction in his or her work. *The ultimate objective is to assure the delivery of the most effective and efficient client services.*

Social workers who are administrators should take reasonable steps to ensure that adequate agency or organizational resources are available to provide appropriate staff supervision.

Competence is essential for ethical social work practice and social workers must be competent in the services that they are providing (NASW *Code of Ethics, 1999–1.04 Competence*). In order to be competent, they must keep abreast of new developments in the field and obtain supervision.

Social workers should provide services and represent themselves as competent only within the boundaries of their education, training, license, certification, consultation received, supervised experience, or other relevant professional experience (NASW *Code of Ethics, 1999–1.04 Competence*).

Social workers should provide services in substantive areas or use intervention techniques or approaches that are new to them only after engaging in appropriate study, training, consultation, and supervision from people who are competent in those interventions or techniques (NASW *Code of Ethics, 1999–1.04 Competence*).

When generally recognized standards do not exist with respect to an emerging area of practice, social workers should exercise careful judgment and take responsible steps (including appropriate education, research, training, consultation, and supervision) to ensure the competence of their work and to protect clients from harm (NASW *Code of Ethics, 1999–1.04 Competence*).

If a supervisor needs to talk with a social worker about a problem situation, he or she should meet privately with the social worker to discuss the matter.

USE OF PROFESSIONAL DEVELOPMENT TO IMPROVE PRACTICE

Professions enjoy a high social status, regard, and esteem conferred upon them by society. This high esteem arises primarily from the higher social function of their work, which is regarded as vital to society as a whole and, thus, special and valuable in nature. All professions involve technical, specialized, and highly skilled work, often referred to as "professional expertise." Training for this work involves obtaining degrees and professional qualifications (i.e., licensure) without which entry to the profession is barred. Training also requires regular updating of skills through continuing education.

Professional development refers to skills and knowledge attained for effective service delivery and career advancement. Professional development encompasses all types of learning opportunities, ranging from formal coursework and conferences to informal learning opportunities situated in practice. There are a variety of approaches to professional development, including *consultation, coaching, communities of practice, mentoring, reflective supervision, and technical assistance.*

Social workers often go through various stages of professional development, including:

1. Orientation and job induction
2. Autonomous worker
3. Member of a service team (independence to interdependence)
4. Development of specialization
5. Preparation to be mentor or supervisor

PROFESSIONAL BOUNDARIES

Many standards speak to the professional boundaries that social workers should maintain with clients. These include those related to sexual relationships, physical contact, and sexual harassment.

The standards that govern social work practice address the use of physical contact with clients. Setting clear, appropriate, and sensitive boundaries that govern physical contact are essential for professional practice *(NASW Code of Ethics, 1999–1.10 Physical Contact)*. Social workers should not engage in physical contact with clients when there is a possibility of psychological harm to a client as a result of the contact (such as cradling or caressing clients).

Physical contact or other activities of a sexual nature with clients are clearly not allowed by social workers.

Social workers should under no circumstances engage in sexual activities or sexual contact with current clients, whether such contact is consensual or forced *(NASW Code of Ethics, 1999–1.09 Sexual Relationships)*.

Social workers should not engage in sexual activities or sexual contact with clients' relatives or other individuals with whom clients maintain a close personal relationship when there is a risk of exploitation or potential harm to a client. Sexual activity or sexual contact with clients' relatives or other individuals with whom clients maintain a personal relationship has the potential to be harmful to a client and may make it difficult for a social worker and client to maintain appropriate professional boundaries. Social workers—not their clients, their clients' relatives, or other individuals with whom a client maintains a personal relationship—assume the full burden for setting clear, appropriate, and culturally sensitive boundaries *(NASW Code of Ethics, 1999–1.09 Sexual Relationships)*.

Social workers should not engage in sexual activities or sexual contact with former clients because of the potential for harm to a client. If social workers engage in conduct contrary to this prohibition or claim that an exception to this prohibition is warranted because of extraordinary circumstances, it is social workers—not their clients—who assume the full burden of demonstrating that the former client has not been exploited, coerced, or manipulated, intentionally or unintentionally *(NASW Code of Ethics, 1999–1.09 Sexual Relationships).*

Social workers should not provide clinical services to individuals with whom they have had a prior sexual relationship. Providing clinical services to a former sexual partner has the potential to be harmful to the individual and is likely to make it difficult for a social worker and individual to maintain appropriate professional boundaries *(NASW Code of Ethics, 1999–1.09 Sexual Relationships).*

In addition, social workers should not sexually harass clients, including sexual advances, sexual solicitation, requests for sexual favors, and other verbal or physical conduct of a sexual nature *(NASW Code of Ethics, 1999–1.11 Sexual Harassment).*

Confidentiality

10

LEGAL AND ETHICAL ISSUES REGARDING CONFIDENTIALITY, INCLUDING ELECTRONIC COMMUNICATION

Social workers should respect clients' right to privacy. Social workers should not solicit private information from clients unless it is essential to providing services or conducting social work evaluation or research. Once private information is shared, standards of confidentiality apply (NASW Code of Ethics, 1999–1.07 Privacy and Confidentiality).

Social workers may disclose confidential information when appropriate with valid consent from a client or a person legally authorized to consent on behalf of a client (NASW Code of Ethics, 1999–1.07 Privacy and Confidentiality).

Social workers should protect the confidentiality of all information obtained in the course of professional service, except for compelling professional reasons. The general expectation that social workers will keep information confidential does not apply when disclosure is necessary to prevent serious, foreseeable, and imminent harm to a client or other identifiable person. In all instances, social workers should disclose the least amount of confidential information necessary to achieve the desired purpose; only information that is directly relevant to the purpose for which the disclosure is made should be revealed (NASW Code of Ethics, 1999–1.07 Privacy and Confidentiality).

Social workers should inform clients, to the extent possible, about the disclosure of confidential information and the potential consequences, when feasible, before the disclosure is made. This applies whether social workers disclose confidential information on the basis of a legal requirement or client consent (NASW Code of Ethics, 1999–1.07 Privacy and Confidentiality).

Social workers should discuss with clients and other interested parties the nature of confidentiality and limitations of clients' right to confidentiality.

Social workers should review with clients circumstances where confidential information may be requested and where disclosure of confidential information may be legally required. This discussion should occur as soon as possible in a social worker–client relationship and as needed throughout the course of the relationship (*NASW Code of Ethics, 1999–1.07 Privacy and Confidentiality*).

When social workers provide counseling services to families, couples, or groups, social workers should seek agreement among the parties involved concerning each individual's right to confidentiality and obligation to preserve the confidentiality of information shared by others. Social workers should inform participants in family, couples, or group counseling that social workers cannot guarantee that all participants will honor such agreements (*NASW Code of Ethics, 1999–1.07 Privacy and Confidentiality*).

Social workers should inform clients involved in family, couples, marital, or group counseling of a social worker's, employer's, and agency's policy concerning a social worker's disclosure of confidential information among the parties involved in the counseling (*NASW Code of Ethics, 1999–1.07 Privacy and Confidentiality*).

Social workers should not disclose confidential information to third-party payers unless clients have authorized such disclosure (*NASW Code of Ethics, 1999–1.07 Privacy and Confidentiality*).

Social workers should not discuss confidential information in any setting unless privacy can be ensured. Social workers should not discuss confidential information in public or semipublic areas such as hallways, waiting rooms, elevators, and restaurants (*NASW Code of Ethics, 1999–1.07 Privacy and Confidentiality*).

Social workers should protect the confidentiality of clients during legal proceedings to the extent permitted by law. When a court of law or other legally authorized body orders social workers to disclose confidential or privileged information without a client's consent and such disclosure could cause harm to a client, social workers should request that the court withdraw the order or limit the order as narrowly as possible or maintain the records under seal, unavailable for public inspection (*NASW Code of Ethics, 1999–1.07 Privacy and Confidentiality*).

A subpoena and court order are not the same. When receiving a subpoena, a social worker should respond and claim privilege, but not turn over records unless the court issues a subsequent order to do so. As stated, when a social worker gets a court order, he or she should try to limit its scope and/or ask that the records be sealed.

Social workers should protect the confidentiality of clients when responding to requests from members of the media (*NASW Code of Ethics, 1999–1.07 Privacy and Confidentiality*).

Social workers should protect the confidentiality of clients' written and electronic records and other sensitive information. Social workers should take reasonable steps to ensure that clients' records are stored in a secure location and that clients' records are not available to others who are not authorized to have access *(NASW Code of Ethics, 1999–1.07 Privacy and Confidentiality).*

Social workers should take precautions to ensure and maintain the confidentiality of information transmitted to other parties through the use of computers, electronic mail, facsimile machines, telephones and telephone answering machines, and other electronic or computer technology. Disclosure of identifying information should be avoided whenever possible *(NASW Code of Ethics, 1999–1.07 Privacy and Confidentiality).*

Social workers should transfer or dispose of clients' records in a manner that protects clients' confidentiality and is consistent with state statutes governing records and social work licensure *(NASW Code of Ethics, 1999–1.07 Privacy and Confidentiality).*

Social workers should take reasonable precautions to protect client confidentiality in the event of a social worker's termination of practice, incapacitation, or death *(NASW Code of Ethics, 1999–1.07 Privacy and Confidentiality).*

Social workers should not disclose identifying information when discussing clients for teaching or training purposes unless a client has consented to disclosure of confidential information *(NASW Code of Ethics, 1999–1.07 Privacy and Confidentiality).*

Social workers should not disclose identifying information when discussing clients with consultants unless a client has consented to disclosure of confidential information or there is a compelling need for such disclosure *(NASW Code of Ethics, 1999–1.07 Privacy and Confidentiality).*

Social workers should protect the confidentiality of deceased clients consistent with the preceding standards *(NASW Code of Ethics, 1999–1.07 Privacy and Confidentiality).*

If a client sues a social worker, a social worker has the right to defend himself/herself and may need to release client information as part of this defense. A social worker should limit this disclosure only to information required for defense.

Confidentiality of minor records can be challenging, especially if a parent wants access to them and/or consents to their release. Social workers must be knowledgeable about ethical standards and laws that relate to the protection and release of minor records. Parents may have access to these records depending upon the age of the minor and the type of treatment or setting. Social workers treating minors with parents who may have joint or limited custody must also be aware of the rights of all parties to access and/or consent to their release.

USE OF CLIENT RECORDS

Social workers should provide clients with reasonable access to their records. Social workers who are concerned that clients' access to their records could cause serious misunderstanding or harm to a client should provide assistance in interpreting the records and consultation with a client regarding the records. Social workers should limit clients' access to their records, or portions of their records, **only in exceptional circumstances when there is compelling evidence that such access would cause serious harm to a client.** Both clients' requests and the rationale for withholding some or all of the record should be documented in clients' files *(NASW Code of Ethics, 1999–1.08 Access to Records).*

When providing clients with access to their records, social workers should take steps to protect the confidentiality of other individuals identified or discussed in such records.

ETHICAL AND LEGAL ISSUES REGARDING MANDATORY REPORTING

Social workers are required to disclose confidential information, sometimes against a client's wishes, to comply with mandatory reporting laws. Laws not only require social workers to report suspected cases of abuse and neglect, but there can be varying levels of civil and criminal liability for failing to do so.

This mandate causes ethical issues for social workers who have a commitment to their clients' interests as well as a responsibility to the larger society.

The majority of all reports of abuse and/or neglect came from professionals including medical personnel, law enforcement agents, educators, lawyers, and social workers.

OBTAINING INFORMED CONSENT

In instances when clients are not literate or have difficulty understanding the primary language used in the practice setting, social workers should take steps to ensure clients' comprehension. This may include providing clients with a detailed verbal explanation or arranging for a qualified interpreter or translator whenever possible *(NASW Code of Ethics, 1999–1.03 Informed Consent).*

In instances when clients lack the capacity to provide informed consent, social workers should protect clients' interests by seeking permission from an appropriate third party, informing clients consistent with clients' level of understanding. In such instances, social workers should seek to ensure that the third party acts in a manner consistent with the clients' wishes and interests.

Social workers should take reasonable steps to enhance such clients' ability to give informed consent *(NASW Code of Ethics, 1999–1.03 Informed Consent)*.

Social workers who provide services via electronic media (such as computer, telephone, radio, and television) should inform recipients of the limitations and risks associated with such services *(NASW Code of Ethics, 1999–1.03 Informed Consent)*.

Social workers should obtain clients' informed consent before audiotaping or videotaping clients or permitting observation of services to clients by a third party *(NASW Code of Ethics, 1999–1.03 Informed Consent)*.

When social workers act on behalf of clients who lack the capacity to make informed decisions, social workers should take reasonable steps to safeguard the interests and rights of those clients *(NASW Code of Ethics, 1999–1.14 Clients Who Lack Decision-Making Capacity)*.

In order to obtain informed consent, social workers must use clear and understandable language related to service purpose, risks, limits due to third-party payers, time frame, and right of refusal or withdrawal. If the client lacks capacity or is a minor, informed **consent** must be obtained by a responsible third party and **assent** must be obtained from the client.

11

Social Worker Roles
and Responsibilities

SOCIAL WORKER–CLIENT RELATIONSHIP PATTERNS

A social worker–client relationship is an emotional or connecting bond. The relationship is the communication bridge whereby messages pass over the bridge with greater or lesser difficulty, depending on the nature of the emotional connection or alliance.

A positive relationship is an important tool of helping. Social workers must create a warm, accepting, trustworthy, and dependable relationship with clients.

In working with a client, a social worker must convey a sense of respect for a client's individuality, as well as his or her right and capacity for *self-determination* and for being fully involved in the helping process from beginning to end.

The most consistent factor associated with beneficial outcomes of a helping relationship is a positive relationship between a social worker and a client, but other factors, such as a social worker's competence and the motivation and involvement of a client, are also influential.

CONCEPT OF EMPATHY

Empathic understanding involves being nonjudgmental, accepting, and genuine.

Empathic Communication

- Establishes rapport with clients—empathic communication is one means of bridging the gap between a social worker and client
- *Starts where a client is* and stays attuned to a client throughout the encounter (being perceptive to changes in frame of mind)
- Increases the level at which clients explore themselves and their problems
- Responds to a client's nonverbal messages (a social worker can observe body language and make explicit a client's feelings)
- Decreases defensiveness and engages a client in processing and testing new information
- Defuses anger that represents obstacles to progress

Empathic responding encourages more rational discussion and sets the stage for problem-solving. For those clients who have learned to cope with feelings of helplessness and frustration by becoming angry and/or violent, an empathic response may be the first step in engaging in helping relationships.

PROCESS OF ENGAGEMENT IN SOCIAL WORK PRACTICE

The beginning of the problem-solving process includes activities of a social worker and a client to be helped that are directed at (a) *becoming engaged with each other (engagement)*, (b) assessing a client's situation in order to select appropriate goals and the means of attaining them (assessment), and (c) planning how to employ these means (planning). During engagement, the limits to confidentiality must be explicitly stated at the beginning of this stage.

It is important to consider how a client feels about coming for help and to deal with any negative feelings a client may feel (particularly if a client is involuntarily seeking help). A social worker must be open to discussing these feelings openly, because very little in a client can be changed until negative feelings are addressed. If a social worker is empathic with a client, it may be possible to find a common ground between what a client wishes and what a social worker can legitimately do.

A social worker and a client establish a therapeutic alliance in which a client views himself or herself as an ally of a social worker. A working alliance or a willingness by a client to work with a social worker should be established. A working alliance is sometimes referred to as a treatment alliance.

A social worker should express hopefulness that change can occur.

Resistance may occur during this stage. If clients are resistant to engage, social workers should clarify the process or specify what will happen and discuss this ambivalence.

CONCEPT OF A HELPING RELATIONSHIP

The aim of helping varies with different situations. The purpose is to assist a client to develop new skills. The intent may be to stimulate or to bolster the self-confidence of a client. Again, a client may have requested assistance to think through a problem or to make a decision. In a helping relationship, a social worker is trying to constructively assist a client—that is, to have an impact on or to influence his or her thinking and acting. The influence is further presumed to be in the direction of increasing the autonomy, understanding, effectiveness, and skill of a client.

Helping is distinguished from the more common concepts of advice giving, reprimanding, or punishing. These often involve threats and seldom result in more than outward conformity or superficial change. They generally do not increase strength or willingness and ability to carry responsibility.

The core of the helping process is the relationship between a social worker and a client.

The relationship between a social worker and a client is expressed through *interaction*. This interaction is commonly thought of in terms of *verbal communication*, which is natural, because the greater part of treatment consists of talking. However, *nonverbal behavior* is also very important. Body posture, gestures, facial expressions, eye movements, and other reactions often express feelings and attitudes more clearly than do spoken words. It is often for these reasons that a social worker must be aware of his or her own feelings, attitudes, and responses, as well as those of a client if he or she is to understand what is taking place and be of assistance.

PRINCIPLES OF RELATIONSHIP BUILDING

A social worker cannot be useful in helping others unless he or she understands and is willing to accept the difficulties that all human beings encounter in trying to meet their needs. A social worker must know that the potential for all the weaknesses and strengths known to humanity exists at some level in every person. Social workers must also understand that human beings become more capable of dealing with their problems as they feel more adequate. Social workers recognize positive, as well as negative, aspects of a client, which will influence efforts to change and successful achievements of goals.

The interaction between a social worker and a client that takes place about a problem involves and is affected by the relationship between the two persons. Human beings act in terms of their feelings, attitudes, and understandings; hence, these must be taken into account and explored if the helping process is to result in change. Both a social worker and a client have objectives; a social worker's perceived objective is to be of assistance. *Clarification and definition of these objectives often become important parts of the helping process.* Both a social worker and a client have a degree of power (i.e., ability to influence the situation and the results).

PROFESSIONAL OBJECTIVITY IN THE SOCIAL WORKER–CLIENT RELATIONSHIP

Social worker communication should not be burdened with emotional investment; instead, social workers should be interested, genuinely concerned, and encouraging, while neither condemning nor praising.

The relationship between a social worker and a client must be productive, and must have certain characteristics. There must be *mutual acceptance and trust.* A client must feel he or she is understood and valued as a person, though his or her performance may be unsatisfactory. *If a client feels judged, he or she will not speak freely,* and his or her response will be to find ways to defend himself or herself and his or her acts.

A social worker accepts and understands a client's problems, recognizes the demands and the requirements of the situation, and assists a client to examine alternatives and potential consequences. A social worker does not tell a client what he or she should do. Only a client can and will decide, because he or she acts upon his or her feelings, insights, and/or understanding of himself or herself and the problem.

CONCEPTS OF TRANSFERENCE AND COUNTERTRANSFERENCE

Transference refers to redirection of a client's feelings for a significant person to a social worker. Transference was first described by Sigmund Freud, who acknowledged its importance for a better understanding of a client's feelings.

Transference is often manifested as an erotic attraction toward a social worker, but can be seen in many other forms such as rage, hatred, mistrust, parentification, extreme dependence, or even placing a social worker in an esteemed status.

When Freud initially encountered transference in his therapy with clients, he felt it was an obstacle to treatment success. But what he learned was that the analysis of the transference was actually the work needed to be done. The focus in psychoanalysis is, in large part, a social worker and a client recognizing the transference relationship and exploring the relationship's meaning.

Since the transference between a client and a social worker happens on an unconscious level, a social worker doing psychoanalysis uses transference to reveal unresolved conflicts a client has with childhood figures.

Countertransference is defined as redirection of a social worker's feelings toward a client, or more generally, as a social worker's emotional entanglement with a client. A social worker's recognition of his or her own countertransference is nearly as critical as understanding his or her transference. Not only does this help a social worker regulate his or her emotions in the therapeutic relationship, but it also gives a social worker valuable insight into what a client is attempting to elicit in him or her.

For example, a social worker who is sexually attracted to a client must understand this as countertransference, and look at how a client may be eliciting this reaction. Once it has been identified, a social worker can ask a client what his or her feelings are toward a social worker, and/or explore how they relate to unconscious motivations, desires, or fears.

USE OF SOCIAL WORKER–CLIENT RELATIONSHIP AS AN INTERVENTION TOOL

The therapeutic process calls for several basic conditions.

There must be trust with a social worker. Unless this condition exists, facts will be withheld and there will be no real exploration of problems. Trust grows as clients talk about themselves and their circumstances, revealing things they do not ordinarily disclose, and discovering that social workers do not condemn them. Trust does not come quickly.

There must be recognition that *the therapeutic process is a joint exploration.* Both a social worker and client must be willing to examine problems, attitudes, and feelings.

There must be *listening* on *both sides.* However, a social worker must listen more than a client does. There is no movement when a social worker is doing all the talking and a client listens passively. A social worker must behave in a manner that makes it easier for a client to speak freely by listening attentively, by *accepting what is said in a nonjudgmental manner*, and by giving occasional support or encouragement.

A social worker may be encouraging by simply repeating reflectively or paraphrasing what a client has said. A social worker may, without other comment, say, "Tell me more" or show acceptance when a client reveals ideas, attitudes, or behaviors that are generally viewed unfavorably. A social worker may also point out that other persons also have such attitudes or make similar mistakes. By assisting a client to speak more freely, a social worker not only furthers mutual exploration of the problem, but also frees a client of anxieties that stand in the way of readiness to accept suggestions. A social worker is also obligated to respect the confidence a client has placed in him or her and to refrain from sharing the information with others.

SOCIAL WORKER–CLIENT RELATIONSHIPS IN WORK WITH COMMUNITIES AND ORGANIZATIONS

The beginning phase of intervention involves *problem recognition, problem definition, and assessment of information pertaining to a problem.*

- Problem recognition is when a community identifies a problem. For instance, "Nobody knows each other around here" is redefined as a problem of community cohesion.

- Problem definition seeks to focus and identify the causes of particular community problems.

- Information gathering seeks to put factual information together based on the problem definition. Facts may or may not bear out the causal assumptions. Needs assessments are sometimes done first in order to provide the basis for problem recognition. Information gathering can range from very simple (information from informal discussions with community members) to more detailed and factual (i.e., statistics to provide a set of specific and empirical bases for community discussion). In the beginning phase, the needs assessment serves a dual purpose—(a) it generates facts and (b) it involves community members in activities that concern the community.

The middle phase emphasizes *goal selection, prioritization, and goal achievement.*

- By the beginning of this phase, a number of possible action steps will have been suggested by various members of the community. Frequently, the very process of discussion of goal alternatives results in the clear selection or desirability of one particular goal over others.

- A social worker needs to continue a process of interaction and encouragement with community members around the process of selecting a goal and prioritizing the efforts needed to get to that goal.

- A social worker helps a decision to occur, but also raises questions and concerns about particular courses of action to be sure that all implications have been taken into consideration. Social workers must continually work with clients and client systems to help them understand the impact of the particular actions that they are contemplating.

- Also, a social worker raises questions about the specific steps needed to move toward implementation. *Community members must take primary responsibility in carrying out the community's goal.*

The ending phase contains two subparts: *(a) operation* and *(b) termination.*

- Operation involves the implementation of the actual activities decided on in goal selection. A social worker assists the community in the actual carrying out of the plan and may even take part in operationalizing the plan, but does not become the implementer in lieu of community involvement.

- Goal implementation always represents a high point for the community and is frequently the result of months or even years of community change effort. However, this may also present a problem since the process is not over.

- *Evaluations must occur* and can range from simple debriefings of community members to complex numerical and statistical presentations about impact, percent of change, and so on.

- A community will be able, using its own leadership that has been developed, to continue the kinds of activities it has just completed.

SOCIAL WORKER–CLIENT RELATIONSHIPS IN WORK WITH SMALL GROUPS

Task groups are an essential means by which the goals of a social worker are accomplished. They provide a forum to exchange information and give and receive feedback; for the distribution of tasks; for planning, decision making, and problem-solving; and for the provision of needed support.

Two elements are critical to the success or effectiveness of task groups: *task accomplishment and group maintenance.* Task accomplishment emphasizes the group's productivity and requires that groups be well-organized and goal-oriented.

Group maintenance refers to members' satisfaction with the group and includes both emotional and social components.

There are techniques that social workers will need to employ in their work and when resolving conflicts within task groups:

Bargaining: Bargaining involves exchanging alternatives until an agreement is reached. Bargaining is useful only when there are several acceptable alternatives.

Persuasion: One member may attempt to persuade another member to change his or her position by providing factual information that is relevant to the conflict. This technique works only when the receiving member is willing to consider the information.

Problem-solving: Problem-solving involves a more flexible and open approach than bargaining and requires that both parties have a minimum level of mutual trust and a willingness to consider the other's point of view. Problem-solving is most effective when there is at least one solution to the conflict that is equally beneficial to those who disagree.

Superordinate goals: Conflicts can sometimes be defused by deemphasizing the current conflict and focusing, instead, on the overriding goals that the parties can achieve only through cooperation with one another.

METHODS USED TO CLARIFY ROLES OF THE SOCIAL WORKER

Problems can arise when a client is not clear on a social worker's role. Initial clarification should be made during engagement and should be discussed during the therapeutic process if the role of a social worker changes.

Role is a behavior prescribed for an individual occupying a designated status.

Social role theory has some important terms that relate to role issues.

- *Role ambiguity*: lack of clarity of role
- *Role complementarity*: the role is carried out in an expected way (i.e., parent–child; social worker–client)
- *Role discomplementarity*: the role expectations of others differs from one's own
- *Role reversal*: when two or more individuals switch roles
- *Role conflict*: incompatible or conflicting expectations

SOCIAL WORKER'S ROLES IN THE PROBLEM-SOLVING PROCESS

People generally like to give advice. It gives them the feeling of being competent and important. Hence, social workers may easily fall into this *inappropriate* role without taking into account the abilities, the fears, and the interests of clients and/or their circumstances.

Social workers should also not be insensitive to clients' resistance. When a client does not claim any difficulties, is unable or refuses to talk, explains that it is someone else's fault, and/or denies what has happened, a social worker may try to argue or in other ways exert pressure. This response tends to increase a client's resistance. This approach does nothing for a client.

A social worker may also confuse the situation and hinder clarification of the problem. In an effort to establish a relationship, a social worker may overpraise or fail to confront a client. A client must look at his or her own role in the situation and recognize his or her own limitations.

Social worker roles in the problem-solving process include consultant, advocate, case manager, catalyst, broker, mediator, facilitator, instructor, mobilizer, resource allocator, and so on.

CLIENT'S ROLES IN THE PROBLEM-SOLVING PROCESS

Clients often tend to think of themselves and their problems as unique. A client may think his or her difficulties are so different from those of others that no one else could ever understand them. He or she may even enjoy this feeling of uniqueness. It may be a defense against the discomfort of exploring his or her fears of being like others. At this point, a client may not be ready to look at the problem. *It is hard to admit difficulties, even to oneself.*

There may also be concerns as to whether social workers can really be trusted. Some people, because of unfortunate experiences in their childhoods, grow up with distrust of others. Furthermore, people are generally afraid of what others will think of them.

A client may only be looking for sympathy, support, and/or empathy, rather than searching for a new way to solve his or her difficulties. A client may not see that change must occur. When a social worker points out some of the ways in which a client is contributing to his or her own problems, he or she stops listening. Solving the problem often requires a client to uncover some aspects of himself or herself that he or she has avoided thinking about in the past and wants to avoid thinking about in the future.

A client may have struggled very hard to make himself or herself an independent person. *The thought of depending on or receiving help from another individual seems to violate something.* A client must constantly defend against a sense of weakness and may have difficulty listening to and using the assistance of another person.

There are also many clients who have strong needs to lean on others. Some spend much of their lives looking for others on whom they can be dependent. In the helping situation, they may constantly and inappropriately seek to repeat this pattern.

INFLUENCE OF THE SOCIAL WORKER'S VALUES ON THE SOCIAL WORKER–CLIENT RELATIONSHIP

Social workers must recognize values that may *inhibit* the therapeutic relationship.

1. **Universalism—There is one acceptable norm or standard for everyone** *versus* there are other valid standards that have been developed by people that they have determined to be most useful to them.

2. **Dichotomous "either-or" thinking; differences are inferior, wrong, bad** *versus* differences are just different and coexist.

3. **Heightened ability/value on separating, categorizing, numbering, "left-brain"** *versus* "right-brain" or "whole picture." Mental activity is highly valued to the exclusion of physical and spiritual experiences. Persons are studied in isolation, not as part of a group or interrelated with their environment.

4. **High value on control, constraint, restraint** *versus* value on flexibility, emotion/feelings, expressiveness, spirituality. What cannot be controlled and definitively defined is deemed nonexistent, unimportant, unscientific, or deviant/inferior. Reality is defined with the assumption of objectivity; subjective reality is viewed as invalid because it cannot be consistently replicated by many people.

5. **Measure of self comes from outside, and is only in contrast to others** *versus* value comes from within—you are worthwhile because you were born, and you strive to live a life that is in harmony with others and the environment. Worth is measured by accumulation of wealth or status (outside measures)—therefore, one can only feel good if one is better than someone else, or accumulates more than someone else, or has a higher status.

6. **Power is defined as "power over" others, mastery over environment** *versus* "power through" or in harmony with others; by sharing power, power can be expanded, and each becomes more powerful.

DUAL RELATIONSHIPS

Social workers must ensure that they do not engage in dual or multiple relationships that may impact on the treatment of clients. The standards related to this area provide guidelines that can assist social workers if such relationships emerge (*NASW Code of Ethics, 1999—1.06 Conflicts of Interest*).

Social workers should be alert to and avoid conflicts of interest that interfere with the exercise of professional discretion and impartial judgment. Social workers should inform clients when a real or potential conflict of interest arises and take reasonable steps to resolve the issue in a manner that makes clients' interests primary and protects clients' interests to the greatest extent possible. In some cases, protecting clients' interests may require termination of the professional relationship with proper referral of clients (*NASW Code of Ethics, 1999—1.06 Conflicts of Interest*).

Social workers should not take unfair advantage of any professional relationship or exploit others to further their personal, religious, political, or business interests (*NASW Code of Ethics, 1999—1.06 Conflicts of Interest*).

Social workers should not engage in dual or multiple relationships with clients or former clients in which there is a risk of exploitation or potential harm to a client. In instances when dual or multiple relationships are unavoidable, social workers should take steps to protect clients and are responsible for setting clear, appropriate, and culturally sensitive boundaries. Dual or multiple relationships occur when social workers relate to clients in more than one relationship, whether professional, social, or business. Dual or multiple relationships can occur simultaneously or consecutively (NASW Code of Ethics, 1999—1.06 Conflicts of Interest).

When social workers provide services to two or more people who have a relationship with each other (for example, couples, family members), social workers should clarify with all parties which individuals will be considered clients and the nature of social workers' professional obligations to the various individuals who are receiving services. Social workers who anticipate a conflict of interest among the individuals receiving services or who anticipate having to perform in potentially conflicting roles (for example, when a social worker is asked to testify in a child custody dispute or divorce proceedings involving clients) should clarify their role with the parties involved and take appropriate action to minimize any conflict of interest (NASW Code of Ethics, 1999—1.06 Conflicts of Interest).

In addition, social workers engaged in evaluation or research should be alert to and avoid conflicts of interest and dual relationships with participants, should inform participants when a real or potential conflict of interest arises, and should take steps to resolve the issue in a manner that makes participants' interests primary (NASW Code of Ethics, 1999—5.02 Evaluation and Research).

INFLUENCE OF CULTURAL DIVERSITY ON THE SOCIAL WORKER–CLIENT RELATIONSHIP

A social worker's self-awareness about his or her own attitudes, values, and beliefs about cultural differences and a willingness to acknowledge cultural differences are critical factors in working with diverse populations. A social worker is responsible for bringing up and addressing issues of cultural difference with a client and is also ethically responsible for being culturally competent by obtaining the appropriate knowledge, skills, and experience.

Social workers should:

1. Move from being culturally unaware to being aware of their own heritage and the heritage of others
2. Value and celebrate differences of others rather than maintaining an ethnocentric stance

3. Have an awareness of personal values and biases and how they may influence relationships with clients

4. Demonstrate comfort with racial and cultural differences between themselves and clients

5. Have an awareness of personal and professional limitations

6. Acknowledge their own racial attitudes, beliefs, and feelings

Practice Test

170 Question Practice Test

This practice test contains 170 questions, but remember that your score on the actual examination will be based on 150 questions because 20 items are being piloted. As you won't know which items will be scored and determine whether or not you pass, you will need to complete all 170 questions. Thus, this practice test has 170 questions so that you can gauge the length of time that it takes you to complete an equivalent number of questions. The questions in each domain or area are in random order on this practice test, as they are on the actual examination, and there is a similar distribution of questions from each section as will appear on your actual examination.

Human Development, Diversity,
and Behavior in the Environment

48 Questions

Assessment and Intervention Planning

41 Questions

Direct and Indirect Practice

36 Questions

Professional Relationships, Values, and Ethics

45 Questions

The best way to use this practice test is as a mock examination, which means:

a. Take it AFTER you have completed your studying—do not memorize answers to these questions.

b. Do not apply the answers to these questions to the actual examination or you may miss subtle differences in each question that can distinguish the correct from the incorrect answer.

c. Take it in its entirety during a 4-hour block of time to show yourself that you can finish in the allotted time period for the examination.

d. Do not look up the answers until you are completely finished with the entire practice test, and do not worry if you get incorrect answers. Remember, this examination is not one in which you can expect to get all of the answers correct. **The number of questions that you will need to answer correctly generally varies from 93 to 106 correct of the 150 scored items.**

1. Which of the following is NOT true about motivation to change?

    A. Motivation fluctuates from one time to another
    B. Motivation can be increased by working to remove barriers to change
    C. Motivation is driven by hope or the belief that life can be different
    D. Motivation that is imposed by external forces is more salient than that which is intrinsic

2. Evidence-based social work practice can BEST be defined as:

    A. Interventions that a social worker has gained training and experience in delivering
    B. Treatment that yields the most cost-effective outcomes according to a cost–benefit analysis
    C. Decision making based on the conscientious, explicit, and judicious use of research knowledge, clinical expertise, social work values, and client wishes
    D. Practice evaluations that adhere to scientific principles

3. What are the stages of change in sequential order?

    A. Precontemplation, preparation, contemplation, action, maintenance, and relapse
    B. Preparation, action, precontemplation, contemplation, maintenance, and relapse
    C. Preparation, precontemplation, contemplation, action, maintenance, and relapse
    D. Precontemplation, contemplation, preparation, action, maintenance, and relapse

4. Which of the following is NOT an essential step in ethical problem-solving?

    A. Identifying the ethical standards that may be compromised
    B. Determining whether there is an ethical dilemma
    C. Weighing ethical issues in light of social work values and principles
    D. Asking a supervisor to monitor practice to identify new ethical issues or dilemmas

5. A young boy is stopped by a police officer and claims that he is a member of the armed forces, though it is obvious that he is not. This assertion by the boy is MOST likely a:

    A. Comorbid thought
    B. Dissociation
    C. Folie à deux
    D. Delusion

6. A social work administrator is having trouble finding a group home manager for a new program scheduled to open in two weeks. Further delays in locating staff will delay clients from moving into the program. The administrator temporarily hires her niece, who just graduated with a social work degree, for this position. This action is:

   A. Ethical because the niece is clearly qualified for the position
   B. Unethical because this is a conflict of interest
   C. Ethical because the position is temporary and ensures clients get the services needed
   D. Unethical because clients will experience staff turnover when a new manager is hired

7. A social worker is interested in seeing the extent to which current clients are satisfied with a new relapse prevention program. The social worker distributes a client satisfaction survey to those in the program. The social worker then collects the surveys and analyzes the results that are presented to a management team in the agency. The social worker is conducting which type of evaluation?

   A. Summative
   B. Experimental
   C. Quasi-experimental
   D. Formative

8. Which of the following is an example of social stratification?

   A. A child is not included in group activities in school because of his or her poor social skills
   B. Children who are violent need to be segregated from their peers
   C. A child with social deficits is assumed to be delayed in cognition without additional assessment
   D. Children from affluent households receive a better public education than those from low-income households

9. During an intake interview, a client reports that she is extremely depressed and has self-destructive thoughts. She has had prior suicide attempts, but tells the social worker not to worry as she won't "do it again." The social worker should FIRST:

   A. Tell the client that her decision not to harm herself is a good one
   B. Explore with the client what is causing her depression
   C. Conduct a safety assessment
   D. Refer the client to a psychiatrist for a medication evaluation

10. A client with a Social Anxiety Disorder will MOST likely be prescribed which of the following medications to take on an ongoing basis?

    A. Zoloft (sertraline)
    B. Mellaril (thioridazine)
    C. Thorazine (chlorpromazine)
    D. Valium (diazepam)

11. A social worker is appointed by the court to conduct a child custody evaluation for a couple that is divorcing. The mother reports that her husband is verbally abusive, controlling, and neglects the children when they are in his care. She reports that the children have missed a lot of school when staying with their father because he does not assist with getting them ready for school or doing their homework. The father states that his wife is lazy, irresponsible, and cannot meet the children's basic needs. He reports that the school frequently has to provide lunch for the children because the mother does not supply it when they are in her care. In order to BEST evaluate the legitimacy of the information, the social worker should:

    A. Ask the husband and wife to put their allegations in writing and sign them, attesting to their accuracy
    B. Determine whether the husband or wife have had any past instances with being untruthful
    C. Always speak to the husband and wife together so that they are more likely to be honest
    D. Obtain information from school personnel and records after obtaining parental consent

12. A social worker is facilitating a psychotherapy group for individuals who are in recovery from substance abuse. After group, a client mentions that she has been having problems dealing with job stress without the use of substances. In order to meet this client's needs, the social worker should:

    A. Recommend that the client see the social worker individually in addition to the group therapy because she appears to need some additional support
    B. Suggest that the client bring this topic up in the group next week to see if others are having similar problems
    C. Evaluate whether group therapy is the best treatment modality for the client due to the issue being mentioned to the social worker outside of the group context
    D. Determine if there is an employee assistance program in the client's work setting to assist

13. An 11-year-old child would like to start helping around the house with chores. She approaches her mother many times, but is told she cannot assist because "she won't do it right." During several attempts to do things on her own, she is scolded. According to psychosocial development theory, she may experience doubts in her abilities due to a crisis in which of the following stages?

   A. Industry versus inferiority
   B. Initiative versus guilt
   C. Autonomy versus shame/doubt
   D. Generativity versus stagnation

14. A social worker employed in a hospital is asked to use a SOAP format in a client's record. In this format, the "A" stands for:

   A. Action plan
   B. Assessment
   C. Active treatment
   D. Adjustments to services needed

15. Aphasia is BEST defined as difficulty with:

   A. Walking or running
   B. Common motor skills such as combing hair, despite normal strength
   C. Understanding language or using language to speak or write
   D. Recognizing familiar objects

16. Culture-bound syndromes in the *DSM-5* are replaced by all of the following concepts EXCEPT:

   A. Cultural syndromes
   B. Cultural stratification
   C. Cultural idioms of distress
   D. Cultural explanations

17. A social worker receives a court order to provide records of a former client. In this instance, the social worker should submit the records:

   A. And try to contact the client to inform her about the disclosure
   B. With the contact information of the client so the court can contact her about the release
   C. But not contact the client as court orders are not to be discussed by anyone other than judges and attorneys
   D. And write to the judge to see if he or she wants the client to know about the court order

18. A family comes into treatment because of their young daughter's behavior. They report, upon intake, that she yells at her parents, doesn't listen, and complains about their behavior. There is little progress during the course of treatment and the girl reports that she has no intention of changing. After the sixth session, a social worker tells the girl that she cannot help with her behavior and she should continue to "do as she wishes." According to strategic family therapy, the social worker's directive is known as a:

A. Paradoxical intent
B. Pretend technique
C. Relabeling paradigm
D. Differentiation response

19. A social worker is leaving one agency to work at another. In order to address this situation ethically, the social worker should:

A. Not inform clients in order to avoid causing them undue stress and harm
B. Advise clients that it would be best for them to transfer services to the social worker's new agency to avoid any interruptions in treatment
C. Inform clients of appropriate options for the continuation of services and the benefits and risks of the options
D. Discontinue services to clients immediately

20. Federal law requires health care facilities that receive Medicare and Medicaid reimbursements to do all of the following with regard to advance directives EXCEPT:

A. Inform clients of their rights to have advance directives that will allow them to make decisions regarding their health care
B. Use a portion of their revenues to assist clients with the costs associated with creating advance directives
C. Ask clients if they have advance directives and document their responses
D. Provide education about advance directives

21. In which of the following circumstances is task-centered treatment NOT recommended?

A. When the client wants to see immediate results or changes in circumstances
B. When the client is anxious to be an active part of the change process
C. When there is a time limited period in which to work with the client
D. When the client is addressing long-standing problems that are complex in nature

22. A client is currently taking Clozaril for the treatment of Schizophrenia. The client is MOST likely going to be required to undergo what medical monitoring due to this medication use?

    A. Weight checks
    B. Blood work
    C. Dietary restrictions
    D. Exercise regimen

23. Which of the following inhibits the establishment of a therapeutic relationship?

    A. A universalism approach or the acceptance of a standard set of norms or standards
    B. A pluralistic approach that values cultural pluralism
    C. Clients examined as being influenced by their environment with problems being seen as resulting from role ambiguity rather than individual deficits
    D. Flexible treatment approaches that take into account the subjective realities of clients

24. Which of the following is NOT an exception to a social worker's duty to protect confidentiality?

    A. When a client poses a serious risk to self and others
    B. When child abuse is suspected
    C. When a client has violated criminal laws and has not been properly prosecuted
    D. When there is an imminent threat by a client to an identifiable third party

25. Which of the following theories is used to explain why clients in battering relationships will not leave until the benefits exceed the risks?

    A. Psychoanalytic
    B. Problem-solving
    C. Functional
    D. Social exchange

26. A social worker is working with a client who is anxious about public speaking. The social worker asks the client to close her eyes, visualize herself speaking to a large group, and describe her feelings related to the imaginary situation in detail. This technique by the social worker is known as:

    A. Covert modeling
    B. Self-modeling
    C. Live modeling
    D. Symbolic modeling

27. Which of the following is an example of role discomplementarity?

    A. A husband complains that his wife does not take responsibility for keeping the house clean and a wife is upset that her husband does not financially provide for the family
    B. A woman states that she does not like working and wants to quit her job
    C. A young child wants to play in the neighborhood unsupervised
    D. A man struggles to fit in time at home with his family due to his hectic work schedule

28. Which of the following is NOT one of six levels of cognition?

    A. Synthesis
    B. Knowledge
    C. Affective
    D. Evaluation

29. Which of the following is NOT a stated purpose of the professional *Code of Ethics*?

    A. To be used by malpractice insurance companies to mitigate liability
    B. To summarize the values on which the profession is based
    C. To be used by the profession to determine whether social workers have acted unethically
    D. To serve as a guide to socialize new social workers in the field

30. Which of the following is an example of role reversal?

    A. A mother who shares her 11-year-old daughter's clothes and collects stuffed animals
    B. A mother expecting her 11-year-old daughter to stay at home unsupervised
    C. A mother with relationship problems who is repeatedly emotionally comforted by her 11-year-old daughter
    D. A mother who arranges a date for her 11-year-old daughter

31. A social worker receives a subpoena from the courts in the mail for a former client's records. In this situation, a social worker should:

    A. Immediately send in the original records to the courts
    B. Prepare a summary of the records to send in immediately
    C. Claim privilege to protect the confidentiality of the client
    D. Ignore the subpoena because it relates to a former client and is not relevant

32. In the *DSM-5*, when a social worker provides a reason why a condition does not qualify for a disorder, it should be noted as:

    A. Not Otherwise Specified
    B. Other Specified

    C. Unspecified

    D. Not Specified Elsewhere

33. A client abruptly stops coming to therapy after the sixth session. She shows up at the office several weeks later demanding a copy of her records. The social worker does not believe that the information in the record could cause harm to the client, but denies access because the client did not provide any reason for the abrupt termination or reason for wanting the copies. The actions by the social worker are:

    A. Unethical because the client should have access to his or her record under *these* circumstances

    B. Ethical because the reason for the release must be disclosed to the social worker

    C. Ethical because the client terminated without notice

    D. Unethical because the client is always able to access his or her record under *any* circumstances

34. A client was referred to a mental health agency for treatment. Upon admission, he reported feeling lethargic and hopeless and had difficulty getting out of bed. Several weeks later, he states that he is sleepless, agitated, and unable to focus. Which of the following medications is the client MOST likely going to be prescribed?

    A. Ativan (lorazepam)

    B. Nardil (phenelzine)

    C. Lithium (lithium carbonate)

    D. Buspar (buspirone)

35. When clients are at high risk for relapse after discharge, all of the following should occur after termination EXCEPT:

    A. Regular assessments to determine whether services are needed

    B. Creation of client contracts that reinforce positive behaviors

    C. Utilization of natural supports and peer support services

    D. Follow-up to see whether discharge plans are being implemented

36. A social worker in private practice designs a standard intake form that includes questions about the client's demographic information including age, gender, marital status, sexual orientation, education, and drug/alcohol use. This form is:

    A. Ethical since it contains important information for the social worker to know in order to work with the client effectively

    B. Ethical since all of this information will be kept confidential

    C. Unethical since this information may not be needed for treatment

    D. Unethical unless the social worker makes it clear that the client has the choice as to whether to complete it

37. A social worker is charged with creating a behavioral objective to assist her client, John, in his educational setting. Which of the following statements is the BEST example of this type of objective?

   A. John will make eye contact during conversations in practical arts class at least 75% of the time
   B. John will be motivated to complete his homework daily in order to achieve a grade of a B or better
   C. The teacher will praise John during class at least 10 times per hour
   D. John will sit in his chair at least 80% of the time

38. A new client enters the office walking slowly, using a cane, and has difficulty picking up objects, swallowing, and speaking as a result of a stroke. The BEST diagnosis for this client is:

   A. Agnosia
   B. Ataxia
   C. Prosopagnosia
   D. Acalculia

39. Echolalia is BEST defined as:

   A. Mimicking another's speech
   B. Spontaneous movement
   C. Repetitive movements
   D. Odd mannerisms or actions

40. A man who is having problems at work finds that he is yelling at his children more and has begun to have marital issues with his wife. The husband is MOST likely using the defense mechanism of:

   A. Reaction formation
   B. Projection
   C. Conversion
   D. Displacement

41. Upon admission, a client reports that he has always feared disapproval and rejection from others in his life. Several weeks later, the client appears anxious and worried. When asked about his behavior, he states that he feels judged by the social worker and that the social worker is being critical of him when he sees her. The client's feelings are an example of:

   A. Countertransference
   B. Psychosis
   C. Paranoia
   D. Transference

42. Which of the following is the MOST significant change in the *DSM-5* concerning substance-related disorders?

    A. Substance Abuse and Substance Dependence have been combined into a single Substance Use Disorder

    B. Recurrent legal problems were added to the criteria for Substance Use Disorders

    C. Craving or a strong desire to use a substance was deleted from Substance Dependence

    D. Recurrent legal problems were deleted from the criteria for Substance Abuse

43. A social worker sees that a colleague is distracted when interacting with clients and is showing up for appointments late. The social worker learns that this behavior began several weeks earlier, after the death of her colleague's husband. In this instance, the social worker should:

    A. Give the colleague additional time to grieve and monitor the colleague's actions to see if the behavior subsides on its own

    B. Speak to a supervisor to see if the colleague's workload could be reduced for a period of time

    C. Contact the human resources department to see if there are employee assistance services available

    D. Speak to the colleague directly about the observations to see if additional assistance is needed

44. Which of the following is NOT true of life crises?

    A. They must be precipitated by major life events

    B. The ways in which they are addressed have a significant role in subsequent functioning

    C. They can produce healthier behavior if understood and overcome

    D. They produce anxiety, tension, and disequilibrium

45. Which of the following is true of BOTH networking in business and networking in social work practice?

    A. It aims to educate about the problems experienced by others and thereby help to effect system changes

    B. It aims to attract more individuals to organizations so that these entities can prosper

    C. It is beneficial for clients as it keeps the costs down through sharing of resources

    D. It creates a community and builds alliances around a common interest or goal

46. Which of the following is the MOST important benefit of community participation in social work practice?

    A. It puts the decision-making power partly or wholly with community members
    B. It shows the media that individuals want to get involved when there is a good cause
    C. It informs community members about the work that needs to be done to make change
    D. It divides the workload so that it can be distributed across a larger group

47. If a client has a Substance Use Disorder in addition to Schizophrenia, these two disorders are considered to be:

    A. Premorbid
    B. Comorbid
    C. Contraindicated
    D. Dissociated

48. A woman complains that her 7-year-old son "makes things up and exaggerates." He often adds information when recalling experiences and talks about knights and dragons being part of his everyday world. The woman is angry about this behavior and worried that it is an indication of some mental health problem. In order to best assist, the social worker should:

    A. Explain that the behaviors are associated with the preoperational thought stage of cognitive development
    B. Conduct a mental status examination on the child
    C. Refer the child for a mental health evaluation based upon the mother's concerns
    D. Determine whether this behavior is a concern to others, including his teachers

49. A social worker notices what appears to be burns on a child's arm and asks the child about these markings. The child responds that "grandma burned me, but mommy isn't going to let me go over there anymore so it's OK." The social worker should:

    A. Document the conversation in the file and make sure to check the child regularly in the future for burns or bruises
    B. Report the conversation immediately to child protective services
    C. Discuss the conversation with a supervisor at the next supervision session
    D. Contact the grandmother to validate this report by the child

50. A client has been in therapy for about 4 months and has made substantial progress toward achieving his goals. The social worker and client believe that continued treatment would be beneficial. However, the client recently lost his job and has been informed that his insurance coverage, which has been paying for the services, will end immediately. The client states that he cannot afford to pay the rate paid by the insurance company. In order to facilitate continued progress, the social worker should:

A. Suggest that the client now only pay the amount of the copay and keep track of what would have been paid by an insurance company so a payment plan can be put in place once the client is employed again

B. Brainstorm with the client about services that the client can provide in exchange for treatment

C. Terminate therapy immediately, but with the understanding that it will begin immediately upon enrollment in a new insurance plan

D. Discuss a feasible amount to be paid by the client while he is uninsured

51. Which of the following is NOT a key diagnostic criterion of paraphilic disorders according to the *DSM-5*?

A. Atypical sexual interests

B. Personal distress about sexual interests not strictly due to societal disapproval

C. Sexual desire or behavior that involves another person's psychological harm or from persons who are unwilling or unable to consent

D. Legal involvement due to sexual interests or behaviors

52. Which of the following is a limitation when using existing case records as the data source for the evaluation of client progress?

A. It saves time because the information is already available and does not have to be gathered

B. There are financial benefits because there are no additional costs associated with data collection

C. The scope of the evaluation is restricted to that which is explicitly stated in the file

D. It cannot be done unless the client consents in writing to allow such use

53. A client needs to access services from another organization. In order to BEST assist this client, a social worker should:

A. Let the client identify and contact agencies independently to avoid interfering with the client's right to self-determination

B. Refer the client to an agency that the social worker has a relationship with to ensure an easy transition

C. Work with the client to evaluate options and select an agency that the client thinks will best meet his or her needs

D. Contact the client's insurance company to see which agencies are participating providers

54. During an intake interview, a client uses derogatory language to refer to individuals of a particular ethnic group. This language causes the social worker to become angry. In order to appropriately deal with the anger, the social worker should:

A. Explain to the client in a professional manner that this language is inappropriate and upsets the social worker

B. Suggest that the client see another social worker in the agency without giving the client an explanation

C. Recognize the anger and discuss it later with the supervisor

D. Tell the client about the reaction so that a decision can be made by the client about whether the social worker is the best match for the client

55. A client who has Schizophrenia has not been taking his medication. He is in crisis, but does not pose a danger to himself or others. The client was recently discharged from an inpatient hospitalization after an involuntary commitment. In the social worker's opinion, the client would benefit from rehospitalization, but the client does not want to be readmitted. The social worker should:

A. Identify community resources to meet his immediate needs

B. Contact the hospital to see if he can be readmitted

C. Recommend that the client be involuntarily committed again to get the medication needed

D. Determine if he has a family member or someone who can persuade him to enter the hospital again

56. A client's insurance company threatens to discontinue to pay for services immediately if it does not receive the current treatment goals of the client. The social worker sends these goals without written consent from the client. This action by the social worker is:

A. Ethical since the client would not be able to continue services without the insurance payments

B. Unethical because such a release requires written consent

C. Ethical since treatment goals can be sent to an insurance company without written consent

D. Unethical or ethical, depending upon whether the social worker spoke to the client about insurance requirements at the beginning of treatment

57. A social worker is running a group with adolescents. One of the group members calls the social worker because she is very upset that

something that she said in group was disclosed to others in her school by another group member. The BEST method for the social worker to address this situation is to:

A. Individually contact the group member who disclosed the information to discuss the concern

B. Terminate the group member who disclosed the information in order to create a "safe" environment for the other participants

C. Suggest that the upset group member bring up her concern at the next group session

D. Develop a confidentiality agreement to be signed by all members at the next group session

58. Which of the following is NOT one of Freud's stages of psychosexual development?

A. Genital

B. Latency

C. Castration

D. Oral

59. Which is NOT true when an agency uses the services of a consultant?

A. The agency retains formal authority over agency practices, whereas a consultant has informal authority based on skills and knowledge

B. The agency must get consent for releases of information when sharing client information with a consultant

C. The agency is mandated to follow a consultant's recommendations

D. The agency must use a consultant who has demonstrated knowledge, expertise, and competence

60. A client expresses an attraction to the social worker during a therapy session. In order to address this issue ethically, the social worker should:

A. Explore it as a therapeutic issue, seek supervision, and document the disclosure in the client file

B. Ignore the overture and hope that the client does not express this attraction again

C. Immediately refer the client to another social worker in the agency because the current social worker cannot be objective once such a disclosure has occurred

D. Terminate services immediately in case a personal relationship develops

61. An agency that employs social workers has detailed job descriptions that delineate the best way to perform functions, closely supervises its employees, and ties employee pay increases to behaviors that promote

the goals of the organization. This agency is MOST likely using which of the following approaches to manage its workers?

A. Scientific management
B. Human relations
C. Systems
D. Contingency

62. Projective tests are based on which of the following theoretical approaches?

A. Behavior management
B. Psychoanalytic
C. Cognitive behavioral
D. Self psychology

63. Most models of spiritual development move from an individual being egocentric to eventually becoming a(n):

A. Conformist
B. Integrated being
C. Dichotomous thinker
D. Follower of blind faith

64. All of the following are true about empathetic communication EXCEPT:

A. Empathetic communication bridges the gap between the social worker and client by establishing rapport
B. Empathetic communication is nonjudgmental, accepting, and genuine
C. Empathic communication is verbal communication in which the client is engaged in oral problem-solving and processing of new information
D. Empathetic communication decreases defensiveness and encourages a more rational discussion of problems

65. A new client comes to the first appointment and is extremely anxious. She paces while in the waiting room and states that she "just needs to get some sleep." During the intake interview, the client reports that she is a recreational drug user. Based on her behavior, the client is MOST likely using:

A. Heroin
B. Cocaine
C. Marijuana
D. Oxycontin

66. A woman who is in a relationship that is physically abusive would like to begin couples counseling because she believes that helping her boyfriend to see her point of view may assist in decreasing the violence. In order to appropriately address this request, the social worker should:

    A. Suggest that she ask her boyfriend to come to the next session
    B. Ask if the social worker can contact the boyfriend to assess his interest in receiving couples counseling
    C. Explain to the woman that couples counseling should not take place at this time, given the physical abuse
    D. Contact the boyfriend about coming in for individual counseling with the suggestion that there be joint sessions with the two of them at times

67. A client has just been diagnosed with terminal cancer. Using a systems approach, the social worker should:

    A. Develop a plan for long-term care aimed at meeting the client's medical needs
    B. Work with the client on addressing the impacts of this prognosis on his or her psychological and spiritual well-being
    C. Consider whether continuing to treat the client is in the client's best interest given this prognosis
    D. Reexamine the treatment goals to see if they are still relevant or need to be revised given this health information

68. According to Freud, an adolescent in puberty is in which stage of psychosexual development?

    A. Genital
    B. Phallic
    C. Latency
    D. Anal

69. Which of the following is the BEST definition of empowerment?

    A. Obtaining resources to assist in improving a client's financial and social status
    B. Building skills and obtaining resources that will assist a client in controlling and making changes, if desired, in his or her own well-being
    C. Meeting basic needs in a client's life to facilitate growth toward self-actualization
    D. Creating alliances or power networks that can be used by a client to increase his or her social standing

70. A client is starting a new business and really needs a partner to assist with start-up activities. Without this help, the client will experience extreme financial hardship because she will not be able to bring in needed income to her household. The social worker has a lot of

business expertise that would be valuable to the client. In this situation, the social worker should:

A. Continue to serve the client, providing only emotional support during this crisis

B. Terminate services to the client to assist with the start-up business so that the client does not experience financial loss

C. Continue to serve the client, providing financial support in addition to emotional support during this crisis

D. Stop billing the client for a short period while assisting the client with business start-up, with the understanding that this arrangement is time limited

71. Which of the following is NOT considered as part of culturally informed intervention planning?

A. Involvement of family members in treatment

B. Use of individual versus group treatment modalities

C. Incorporation of alternative treatment approaches

D. Need for informed consent procedures

72. Which of the following statements about gender identity and/or sexual orientation is TRUE?

A. Pansexual refers to being attracted to individuals outside or independent of gender

B. Individuals who crossdress usually identify as homosexual

C. Sexual orientation and gender identity are related

D. Gender expression and gender identity must be congruent

73. A deceased client has:

A. All of the same rights to confidentiality as a living client, with the exception of billing records

B. Some of the same rights to confidentiality as a living client as decided by the executor of the estate

C. None of the same rights to confidentiality as a living client

D. All of the same rights to confidentiality as a living client

74. A social worker cannot limit a client's right to self-determination in the following circumstances EXCEPT:

A. When a client's actions violate policies set forth by the social worker's agency

B. When the social worker does not believe that a client is making appropriate decisions

C. When a client poses a serious and imminent risk to himself or herself or others

D. When there are alternatives that will enhance the client's well-being

75. Trichotillomania is classified under which of the following in the *DSM-5*?

    A. Disruptive, Impulse-Control, and Conduct Disorders
    B. Anxiety Disorders
    C. Trauma- and Stressor-Related Disorders
    D. Obsessive-Compulsive and Related Disorders

76. Group therapy is not appropriate for all of the following client groups EXCEPT those who are:

    A. Actively in crisis
    B. Paranoid or psychotic
    C. Compulsively in need of attention
    D. Isolated from others

77. A client is referred to a social worker by an employee assistance program for problems at work including insubordination and not following company policies. Upon intake, the client states that he is not the one that needs help and that the social worker should be trying to "fix" his boss, who is the real problem. The client reports that his difficulties are a result of jealousy by his boss because the client "knows more and is more successful." The client dominates the conversation during the session and spends most of the time describing his achievements, including the amount of money that he earns and spends on his possessions. The BEST diagnosis of the client is:

    A. Narcissistic Personality Disorder
    B. Histrionic Personality Disorder
    C. Avoidant Personality Disorder
    D. Obsessive-Compulsive Personality Disorder

78. A client enters a social worker's office and is outraged at an interaction that has just taken place with another agency staff member. The client is indignant and demands that the social worker "do something." In this situation, the social worker should FIRST:

    A. Explain to the client that it would be best for the client to address the issue directly with the staff member
    B. Get the staff member so that the client can speak to him or her and resolve the issue immediately
    C. Tell the client to go to the agency director who is in a position to take action
    D. Listen to the client's account of the situation

79. Which of the following statements is true?

    A. Consent and assent have the same legal meaning
    B. When treating those who lack capacity to provide informed consent, consent should be obtained by the responsible third party and assent should be obtained by the client

C. All clients must receive social work services voluntarily
D. There is no need to get consent to audiotape or videotape services because it is always permitted if a client signs a consent form

80. A mother comes in to see a social worker because she is concerned about cognitive delays in her child. The child is far behind her peers in academic achievement. A social worker refers this child for diagnostic testing. Given the mother's concerns, the child will MOST likely be given which of the following assessments?

A. The Minnesota Multiphasic Personality Inventory
B. The Myer-Briggs Type Indicator
C. The Thematic Apperception Test
D. The Wechsler Intelligence Scale

81. A client is very worried about her financial situation. She buys a new car and tells the social worker that she made the purchase "because the car is much less likely to break down and will save money in the long run." This statement MOST likely results from:

A. Ego-syntonic beliefs
B. Isolation of affect
C. A double bind
D. Cognitive dissonance

82. A social worker's ex-husband comes to her agency for therapy services. The ex-husband asks that the social worker provide these services because she is aware of his history and he feels comfortable speaking to her about his problems. They have been divorced for 15 years. The social worker refuses. Based on the professional *Code of Ethics*, this action by the social worker is:

A. Unethical because it has been more than 10 years since they were married
B. Ethical because she had a prior sexual relationship with the client
C. Unethical because the social worker did not respect the client's wishes with regard to the provision of treatment
D. Ethical because the social worker does not want the client to know anything about her current life circumstances

83. A teenager is having problems initiating conversation with peers. In order to BEST assist the teenager, the social worker should:

A. Ask the teenager to keep a journal documenting thoughts that can be used in later conversations with peers
B. Explore with the teenager the underlying reasons for his or her problems with peer relationships

    C. Assess whether there are other social deficits that may result in appropriate diagnosis

    D. Engage in a role-play with the teenager so that he or she can practice needed communication skills

84. Which of the following represents the order of client needs within a hierarchy?

    A. Physiological, safety, social, esteem, and self-actualization
    B. Physiological, safety, esteem, social, and self-actualization
    C. Safety, physiological, social, esteem, and self-actualization
    D. Safety, physiological, esteem, social, and self-actualization

85. A client reports that he has experienced some "ringing" in his ears for the last week, which is causing him great distress. The social worker should FIRST:

    A. Refer the client for a neurological evaluation
    B. Provide the client with coping skills to address his distress
    C. Identify whether he is reporting an auditory hallucination
    D. Explore with the client what changes in his life may have coincided with this symptom

86. Which of the following is the basic premise of groupthink?

    A. Groups make faulty decisions because they ignore alternatives due to group pressures
    B. Groups with similar membership tend to be more cohesive and effective
    C. Decision making by groups takes longer than individual decision making
    D. Groups come up with creative solutions to problems using their diverse perspectives

87. When working with an involuntary, court-mandated client, it is useful for a social worker to FIRST do which of the following to address resistance?

    A. Show the client a copy of the court order so that he or she can understand the reasons for treatment
    B. Make sure that the client sees all reports given to the court to build trust between the client and social worker
    C. Include some of the client's own goals in the service plan in addition to those that must be addressed as mandated by the court
    D. Acknowledge the client's circumstances and lack of choice in receiving services

88. A client who has been experiencing severe depression and previously expressed thoughts aimed at hurting herself appears less hopeless and

to have a more positive affect. In this situation, the social worker should FIRST:

A. Acknowledge the recent improvement in depressive symptoms to the client
B. Determine the coping skills that the client is using to bring about change
C. Focus on other immediate goals that are a concern to the client
D. Conduct a suicide risk assessment

89. Which of the following stages is often described as "a midlife crisis" where individuals struggle between guiding the next generation and becoming self-absorbed?

A. Generativity versus stagnation
B. Ego integrity versus despair
C. Intimacy versus isolation
D. Identity versus role confusion

90. A mother and teenage child yell at each other almost the entire time of a session. The mother says that she is upset with her daughter's choice in boyfriend, her grades in school, her inappropriate dress, and her lack of help around the house. The daughter says that she is angry as her mother does not listen to her, does not respect her privacy, does not give her any "space," and speaks to the daughter's friends in a demeaning manner. In order to BEST assist with helping them resolve their conflicts, the social worker should:

A. Work with the mother and child to prioritize their concerns
B. Focus on both the mother's and child's strengths and skills
C. Suggest that the mother and child increase the amount of time that they spend with one another to facilitate the problem-solving process
D. Acknowledge the level of conflict and discord between the mother and child

91. Which of the following is NOT congruent communication?

A. Ignoring nonverbal cues that indicate anger
B. Smiling at a person who is being annoying
C. Hugging a person in pain
D. Yelling at an individual when upset

92. Which of the following is NOT an objective of social work supervision?

A. To increase the social worker's capacity to work more effectively
B. To assist the social worker in resolving conflicts or problems
C. To assure the delivery of the most effective and efficient client services
D. To ensure consistent treatment of clients

93. A client is having difficulty finding a career that is fulfilling to her. She has repeatedly taken jobs that she has quit because "they just don't fit." In order to assist the client in resolving this problem, which of the following tests may be used?

    A. Minnesota Multiphasic Personality Inventory
    B. Myers-Briggs Type Indicator
    C. Thematic Apperception Test
    D. Wechsler Intelligence Scale

94. A client is very distressed because she is physically attracted to individuals of the same gender. She has become increasingly upset by these desires and wants to find ways to eliminate them. The feelings that the client is experiencing are:

    A. Latent
    B. Ego alien
    C. Ego-syntonic
    D. Rooted in the pleasure principle

95. A client learns that she may have a genetic condition and would like to be tested as she and her husband are thinking about having children. All of the following are true EXCEPT:

    A. The social worker should make sure that the client is fully informed of all risks/benefits of testing before it is done
    B. The insurance provider must authorize these tests in order for them to be completed
    C. Self-determination of the client should be respected in this situation
    D. The social worker should be aware of the process of genetic inheritance and develop a genogram to assist in decision making

96. A client who has repeatedly stated that she hates her sister tells a social worker that she has just asked her sister to be the maid of honor in her wedding. The social worker points out that this action appears contradictory to her feelings about her sister. This statement by the social worker is known as a:

    A. Clarification
    B. Generalization
    C. Paradoxical instruction
    D. Confrontation

97. Which of the following is NOT a component of a client contract?

    A. The problem to be worked on and the goals to reduce the problem
    B. Authorization letter approving services by the client's insurance company

C. Means of monitoring progress

D. Fees and frequency of meetings

98. Which of the following does NOT have to be done in order for a social worker to provide services in areas that are new to him or her?

A. The social worker must engage in appropriate study of the area

B. The social worker must receive supervision for someone who is competent in the area

C. The social worker must receive training and consultation in the area as needed

D. The social worker must add it to his or her résumé to reflect practice in this area

99. Which of the following statements is TRUE about the relationship between ethical and legal actions of social workers?

A. All legal behaviors are ethical

B. All illegal behaviors are unethical

C. Some behaviors are legal, but unethical

D. A behavior that is illegal can never be ethical

100. According to the Tarasoff decision, in order for a social worker to have a duty to warn, all of the following must be present EXCEPT:

A. The threat of danger

B. An identifiable third party

C. A client history of violence against others

D. Personal harm must be imminent

101. A social worker has been asked to evaluate client progress using a single-subject design. Which of the following designs has the fewest threats to internal validity?

A. AB

B. A

C. ABAB

D. BAB

102. A client became depressed a month ago due to the ending of her marriage. The BEST diagnosis for the client is:

A. Major Depression

B. Endogenous Depression

C. Major Depressive Disorder with Mixed Features

D. Exogenous Depression

103. The social worker learns from a client who is HIV positive that he is having unprotected sexual contact with his girlfriend who is unaware

of his HIV status. In order to address this situation ethically, the social worker should:

A. Disclose to the client that the social worker must try to contact the girlfriend in this situation under the obligation of duty to warn and ask for her contact information

B. Try to locate the girlfriend without informing the client because such notification is required under the Tarasoff decision

C. Make no attempt to contact the girlfriend to disclose the client's HIV status

D. Tell the client that services will need to be terminated unless this behavior ceases

104. Which of the following is associated with negative body image?

A. Self-worth is not tied to appearance

B. Time is not spent on worrying about food or weight

C. Confidence with one's body

D. Believing physical appearance is tied to the value of a person

105. All of the following are true about crisis intervention EXCEPT:

A. It is time limited

B. It focuses on the "here and now"

C. It must follow a major life event

D. It involves a high level of intervention and activity by the social worker

106. A social worker providing psychotherapy in a mental health agency is concerned about protecting the confidentiality of client records. In order to provide the greatest protection for clients while adhering to best clinical practices, the social worker should:

A. Keep all psychotherapy notes in the client file in a secure and locked location

B. Take the psychotherapy notes home to ensure that they are only seen by the social worker

C. Store the psychotherapy notes in a secure and locked location separate from the client file

D. Not keep any documentation, including psychotherapy notes

107. A social worker finds that a client has poor interpersonal skills. The BEST intervention that a social worker can use to address these issues is:

A. Engaging the client in a psychoeducational group aimed at providing information about communication skills

B. Modeling appropriate verbal and nonverbal communication skills

    C. Conducting intensive psychotherapy aimed at addressing the communication deficits

    D. Providing the client with individual instruction on appropriate interpersonal skills

108. A school social worker is using an intervention aimed at enhancing the social functioning of an adolescent student who is acting out. The social worker collects data daily prior to the intervention and during treatment. During the holiday break, the social worker asks the parents to write down the frequency of the behaviors each day in a journal. This journal is reviewed by the social worker upon return to school, at which time the intervention is restarted and behavior is monitored. Which of the following single-subject designs is reflective of the social worker's intervention?

    A. AB

    B. A

    C. ABA

    D. ABAB

109. Which of the following will MOST likely produce emotional or psychological trauma?

    A. Events that happen in adulthood

    B. Events that were expected

    C. Events that could have been prevented

    D. Events that occur unexpectedly without preparation

110. A mother states that her 12-year-old son is now able to stay home alone because he is aware of dangers, meets his basic needs, and problem-solves when needed. This child has reached which stage of cognitive development?

    A. Sensorimotor

    B. Formal operations

    C. Concrete operations

    D. Preoperational

111. Which of the following is NOT always true when using a token economy?

    A. Points or rewards must be consistently given when the targeted behavior is exhibited

    B. For the system to be effective, a substantial number of points or rewards must be taken away for undesirable behavior

    C. Rewards must be of value to the client

    D. It works best when a client can see the points earned toward a reward

112. A child in an after-school program comes into a social worker's office and shows the social worker a burn that appears to have been caused by an iron. The child reports that her mother did it as punishment because she was "being bad." The social worker's colleague overhears the child and tells the social worker that the child has lied many times in the past. The social worker should:

    A. Make a note in the file of the incident, including the observation and the colleague's comment
    B. Ask the colleague to discuss the incident with the social worker and the agency director
    C. Report the incident to the child protection agency
    D. Investigate the incident to see if the child is telling the truth

113. Which of the following is NOT associated with Histrionic Personality Disorder?

    A. Interacting with others using inappropriately seductive or provocative behavior
    B. Using appearance to draw attention to oneself
    C. Being highly suggestible and easily influenced by others
    D. Having close romantic and social relationships with others

114. A social worker who does not provide adolescent services makes referrals to a very reputable agency in her community when she is contacted for such services. In exchange for each of these referrals, the agency provides a $50 gift card to the social worker. This practice is:

    A. Known as fee splitting and is ethical
    B. Known as collateral contact and is unethical
    C. Known as collateral contact and is ethical
    D. Known as fee splitting and is unethical

115. Upon intake, a woman tells a social worker that she was brutally beaten by her boyfriend 6 months ago, but it was an isolated incident and there have been no further acts of violence. Since that time, he has been remorseful and attentive. In this situation, the social worker should FIRST:

    A. Tell the client that the boyfriend's behavior was unacceptable
    B. Document the incident in the assessment, but do not include as a treatment issue since no further incidents have occurred
    C. Explore with the client the degree to which the incident affected her relationship with her boyfriend
    D. Evaluate the need for medical and protective services

116. Upon coming in for an intake interview, a couple reports that they have not had sexual intercourse for more than a year due to the husband's inability to sustain an erection. He reports that he has had a lot of stress at work and feels overwhelmed by the pressures placed upon him. In order to best diagnose the reasons for the husband's sexual dysfunction, a social worker should FIRST:

   A. Ask the husband to provide more information about his job stress
   B. Determine if the physiological changes in the husband occurred at about the same time as his overwhelming feelings
   C. Recommend that the husband see a physician to see if there are any medical problems
   D. Explore whether the couple is having any other problems in the relationship

117. Which of the following is the BEST definition of rapprochement?

   A. A technique used to confront a client in a nonthreatening way
   B. A time in the problem-solving process that indicates the beginning of termination
   C. A feeling experienced by clients who have not formed emotional attachments to others
   D. A stage in childhood development where a small child needs reassurance from a caregiver

118. Which of the following is NOT true regarding Delirium and Dementia?

   A. Clients with Dementia are highly susceptible to Delirium
   B. Many of the same symptoms are shared by Delirium and Dementia
   C. In both Delirium and Dementia, there is a gradual deterioration of memory and intellect, causing confusion
   D. Clients who have Dementia can also experience Delirium

119. A client who has been paying a reduced fee to a social worker in private practice inherits a lot of money from a relative's estate. The client, who was previously poor, is now extremely wealthy and very appreciative of the social worker's services. The client would like to pay the social worker the amount that was discounted for prior services. This action is:

   A. Ethical as long as the client only pays the amount of the discount and no more
   B. Ethical because the client now has the ability to pay for the prior services
   C. Unethical because the social worker agreed to a reduced fee for those services
   D. Unethical unless the social worker can determine that the client can afford this payment for prior services

120. A young man who has a criminal history for violent acts later becomes an acclaimed boxer—which of the following defense mechanisms is the young man MOST likely using?

    A. Sublimation
    B. Incorporation
    C. Introjection
    D. Undoing

121. In the *DSM-5*, which of the following is NOT incorporated into Autism Spectrum Disorder?

    A. Asperger's Disorder
    B. Pervasive Developmental Disorder Not Otherwise Specified
    C. Childhood Disintegrative Disorder
    D. Mental Retardation

122. In instances when clients are not literate or are having difficulty understanding the primary language used in the practice setting, all of the following are acceptable practices by a social worker EXCEPT:

    A. Using a family member to translate information into the client's native language
    B. Assessing the client's comprehension to determine what additional informed consent procedures are needed
    C. Reading documents to the client and providing verbal explanations to written policies as needed
    D. Using a qualified interpretor service when possible to translate information into the client's native language

123. Which of the following is NOT an example of client advocacy?

    A. Working with legislators to craft a bill that would fill a service gap
    B. Speaking to an agency board of directors to change a policy that negatively impacts on clients
    C. Writing a press release for a local paper about a growing community need
    D. Providing community members with a listing of service agencies that can assist them in meeting their needs

124. An agency is experiencing financial hardship and social workers are upset because they have not been able to meet with their supervisors in several weeks because the supervisors have had to assist with other agency administrative tasks. In this situation, the social work administrator should:

    A. Explain to social workers that this situation is not ideal, but necessary in order for the agency to continue to operate
    B. Terminate services to several clients in order to free up social work staff to provide supervision

    C. Explore the use of peer supervision

    D. Instruct the staff to pay for outside supervision if affordable

125. During an initial session, a client complains that she feels like a failure because she is getting divorced and could not "save her marriage." She ends by asking whether she is wrong to feel this way. In order to facilitate the therapeutic alliance, the social work should:

    A. Explore with her why she thinks that the divorce is causing her to feel this way

    B. Find out more about her past relationships

    C. Tell her that such feelings are commonly felt in this situation

    D. Explain that she will have a lot of time to work through these feelings in the coming weeks

126. A social worker is reviewing a client's record and sees that a client was recently taking Zoloft after being switched from Lexapro. The client is MOST likely diagnosed as having:

    A. Major Depressive Disorder

    B. Schizoaffective Disorder

    C. Autism Spectrum Disorder

    D. Attention-Deficit/Hyperactivity Disorder

127. Which of the following is NOT included in the *DSM-5*?

    A. World Health Organization Disability Assessment Schedule (WHODAS)

    B. Global Assessment of Functioning (GAF)

    C. Cultural Formulation Interview Guide (CFI)

    D. *ICD-10* Codes

128. All of the following occur during termination EXCEPT:

    A. Acknowledgement of loss on the part of the social worker and client

    B. Review and update of the client record to ensure completeness

    C. Identification of resources to meet future needs

    D. Review of client accomplishments

129. Which of the following is NOT assessed as part of a routine mental status examination?

    A. Thought processes/reality testing

    B. Psychiatric pathology

    C. Orientation

    D. Judgment/insight

130. According to self psychology, children need all of the following to develop a strong sense of self EXCEPT:

    A. Being around others like themselves in order to feel "belonging"
    B. Someone to look up to who is more capable
    C. Being soothed and validated so they know their feelings matter
    D. Methods to control aggressive drives

131. Which of the following is NOT a form of institutional discrimination?

    A. Not providing translation services or agency paperwork in any language other than English
    B. Only offering therapy and other services on Saturdays
    C. Referring a client to another social worker based on his or her cultural background
    D. Not hiring individuals if they were not born in the United States

132. A woman who uses American Sign Language (ASL) to communicate comes to a community-based agency to see a social worker who is deaf. The woman is in need of mental health services that are not provided at this agency. In this situation, the social worker should:

    A. Provide the services in order to meet the client's need since it is unlikely that she will be able to find a social worker in the mental health agency who knows ASL
    B. Contact a mental health agency with the woman to see what accommodations are available
    C. Provide whatever services are available in the agency so the woman gets some help
    D. Make a referral to an advocacy organization for those who are deaf to see if they can assist

133. What is the immediate goal of social work services for a client in crisis?

    A. To assist the client to return to the previous level of functioning
    B. To provide the client with strategies to prevent future crises from occurring
    C. To determine whether the emotional stressors have caused the client to be a danger to self or others
    D. To develop a long-term strategy to assist the client in dealing with the impacts of the trauma caused by the crisis

134. Which of the following target populations would BEST have their needs fulfilled by participation in a psychoeducational group?

    A. Older adults with high blood pressure who need to learn about healthy eating methods
    B. Teens who need peer support to address issues of addiction

    C. Mothers who feel isolated and want to meet other mothers in their area

    D. Couples who have experienced loss and are having trouble coping

135. Which of the following is TRUE about psychodynamic treatment modalities or approaches?

    A. They are good for use in a managed care environment where change has to occur in a limited time period

    B. They are focused only on the information that a person is paying attention to at a given time

    C. They use dynamic intervention methods that are hands on, such as play therapy

    D. They emphasize unconscious motives and desires, as well as the importance of childhood experiences, in shaping personality

136. A married couple reports that they feel disconnected from one another and rarely speak or provide each other with any kind of support. This is known as:

    A. Negative entropy

    B. Entropy

    C. Differentiation

    D. Equifinality

137. Which of the following observation roles poses the MOST ethical challenges for social workers?

    A. Complete participant

    B. Participant as observer

    C. Complete observer

    D. Observer as participant

138. Which of the following is NOT a dual relationship for a social worker?

    A. Providing therapy to a friend

    B. Hiring a client to do repairs on the social worker's home

    C. Being an agency supervisor to a family member

    D. Going to the same outside clinical supervisor as a friend

139. Which of the following is NOT a physical symptom of trauma?

    A. Insomnia

    B. Feeling disconnected

    C. Muscle tension

    D. Aches and pains

140. A client has recently learned that her child has been diagnosed with a life-threatening condition that will substantially affect her abilities in

the future. For an hour, she talks to the social worker in detail about the medical condition without showing any emotion. The defense mechanism that BEST describes the client's response is:

A. Devaluation
B. Substitution
C. Intellectualization
D. Rationalization

141. At the beginning of the initial session, a client states, "I am so glad that I am here because I really need you to tell me how to solve my problems." The social worker should:

A. Clarify the social worker's role in the problem-solving process with the client
B. Not respond to the comment, but make a note to clearly delineate the social worker's role in the treatment plan
C. Praise the client for her willingness to be open to feedback
D. Suggest to the client that her need to solve her own problems may be an area to explore further in therapy

142. Which of the following is NOT an aim of case management?

A. To avoid duplication and gaps in treatment in care
B. To coordinate and monitor multiple services to ensure efficient and effective utilization
C. To treat emotional or mental dysfunction in order to maximize well-being
D. To link to services as needed to optimize functioning

143. Which of the following is NOT a practice that promotes cultural competence within social work organizations?

A. Recruiting multiethnic staff
B. Including cultural competence requirements in job descriptions and performance/promotion measures
C. Advocating for clients as major stakeholders in the development and monitoring of the service delivery system
D. Ensuring employees get a copy of the professional *Code of Ethics* to review upon hiring and as needed thereafter

144. A private pay client has made substantial progress and achieved all stated treatment goals, but wants to continue to see a social worker "in case something comes up." In this situation, the social worker should:

A. Continue to see the client at the regular fee in order to respect the client's self-determination
B. Begin termination with the client

C. Continue to see the client, but reduce the fee since the treatment goals have been achieved

D. Refer the client to another social worker because it appears that the client may have become dependent on the social worker

145. A social work administrator is part of a management team who decides to close an agency program due to financial pressures. The management team receives many letters from program supporters asserting that this program is essential for other agency operations. The team does not consider other alternatives and closes the program anyway, only to encounter major problems in agency operations weeks later. The actions by the management team are an example of:

A. Groupthink
B. Homogeneity
C. Interdependence
D. Group polarization

146. Members of a community are concerned about rising crime rates, drug problems, and high unemployment in their neighborhood. When engaging in community organizing with this group, the social worker should FIRST:

A. Tell community members about strategies that have worked well to address these issues in other locations
B. Work with the citizens to prioritize their concerns
C. Contact local legislators to make them aware of the problems
D. Identify an individual who can lead the other community members in taking action

147. An agency hires a consultant to assist a social worker to become more competent in addressing substance use issues. The social worker shows the consultant a few client assessment documents and case notes to provide needed background on the kinds of substance use problems that the social worker is facing in practice. The social worker's actions are:

A. Unethical because the clients need to consent to disclosure of this information
B. Ethical because the consultant was hired by the agency and therefore can see this information without client consent
C. Ethical because this information is accessible to anyone in the agency and available for teaching or training purposes
D. Unethical because the social worker should have shown the records of all clients with substance use problems to give the consultant complete information related to all the problems that the social worker is treating

148. Which of the following is TRUE about sexual development of individuals?

    A. Children are not sexual before birth
    B. Humans are sexual beings throughout life
    C. Same-gender sexual behavior during childhood is directly related to sexual orientation later in life
    D. Adults lose their desire for sexual expression later in life

149. Which of the following is NOT a separate stage experienced in the five stages of grief?

    A. Hope
    B. Acceptance
    C. Bargaining
    D. Anger

150. A client barges into a social worker's office yelling in a loud and hostile manner. The MOST effective method for the social worker to address the situation is to:

    A. Tell the client that it is not possible to speak now, but his or her concerns can be discussed during a scheduled appointment
    B. Listen to the client's concerns and provide other methods to reach the social worker in the future if problems arise
    C. Contact agency security immediately to remove the client in order not to reinforce the behavior
    D. Instruct the client on appropriate tone and voice volume when interacting with others

151. A client who is suffering from depression asks a social worker to read her journal. After reading it, the social worker identifies major themes of her writings including feeling isolated, not understood, and rejected by her family. The social worker speaks with the client about these issues and they decide to include them as treatment goals. These goals are based on which of the following in the journal?

    A. Latent content
    B. Manifest content
    C. Explicit communication
    D. Overt writings

152. Which of the following does NOT have to occur in order for a social worker who is in private practice to terminate services to a client who is not paying an overdue balance?

    A. A safety assessment to determine if the client is a danger to self or others
    B. A signed agreement that the client is willing to be seen by another social worker

    C. Documentation of conversations in which the nonpayment has been discussed with the client

    D. Billing for overdue balances

153. Which of the following systems in the body is responsible for the production of hormones that control metabolism and growth?

    A. Digestive

    B. Nervous

    C. Lymphatic

    D. Endocrine

154. Which of the following is NOT a social work role?

    A. Being a client's support system

    B. Advocating for change to address a social problem

    C. Assisting with locating services for a client

    D. Educating a client to assist with problem solving

155. Tardive dyskinesia is associated with the prescribing of:

    A. Antipsychotics

    B. Antidepressants

    C. Antianxiety medications

    D. Mood stabilizers

156. A client sees a woman get brutally beaten and killed during an incident of domestic violence. Shortly after the incident, the client reports the inability to see. This client is MOST likely experiencing the defense mechanism of:

    A. Conversion

    B. Acting out

    C. Compensation

    D. Reaction formation

157. Which of the following is NOT an appropriate task for a social worker facilitating a group?

    A. Modeling methods for the group in dealing with dilemmas or situations

    B. Identifying assumptions made by, or unconscious communication used by, the group

    C. Opening up new avenues of exploration to the group

    D. Providing solutions to problems that are raised by the group

158. A woman has strong feelings of resentment toward her sister. These feelings are rooted in her childhood and she has always believed that her sister was a mean person. However, throughout her childhood, she reports being inseparable from her sister and "doing everything

together." She also reports buying a necklace for her recently that states "Best Sister Ever." This behavior by the woman is an example of:

A. Substitution
B. Splitting
C. Projective identification
D. Reaction formation

159. As required by law, Individual Educational Plans (IEPs) for children with disabilities must be reviewed and revised by schools at least:

A. Daily
B. Yearly
C. Monthly
D. Weekly

160. A social worker who is in a private mental health practice recently earned a doctorate from an accredited university in an unrelated field. She adds "Dr." to her name on her private practice business card. This practice is:

A. Unethical since it is not related to mental health treatment
B. Ethical since she earned a doctorate that entitles her to list it
C. Unethical unless she discloses that it is in another field when asked
D. Ethical since it was from an accredited university

161. A husband complains that his wife nags him too much about working around the house. Once she stops this behavior, he begins to spend more time on house maintenance. This is an example of:

A. Shaping
B. Negative reinforcement
C. Aversion treatment
D. Positive reinforcement

162. Which of the following is NOT one of social work's core values as stated in the professional *Code of Ethics*?

A. Service
B. Integrity
C. Loyalty
D. Competence

163. A client who struggles with alcoholism is prescribed a medication that makes him feel sick every time he drinks while taking it. The use of this medication is what type of operant technique?

A. Extinction
B. Flooding

C. Aversion therapy

D. In vivo desensitization

164. Which of the following is a TRUE statement about the relationship between expressive and receptive communication?

  A. Receptive communication usually develops at an earlier age than does expressive communication

  B. Receptive and expressive communication skills are usually equally developed in young children

  C. Expressive communication usually develops at an earlier age than does receptive communication

  D. Some young children develop receptive communication skills before developing expressive communication skills; for other children, it is the reverse

165. Which of the following is the MOST critical factor for the delivery of effective culturally competent services?

  A. The social worker and client must be from the same cultural group

  B. The social worker must have self-awareness about cultural differences with the client

  C. The social worker must have worked with a cultural group for at least 5 years

  D. The social worker must have a supervisor who is from a different cultural group

166. Which of the following is NOT essential for implementing a strengths perspective?

  A. Opportunities are created so that clients can learn or display competencies

  B. There is collaboration and partnership with the client

  C. There is an assumption that clients can change and adapt

  D. The inner psychological struggles that clients are experiencing must be a focus of treatment

167. During a session, a client is reporting on her daily activities during the last week. She looks down at the ground, not making eye contact. She also pauses repeatedly with periods of silence. The social worker should:

  A. Ask the client if there is something that is bothering her

  B. Listen attentively to show acceptance of her feelings

  C. Accept this behavior as part of her communication style

  D. Document this behavior in the client's record

168. Which of the following statements is NOT true about cultural, racial, and ethnic identity development?

A. Individuals can share the same race, but have different ethnicities
B. The ways in which races have been defined have been fixed over time
C. Some ethnic and racial identities confer privilege
D. Cultural, racial, and ethnic identity is not passed from one generation to the next

169. In the precontemplation stage of change, resistance is BEST addressed by a social worker:

A. Looking at the pros and cons of behavior change
B. Acknowledging a client's fears and concerns
C. Assessing whether new developments in a client's life are causing barriers to the plan
D. Reviewing the appropriateness of the intervention

170. During an initial session, a client appears reluctant to speak and states, "I am not sure if this is going to work out." The BEST response for the social worker to take is to:

A. Use this as an opening to address this hesitancy as a therapeutic issue
B. Ignore the comment because this is only the first interaction and such feelings are likely to subside over time
C. Ask the client to speak about other situations in which the client had similar feelings
D. Clarify what the client can expect, including the social worker's role and confidentiality practices

Practice Test

Answers

1. D

Motivation is a state of readiness or eagerness to change, which fluctuates from one time to another. The role of the social worker is to create an atmosphere that is conducive to change and to increase a client's intrinsic motivation, so that change arises from within rather than being imposed from without. If a client is driven to change internally, it is much more likely that the change effort will be sustained. A technique to increase motivation is to work to remove barriers and instill hope or the belief that life can be different.

2. C

Evidence-based practice (EBP) combines well-researched interventions with clinical experience and ethics, as well as client preferences and culture, to guide and inform the delivery of treatments and services. Social workers, clients, and others must work together in order to identify what works, for whom, and under what conditions. This approach ensures that the treatments and services, when used as intended, will have the most effective outcomes as demonstrated by the research.

3. D

Precontemplation is denial or ignorance of the problem. It is followed by contemplation in which there is ambivalence about making change. Then comes preparation or experimenting with small changes. Action moves toward achieving a goal, whereas maintenance sustains a new behavior and avoids relapse, which can lead to feelings of frustration and failure.

4. D

A social worker, not his or her supervisor, should monitor practice to identify whether new issues or dilemmas arise.

5. D

A delusion is a false, fixed belief despite evidence to the contrary (i.e., believing something that is not true).

Comorbid means existing at the same time. Dissociation is a change in memory, perception, or consciousness. Folie à deux is a shared delusion.

6. B

Social workers should avoid situations interfering with impartial judgment. Hiring a family member creates a dual relationship and should be avoided.

7. D

Formative evaluations examine the process of delivering services, whereas summative evaluations examine the outcomes. Formative evaluations are ongoing processes that allow for feedback to be implemented during service delivery. These types of evaluations allow social workers to make changes as needed to help achieve program goals. Summative evaluations occur at the end of services and provide an overall description of their effectiveness. Summative evaluation examines outcomes to determine whether objectives were met.

The design described is not experimental—which requires a control group and randomization of assignment—or quasi-experimental, which does not require randomization, but has more support for causal inferences than does pre-experimental designs.

8. D

Stratification refers to structured inequality of entire categories of people in society who have unequal access to social rewards. Stratification applies to individuals based on ethnic and racial background, social status, and/or other factors.

9. C

Despite the client's report that she will not act on her thoughts, she is at risk because she has had these feelings and has acted on them in the past. The case vignette does not describe the social worker taking any action yet. A safety assessment will determine the severity of the depression and whether the client is at risk for a suicide attempt. It must be done FIRST before any other action is taken.

10. A

The primary medications used to treat social anxiety disorder are selective serotonin reuptake inhibitors (SSRIs), which were first developed to treat depression. They have been found to be effective in the treatment of a wider range of disorders. Zoloft (sertraline) is an SSRI.

Benzodiazepines, such as Valium (diazepam), reduce levels of anxiety. However, they are habit-forming and sedating, so they are typically prescribed for only short-term use.

Mellaril (thioridazine) and Thorazine (chlorpromazine) are antipsychotic medications for the treatment of psychosis.

11. D

The use of collateral information is often used when the credibility and validity of information obtained from a client or others is questionable. For example, child custody cases are inherently characterized by biased data within an adversarial process. Social workers should use data from neutral parties, such as the school, because this information has higher integrity.

12. B

In group therapy, the group is the major helping agent. Issues should be brought back to the group to address. There is no need for the client to see the social worker for individual therapy. Contacting an employee assistance program would breach confidentiality.

13. A

Industry versus inferiority—From age 6 to puberty, children begin to develop a sense of pride in their accomplishments. If children are encouraged and reinforced for their initiative, they begin to feel industrious and feel confident in their ability to achieve goals. If this initiative is not encouraged and is restricted, children begin to feel inferior, doubting their abilities.

14. B

SOAP stands for Subjective, Objective, Assessment, and Plan. In the Assessment portion, a social worker pulls together subjective and objective findings and consolidates them into a short assessment.

15. C

Aphasia is a change in cognition (mental ability) that is characterized by difficulty understanding language or using language to speak or write.

Difficulty with common motor skills is known as ataxia. Inability to recognize familiar objects is labeled agnosia.

16. B

In the *DSM-5*, there is recognition that every disorder is inherently culture-bound. These new guidelines help a social worker be more sensitive to cultural differences and understand that a client is manifesting symptoms in a way that his or her culture experiences them. Cultural syndromes are clusters of invariant symptoms in a specific cultural group. Cultural idioms of distress are a way of talking about suffering among people in a cultural group, and cultural explanations or perceived causes for symptoms, illness, or distress have been added to assist with diagnosing.

17. A

Social workers should inform clients, to the extent possible, about the disclosure of confidential information and the potential consequences, when feasible, before any disclosure is made. This applies whether social workers disclose confidential information on the basis of a legal requirement or client consent.

18. A

A paradoxical intent or directive prescribes the symptomatic behavior so the client realizes control over it and uses the strength of resistance to change.

19. C

Social workers who are leaving an employment setting should inform clients of appropriate options for the continuation of services and of the benefits and risks of the options.

20. B

The Patient Self-Determination Act of 1991 specifies facilities that receive Medicare and Medicaid inform clients of their rights to make decisions concerning their own health care, ask and document whether clients have advance directives, and provide education for staff and the community.

21. D

A task-centered approach aims to quickly engage clients in the problem-solving process because it is usually delivered in a time-limited environment. The client is an active part of the change process and the approach is highly structured to attempt to achieve immediate results as goals are broken into defined tasks. Termination begins in the first session. This approach is too brief to address long-standing problems that are complex.

22. B

Clozaril increases the risk of agranulocytosis (low white blood cell count). Monitoring of the white blood cell count through regular blood work is required.

23. A

Universalism is based on one acceptable norm or standard for everyone versus many valid standards that have been developed by clients that they have determined to be most useful to them.

24. C

In all other instances, there is a serious threat to the health and safety of self or others. D is required under duty to warn (Tarasoff decision).

25. D

Social exchange theory is based on the idea of totaling potential benefits and losses to determine behavior. A client will leave a battering relationship when the alternative is seen as better than the current situation (rewards outweigh costs).

26. A

Covert modeling is when clients are asked to use their imagination, visualize the desired behavior, and describe it in detail.

Self-modeling is when clients are videotaped demonstrating the desired behavior and this tape is watched and discussed. Live modeling refers to watching a real person performing the desired behavior. Symbolic modeling includes watching others who have been videotaped perform the desired behavior.

27. A

Role discomplementarity results when roles conflict or when the role expectations of others differ from one's own. In this situation, the husband and wife do not have the same expectations with regard to the tasks for which each other should be responsible.

28. C

The six levels of cognition are, in sequential order—knowledge, comprehension, application, analysis, synthesis, and evaluation. Teaching techniques should match the cognitive objective, such as knowing specific facts, theories, or information (knowledge) or creating something new/ integrating it into a solution (synthesis). Learning aimed at judging the quality of something is known as evaluation.

29. A

It also provides ethical standards to which the general public can hold the profession accountable and social workers can consult if professional obligations conflict. These functions of the Code are printed immediately after the preamble. The mitigation of liability by third-party payers is not based on the values of the profession and is not a stated purpose of the Code.

30. C

A role reversal is when two people switch or reverse roles. In this answer, the mother is emotionally dependent and the child is the comforter. These behaviors are usually reversed in a parent–child relationship. The other response choices may relate to roles, but are not reversals.

31. C

A subpoena is not a court order and no documents should be sent unless ordered by the court. However, a social worker does have to respond and should not send in the records when receiving a subpoena unless the client has provided a written release.

32. B

In the *DSM-5*, "Not Otherwise Specified" (NOS) categories for disorders that do not fit under specific disorder categories are replaced. "Other Specified" (i.e., "Other Specified Depressive Disorder") categories are used when a social worker provides the *reason why* the condition does not qualify for a specific diagnosis (i.e., short duration). "Unspecified" is used when no additional explanation is provided as to why the disorder does not meet the usual criteria.

33. A

A social worker who is concerned that client access to his or her records could cause serious harm to the client can limit access to the record or portion of the record when the rationale for the request is documented in the file. This case vignette clearly states that the social worker is not concerned that releasing the record to the client would be harmful, so it must be released and to not do so is unethical.

34. C

Ativan and Buspar are antianxiety medications and Nardil is an antidepressant. Lithium is a mood stabilizer, and this client appears to be experiencing depression upon admission, as well as mania later in treatment. A mood stabilizer is used for the treatment of Bipolar Disorder.

35. B

Clients who are at high risk for developing problems after services have ended should receive regular assessments to see if additional services are needed and/or discharge plans are being implemented. Natural supports and peer supports, such as 12-step programs, are good resources to assist with sustaining progress made. The creation of a contract is not done after termination because it indicates the presence of an intervention in a therapeutic relationship. It is incorrect given the order of the problem-solving process.

36. C

Social workers should respect clients' right to privacy. Social workers should not solicit private information from clients unless it is essential to providing services or conducting social work evaluation or research. Information about the client's sexual orientation and/or drug or alcohol use may not be relevant to the presenting problem or treatment.

37. A

A behavioral objective should be client-oriented and emphasize what a client needs to do. C is excluded as it focuses on the teacher's actions. An important element of behavioral objectives is that they are observable. Motivation is not easily observed. The conditions under which the behavior will be performed should also be included. D does not indicate if the expectation regarding sitting is to take place during class or all of the time. A has all of the elements—it specifies the target behavior, the conditions under which the behavior will be performed, and the criteria for determining when the acceptable performance of the behavior occurs.

38. B

Ataxia describes a lack of muscle control during voluntary movements, such as walking or picking up objects. A sign of an underlying condition, ataxia can affect movement, speech, eye movement, and swallowing.

Persistent ataxia usually results from damage to the cerebellum—the part of the brain that controls muscle coordination. Many conditions can cause ataxia, including alcohol abuse, stroke, tumor, cerebral palsy, and multiple sclerosis.

An inability to recognize familiar objects is agnosia, and an inability to recognize familiar faces is prosopagnosia. Acalculia is the inability to do simple arithmetic.

39. A

Echolalia is repeating noises and phrases. It is sometimes associated with Catatonia, Autism Spectrum Disorder, Schizophrenia, and other disorders.

40. D

Displacement is directing an impulse, wish, or feeling toward another person or situation that is less threatening. The man unconsciously realizes that he cannot express his anger on the job or it may have negative consequences, so he goes home and yells at his wife and children.

41. D

Transference refers to redirection of a client's feelings for a significant person to a social worker. Transference is often manifested as an erotic attraction toward a social worker, but can be seen in many other forms such as rage, hatred, mistrust, parentification, extreme dependence, or even placing a social worker in an esteemed status.

42. A

DSM-IV created separate diagnoses for "abuse" and "dependence" although substance-related problems occur on a continuum. The *DSM-5* uses "Substance Use Disorders" as the diagnosis for people with such problems.

"Recurrent legal problems" was deleted as a criteria for Substance Use Disorders and "craving or a strong desire or urge to use a substance" was added to the criteria.

43. D

A social worker with direct knowledge of a colleague's impairment due to personal problems, psychological stress, and so on, that interferes with practice effectiveness should consult with the colleague when feasible and assist the colleague in taking remedial action.

44. A

Life crises do not have to be a major event. They can be the "last straws" in a series of events that exceed the client's ability to cope.

45. D

The first answer is true for social work, but not for business. B is true for business networking, but the aim in social work is not to attract clients for the betterment of the agency. C may not be true in business because lower operating costs are not always passed on to clients; they may mean more profits for a company. In both business and social work, networking provides opportunities to work with others toward the achievement of common goals and helps in establishing professional relationships or alliances.

46. A

The values and principles of social work practice should be used as the basis for selecting the most important benefit. A is based on the belief of self-determination or that individuals and groups should be in charge of taking actions that are best for them. The other response choices may be true, but they are not based on this fundamental concept in social work practice.

47. B

Comorbid refers to two problems, conditions, or disorders that exist at the same time—such as the presence of a mental health and substance use issue, or a mental health and medical problem.

48. A

Magical thinking is a hallmark of Piaget's preoperational thought stage. Understanding that children learn through this process, and that it is typical, may assist the mother in better coping with this behavior. There is no indication that there are any mental health issues, so the social worker should not see the child or take other action based on this report alone.

49. B

Social workers are mandatory reporters and must not delay in reporting or investigating such an incident themselves. All suspected abuse situations should be reported to the child protection agency immediately.

50. D

A social worker can waive or reduce the fee, but cannot barter (B) or create a loan system with the client (A) because it is a conflict of interest. Both parties agree that continued treatment is needed, so C does not appear appropriate.

51. D

Most clients with atypical sexual interests do not have mental disorders. To be diagnosed with paraphilic disorders, *DSM-5* requires that clients with these interests feel personal distress about their interest, not merely distress resulting from society's disapproval, or have a sexual desire or behavior that involves another person's psychological distress, injury, or death, or a desire for sexual behaviors involving unwilling persons or persons unable to give legal consent. These desires and/or behaviors do not need to have resulted in legal involvement.

52. C

The first two answers are correct and are not limitations, but benefits. C is a limitation because there may be gaps in the record or the information that is explicitly stated may not reflect all the progress that has been made. D is not true and is therefore not a limitation; consent is only required for records that are being used in formal evaluation beyond determining individual client progress, which was the circumstance described in this question.

53. C

Social workers want to respect a client's right to self-determination and should not select an agency for the client. In addition, the social worker should assist the client to gather all needed information so that the client can make an informed decision. Working with insurance companies to ensure coverage is a part of the process, but the decision should primarily be based on the ability of the agency to meet the client's needs.

54. C

A client must feel he or she is understood and valued as a person, though his or her performance may be unsatisfactory. If a client feels judged, he or she will not speak freely. Hence, a social worker must be interested, genuinely concerned and encouraging, and at the same time, objective, but neither condemning nor praising. In this case vignette, the social worker should use the supervisor to process the feelings that arise as a result of the client's actions. The other response choices involve telling the client about the anger, which could interfere with the engagement process, or sending the client to another agency that does not assist him or her.

55. A

The case vignette states that the client is not a danger to himself or others, so he cannot be involuntarily committed. The social worker should not contact the hospital because the client is not agreeable to admission. Using a family member or others to convince him is not appropriate. The client is in crisis, so community resources aimed at meeting his immediate needs are the priority.

56. B

Social workers should not disclose confidential information to third-party payers unless clients have authorized such disclosure. Speaking to the client at the onset of treatment about insurance requirements does not constitute informed consent for the release of information requested.

57. C

There is no legal mandate for group members to safeguard information disclosed in groups. However, this disclosure may be a violation of the rules that the group established for itself. It is appropriate for the group to discuss and decide what actions, if any, should take place. Such disclosures may threaten the psychotherapeutic goals of the group, but any confrontation should be done in the group context.

58. C

Freud's psychosexual stages were oral, anal, phallic, latency, and genital. They began in infancy and went through puberty into adulthood. Castration anxiety is a child's fear that his penis will be cut off for desiring his mother. It is not one of the five stages.

59. C

Although a consultant does not have any formal authority over agency decision making, he or she has informal authority as an "expert." Releases of information are needed when disclosing data to a consultant. A consultant should be competent, demonstrating knowledge and expertise. However, the agency is not required to follow the advice given by a consultant. The final decision rests with the agency administration and board of directors.

60. A

A social worker must address this expression within an appropriate therapeutic context. Referring or terminating is not appropriate and ignoring it does not assist the client in understanding why these feelings are occurring. The social worker should *never* act on these feelings and engage in a relationship with a client.

61. A

A scientific management approach finds the one "best way" to perform each task; carefully matches each worker to each task; closely supervises workers, using reward and punishment as motivators; and manages and controls behavior.

A systems approach considers the organization as a system composed of interrelated subsystems. A contingency approach recognizes that organizational systems are interrelated with the environment and different organizational relationships are needed depending upon the larger environmental context. A human relations approach emphasizes creativity, cohesive work groups, participatory leadership, and open communication.

62. B

In a projective test, a client offers responses to ambiguous scenes, words, or images. This type of test emerged from a psychoanalytic approach, which suggested that clients have unconscious thoughts or urges. Projective tests are intended to uncover unconscious desires that are hidden from conscious awareness.

63. B

Individuals usually begin unwilling to accept a will greater than their own and are extremely egotistical. They then move to conforming and having blind faith. In this second stage, things are seen dichotomously— as right or wrong. Individuals then come to develop a deeper understanding of good and evil and do not accept blind faith, but integrate their beliefs into their larger worldview and behaviors.

64. C

Empathetic communication also includes the client's nonverbal messages. A social worker can observe body language and make explicit a client's feelings, as well as communicate, through eye contact and posture, interest and understanding in what the client is saying.

65. B

Cocaine use is indicated by dilated pupils, hyperactivity, euphoria, anxiety, and excessive talking.

Heroin use is indicated by contracted pupils, sleeping at unusual times, sweating, vomiting, twitching, and loss of appetite. Marijuana use is indicated by glassy, red eyes, inappropriate laughter, and loss of interest and motivation. Oxycontin (oxycodone) is an opioid pain medication used to treat moderate to severe pain and its use is indicated by sleepiness, inattention, and loss of appetite.

66. C

Traditional marital and couples therapy are not appropriate in battering relationships. It puts victims in greater danger of further abuse.

67. B

A systems approach states that all parts of well-being are interrelated or interconnected. Thus, a change in physical health will impact on psychological and spiritual functioning. The treatment should not focus on just the health issues, but ensure that these other areas are considered.

68. A

The genital stage begins in puberty and the source of pleasure is the genitals. Sexual urges return after being dormant during the latency stage, which begins at about age 5.

69. B

Empowerment aims to ensure a sense of control over well-being and that change is possible. It is not doing something for a client, but assisting him or her to have skills or resources needed to make desired changes himself or herself.

70. A

Social workers should not terminate services to pursue social, financial, or sexual relationships with clients. Social workers should also not engage in dual relationships with clients.

71. D

A social worker should consider the cultural appropriateness of family involvement, individual versus group treatment, alternative treatment approaches (yoga, aromatherapy, music, and writing), medication (western, traditional, alternative), and/or location/duration of intervention. Informed consent is required for all clients, regardless of cultural background. The procedures used may vary depending upon client culture, but the need for informed consent is universal.

72. A

Pansexuality refers to being attracted to an individual, independent or blind to gender. Most individuals who cross-dress are not homosexual or attracted to those of the same sex. Sexual orientation and gender identity are unique—individuals may view themselves as being male or female (gender identity) and be attracted to those of the same sex or a different sex. Gender expression is the way in which an individual expresses himself or herself. However, just because someone dresses, looks to be, or exhibits characteristics of a particular gender does not mean that this is the basis of his or her identity.

73. D

Social workers should protect the confidentiality of deceased clients consistent with the same ethical standards that apply to those who are living.

74. C

A social worker must respect and promote a client's right to self-determination, even when these decisions may not result in the best outcome in the social worker's opinion or when they violate agency practices. Only in instances that a client poses a serious and imminent risk to himself, herself, or others can self-determination be limited according to ethical standards and applicable laws.

75. D

Trichotillomania is a hair-pulling disorder that was classified in the *DSM-IV-TR* as an Impulse Control Disorder (Not Elsewhere Classified). In the *DSM-5*, it is listed under Obsessive-Compulsive and Related Disorders.

76. D

Clients who are in crisis, suicidal, actively psychotic, or paranoid are not appropriate for group treatment. In addition, those who have a compulsive need for attention are also not good group participants. Clients who are isolated can benefit from the socialization and universality that groups offer.

77. A

There are many features of Narcissistic Personality Disorder described, including not voluntarily coming into treatment, blaming others, having an exaggerated sense of self-importance, being absorbed by fantasies of unlimited success, constantly seeking attention, monopolizing the conversation, and bragging.

78. D

Silence is effective when faced by a client who is experiencing a high degree of emotion. The social worker should not send the client to someone else or take action until the nature of the situation is known. Listening and finding out more is the FIRST step in deciding the appropriate next steps, if any.

79. B

Consent is a legal term that means a client is willing to, and has the legal authority to, give permission to receive treatment. Assent is a willingness to participate, but does not have the same legal meaning because it may be granted by a client who is not his or her own guardian. Some clients receive social work services involuntarily. A specific consent form should be used to outline purpose, storage, and release of audiotaping or videotaping.

80. D

The Wechsler Intelligence Scale (WISC) is designed as a measure of a child's intellectual and cognitive ability.

The Minnesota Multiphasic Personality Inventory (MMPI) is a personality test for the assessment of psychopathology. The Myers-Briggs Type Indicator (MBTI) attempts to classify individuals along four theoretically independent dimensions that describe personality features. The Thematic Apperception Test (TAT) provides information on a client's perceptions and imagination, for use in the understanding of the subject's current needs, motives, emotions, and conflicts, both conscious and unconscious.

81. D

Cognitive dissonance is a state of conflict in the mind, whereby two opposing views are present at the same time. It suggests that the mind naturally wants to eliminate dissonance whenever possible and does so by justifying or changing attitudes and beliefs. Cognitive dissonance is extremely powerful, so justification is used to reduce it.

82. B

Social workers should not provide clinical services to individuals with whom they have had prior sexual relationships.

83. D

Role-playing is a very effective teaching strategy and provides active learning. None of the other answers that may be useful provides the teenager with an intervention (as the question is about the best way *to assist*) that allows him or her to practice communication skills that can be used with peers.

84. A

According to Maslow's hierarchy of needs, the needs of individuals are ordered as physiological, safety, social, esteem, and self-actualization.

85. A

"Ringing" or other sounds originating in the ears (tinnitus) can be a symptom of a neurologic or organic problem. The social worker needs to FIRST rule out a medical cause before determining other etiology.

86. A

Groupthink is when a group makes faulty decisions based on group pressures. Groups affected by groupthink ignore alternatives and tend to take irrational actions. A group is especially vulnerable to groupthink when its members are similar in background, when the group is insulated from outside opinions, and when there are no clear rules for decision making.

87. D

The problem-solving process starts with engagement. Acknowledging the client's circumstances is an action that the social worker can take to show empathy and an understanding of the difficulty of the situation. Some of the other response choices may be useful in working with an involuntary, court-mandated client, but they are not done FIRST.

88. D

A sign of a possible suicide attempt is a recent improvement in depressive symptoms. A client is also at greater risk after being discharged from the hospital or after being started on antidepressants, because he or she may now have the energy to implement a suicide plan. The social worker should assess the client for suicide risk immediately.

89. A

Generativity versus stagnation—During middle adulthood, individuals should develop a sense of being a part of the bigger picture, as well as giving back to society. By failing to achieve these objectives, individuals become stagnant and self-absorbed.

90. A

Given that there is conflict over a number of issues, the social worker should help structure the interactions between the mother and child. Essential is deciding which of the complaints is most salient for the mother and child. Increasing time with one another in the early stages of conflict resolution can exacerbate the situation because coping and communication skills have not improved yet. Acknowledging the conflict and using the strengths and skills of each party during conflict resolution may be useful, but will not assist in helping with resolution like prioritization, given the number of issues raised.

91. B

Congruence is when the communication of an individual matches his or her feelings. An individual who is being annoyed by someone would not smile. If the facial expression matched the individual's feelings, it would be a frown or grimace.

92. D

Social workers may use different treatment approaches with clients and individualized treatment is required. Supervision can assist in ensuring that services are tailored to specific client needs and are delivered in adherence with the *Code of Ethics*.

93. B

The Myers-Briggs Type Indicator (MBTI) attempts to describe personality features. The client may find the MBTI test useful as a way of understanding herself. The client may want to pursue careers that allow her to make use of her natural preferences.

The Minnesota Multiphasic Personality Inventory (MMPI) is a personality test for the assessment of psychopathology. The Thematic Apperception Test (TAT) provides information on a client's perceptions and imagination, for use in the understanding of the subject's current needs, motives, emotions, and conflicts, both conscious and unconscious. The Wechsler Intelligence Scale (WISC) is designed as a measure of a child's intellectual and cognitive ability.

94. B

"Ego alien" means these feelings are experienced as being alien to the ego and not consistent with the client's interests, conflicting with the rest of her view of herself.

95. B

Although there may be some procedures for ensuring preauthorization by the client's insurance in order for the tests to be covered, they can be performed without the insurance company's consent.

96. D

Confrontation is calling attention to something.

Clarification is reformulating a problem in the client's words to make sure there is a mutual understanding of the issue. Generalization or normalization of behavior is often used to show the client that what he or she is feeling or experiencing is typical and understandable. A paradoxical instruction is prescribing the opposite of what you want the client to do; it is commonly referred to as "reverse psychology."

97. B

The contract or service plan specifies problem(s) to be worked on, the goals to reduce the problem(s), a client's and a social worker's roles in the process, the interventions or techniques to be employed, the means of monitoring progress, stipulations for renegotiating the contract, and the time, place, fee, and frequency of meetings.

98. D

Social workers should provide services in substantive areas or use intervention techniques or approaches that are new to them only after engaging in appropriate study, training, consultation, and receiving supervision from those who are competent in those interventions and techniques.

99. C

There are some actions that may be legal, like accepting gifts or going to a movie with a client, but are NOT ethical. In addition, a social worker may engage in public protest, which is not legal in some locations or situations, but this behavior may be ethical.

100. C

Duty to warn has become an important mandate in social work. Generally, a social worker has to believe that a client is a danger to an identifiable third party and that the client is able to act on this danger in order for it to be considered necessary to warn and/or protect the intended victim. For example, if a client states that he or she is going to kill "women," a social worker may consider this client a danger to others and take appropriate action. However, there is not an obligation to notify intended victim(s) because the threat is too broad and does not require notification to women in general. In addition, if a client who is incarcerated and not going to be released makes a threat against someone outside the prison to whom he or she does not have access, there is no imminent threat. A history of violence is not required for a social worker's duty to warn obligation.

101. C

"A" stands for measures taken when treatment is not provided (such as during baseline) and "B" stands for measures taken when treatment is being delivered. Internal validity is the confidence that the treatment is the cause of changes in behavior seen. There are two opportunities using the "ABAB" design to see if the introduction of treatment coincides with changes in behavior. There is only one opportunity in A, none in B, and D does not have a baseline, so it is unclear as to the frequency or severity of the behavior before treatment started. A baseline assessment process is desired in single-subject designs, unless the client is in crisis, which necessitates the immediate starting of treatment (BAB).

102. D

Exogenous depression is caused by external events or psychosocial stressors, such as the ending of a marriage.

Endogenous depression is caused by a biochemical imbalance rather than a psychosocial stressor or external factors.

The criteria for Major Depressive Disorder with Mixed Features are not *explicitly* stated in this case vignette and, thus, this diagnosis cannot be applied.

103. C

This situation does not fall under duty to warn. The allowance to breach confidentiality if a client poses an imminent risk to an identifiable party has not generally been applied to HIV-positive clients who are engaging in unprotected sexual activity. It is the responsibility of all sexually active adults to use "safe sex" procedures or use proper protective measures to reduce the risk of sexually transmitted conditions. Thus, if this client's girlfriend were using such measures, there would be no risk to her.

104. D

If a client believes that his or her physical appearance is linked to his or her value, negative body image is likely to emerge. A client's self-worth should not be defined by appearance.

105. C

A crisis does not need to be triggered by a major life event. Crisis intervention is focused on the "here and now" and is time limited. As the goal is to intervene quickly, there is usually a heightened level of activity by the social worker to assist clients in alleviating stress and returning to the previous level of functioning.

106. C

Psychotherapy notes are specifically discussed in HIPAA. The general rule is that a social worker may not disclose psychotherapy notes for any purpose unless a client's authorization is obtained.

In order to take advantage of this extra protection afforded to psychotherapy notes, notes must be kept "physically separate" from the rest of a client's record. The term "physically separate" is not defined in the HIPAA rules, so it is not clear if this means in a separate file, a separate file cabinet, or simply in a separate part of the same file as the rest of the record. It is safer to *at least* keep the information in a separate file folder.

107. B

Modeling is a very effective method for teaching and should be used whenever possible. Showing a client how to interact is better than providing individual or group instruction. In addition, the social worker should not assume that the skill deficits are a result of a deeper clinical issue.

108. D

The baseline is denoted by "A" and the intervention is denoted by "B." In the case vignette, the social worker collected data prior to the onset of an intervention (AB). However, the holiday break represented a second baseline due to the interruption of treatment. It is an opportunity to see if the behavior changed once the intervention was removed. The intervention was then reinstituted upon the adolescent's return to school. This baseline and reintroduction is also represented as an AB design. Thus, the social worker is using an ABAB design.

109. D

Events will most likely lead to emotional or psychological trauma if they happen unexpectedly, there was no preparation or warning, they happened repeatedly, they were the result of intentional cruelty, or they happened in childhood. Clients who feel that there was no way to prevent such events are also more likely to experience emotional or psychological distress.

110. B

Piaget defined four stages of cognitive development. They are sensorimotor, preoperational, concrete operations, and formal operations. The formal operations stage begins at about age 11 and is characterized by a higher level of abstraction, assuming adult roles, and thinking hypothetically.

111. B

Some token economies do not include the removal of points for undesirable behavior. They only provide points or rewards when the targeted behavior is exhibited. Even when points are deducted for undesired behavior, it is usually done in a manner in which the client does not lose a substantial number, because this may make the client feel hopeless or that the lost points cannot be regained by exhibiting positive behavior in the future.

112. C

A social worker is a mandatory reporter and must contact the child protection agency that is trained to conduct the investigation and determine the child's credibility. The social worker must report even when a colleague or supervisor does not have the same reasonable suspicion.

113. D

Histrionic personality disorder is a pervasive pattern of excessive emotionality and attention seeking. A client with this disorder: interacts with others using inappropriate sexually seductive or provocative behavior; consistently uses physical appearance to draw attention to himself or herself; is highly suggestible or easily influenced by others or circumstances; considers relationships to be more intimate than they actually are in real life.

Clients with this disorder may have difficulty achieving emotional intimacy in romantic relationships, as well as impaired relationships with same-sex friends, because of their sexually provocative behavior or their demands for constant attention.

114. D

A social worker should not receive a fee for making a referral because this creates a conflict of interest.

115. D

The cycle of abuse indicates that this may be the "honeymoon" phase that happens after a battering incident. Just because there has not been any violence in the last 6 months does not mean that the battering will not occur in the future. The "honeymoon" phase leads to "tension building" and then violence in the future. The social worker must address the medical needs and safety issues of the client FIRST according to Maslow's hierarchy of needs.

116. C

It is essential to FIRST determine whether the sexual dysfunction is a result of a medical problem that is preventing the husband's ability to sustain his erection. If medical causes are ruled out by a physician, a social worker can examine psychological and/or social factors that are contributing, including work and other pressures. It also may be helpful to determine whether there are other problems in the relationship, but only after medical/biological etiology has been eliminated.

117. D

This stage in object relations theory generally occurs prior to the second birthday when a small child wants to once again become closer to the caregiver, realizing that mobility causes separateness. The child realizes that the caregiver is a separate entity and needs reassurance.

118. C

Delirium is a medical condition that results in confusion and other disruptions in thinking and behavior, including changes in perception, attention, mood, and activity level. Clients living with Dementia are highly susceptible to Delirium. Unfortunately, it can easily go unrecognized because many symptoms are shared by Delirium and Dementia. Sudden changes in behavior, such as increased agitation or confusion in the late evening, may be labeled as "sundowning" and dismissed as the unfortunate natural progression of one's Dementia.

In Dementia, changes in memory and intellect are slowly evident over months or years. Delirium is a more abrupt confusion and represents a sudden change from the client's previous status. Unlike the subtle decline of Alzheimer's disease, the confusion of delirium fluctuates over the day, at times dramatically.

119. C

A social worker can now charge the client the full amount for services, but cannot charge the client for payments associated with services already rendered.

120. A

Sublimation is when maladaptive feelings or behaviors are diverted into socially acceptable ones. In this instance, the behavior that caused the young man to be arrested in the past is being used to gain accolades in a legitimate sport.

121. D

Using *DSM-IV*, clients could be diagnosed with four separate disorders: Autistic Disorder, Asperger's Disorder, Childhood Disintegrative Disorder, or Pervasive Developmental Disorder Not Otherwise Specified. These separate diagnoses were not consistently applied across practitioners and settings. They now fall under Autism Spectrum Disorder.

Mental Retardation has a new name, "Intellectual Disability (Intellectual Developmental Disorder)."

122. A

In instances when clients are not literate or have difficulty understanding the primary language used in the practice setting, social workers should take steps to ensure clients' comprehension. This may include providing clients with detailed verbal explanations or arranging for qualified interpreters or translators whenever possible. Using family members is not acceptable due to confidentiality concerns, as well as possibilities that interpretations or impressions of family members will be included in the translation.

123. D

All of the response choices aim to affect or initiate change—the goal of client advocacy—except the last one. Examples of client advocacy activities include obtaining services or resources that would not otherwise be provided; modifying or influencing policies or practices that adversely affect groups or communities; or promoting legislation or policies that will result in the provision of requisite resources or services.

124. C

Social workers who are administrators should take reasonable steps to ensure that adequate agency or organizational resources are available to provide appropriate staff supervision. Peer supervision may be a feasible method for receiving feedback and input into treatment decisions that do not result in hardships to either clients or workers.

125. C

These statements are occurring in the first or initial session. The goal of this session is the building of a therapeutic alliance or engagement. Providing her with assurance that her feelings are not unusual and are shared with others in this situation alleviates anxiety and guilt, making her more open to speak about her difficulties. It also shows the client that the social worker understands what she is experiencing. The other response choices may be done, but are not the best responses given that the answer needed to directly relate to an action that would "facilitate the therapeutic alliance."

126. A

These medications are antidepressants. The client may have one of the other diagnoses and/or more than one diagnosis, but he or she is MOST likely taking these medications for depressive symptoms that are associated with Major Depressive Disorder.

127. B

Initially developed as the Health-Sickness Rating Scale, the GAF was introduced as Axis V of the *DSM-III* and *DSM-IV*. The GAF was used to assist in determining medical necessity and level of disability. The APA discontinued use of the GAF in the *DSM-5*, and now suggests the use of the World Health Organization Disability Assessment Schedule (WHODAS) as a measure of disability.

128. B

During termination, there should be discussion of the emotional feelings that may result from the ending of the therapeutic relationship. Termination is a time to examine evaluation results and review client accomplishments, as well as anticipate future needs of the client. The client record should be reviewed and updated on a continual basis and is not a task exclusively associated with termination.

129. B

A mental status examination is a structured way of observing and describing a client's current state of mind, under the domains of appearance, attitude, behavior, mood and affect, speech, thought process, thought content, perception, cognition, insight, and judgment. A mental status examination is a necessary part of any client assessment no matter what the presenting problem. It is not a psychiatric evaluation and does not determine *DSM* diagnosis.

130. D

As a result of receiving empathic responses from early caretakers, a child's needs are met and the child develops a strong sense of self. The needs of a child are mirroring (C), idealization (B), and twinship (A).

131. C

Institutional discrimination is when the policies or practices of an agency are discriminatory to a group of people. If proper translation does not occur, individuals who are not proficient in English will be excluded from understanding. Saturday services will preclude those who observe this day as the Sabbath. Lastly, making employment decisions based on birth location precludes those born outside the United States from being hired. Social workers may refer individuals to others based on cultural factors for appropriate therapeutic reasons. If the reason for the referral is simply based on cultural background, this may be a form of discrimination, but is not institutional discrimination unless it is a repeated practice or policy.

132. B

Choice A calls for the social worker to work outside his or her scope. C does not meet the woman's need, and referring her to an advocacy organization for those who are deaf (D) may just result in an extra step that does not result in service. The woman also may not identify with the deaf culture and may want to go to a generic mental health agency with an accommodation.

133. A

The goals of crisis intervention are to immediately relieve the stress experienced, return the client to a previous level of functioning or assist with regaining equilibrium, and help develop coping mechanisms. A social worker may want to work with a client to identify precursors or deal with the impacts of the trauma, but these actions would occur after the crisis has subsided.

134. A

The aim of a psychoeducational group is education. With improved education about healthy eating, older adults have information needed to make good food choices. The other target populations would benefit from psychotherapeutic groups as they could benefit from interacting with others who have experienced the same difficulties. Realizing that they are not alone can help these individuals with shame or isolation. Peer support is usually associated as a benefit from psychotherapeutic groups, not psychoeducational ones.

135. D

Psychodynamic theories explain the origin of the personality. Although many different psychodynamic theories exist, they all emphasize unconscious motives and desires, as well as the importance of childhood experiences in shaping personality.

136. B

Entropy is a closed system, whereas negative entropy is the opposite (an exchange of energy and resources to promote growth). In this example, the married couple is not using personal resources to ensure the health of their relationship.

137. A

At one end of the continuum, a social worker is a full participant in the activities; at the other end, a social worker is a pure observer, seeking to be as unobtrusive as possible so as not to influence the situation being observed in any way. "Participant as observer" and "observer as participant" fall somewhere along this continuum, since a social worker is either already part of a group or context being researched or seeks to become involved in order to gain access to the information required.

Participation of a social worker raises potential questions of bias and subjectivity that might undermine the reliability and validity of any information gathered. Thus, "complete participant" is the most problematic.

138. D

Social workers should not provide services to or supervise friends or relatives. In addition, hiring a client is prohibited as it creates another relationship (employer/employee) with a client. Using the same supervisor as a friend, relative, or colleague is not a dual relationship.

139. B

All of the options are signs of trauma, but B is an emotional and psychological symptom. It is not physical.

140. C

Intellectualization is when a person avoids uncomfortable emotions by focusing on facts and logic. In this instance, the client is not dealing with the emotions associated with this recent diagnosis, but instead focused on the rational medical details of the condition.

141. A

As part of engagement, the roles of the social worker and client in the problem-solving process should be discussed and clarified, if needed.

142. C

Case management can be defined in many ways and has numerous aims. Most of them are based on the belief that clients need assistance, because the service delivery system is complex, fragmented, duplicative, and uncoordinated. A major case management activity is linking to services. Case management is distinct from psychotherapy.

143. D

Some approaches within organizations to promote cultural competency include recruiting multiethnic staff, including cultural competence requirements in job descriptions and performance/promotion measures, reviewing demographic trends for the geographic area served to determine service needs, creating service delivery systems that are more appropriate to the diversity of the target population, and advocating for clients as major stakeholders in the development of service delivery systems to ensure they are reflective of their cultural heritage.

144. B

It is unethical to continue to treat when services are no longer needed or serve the client's interests. The fee charged is not relevant to this standard.

145. A

Groupthink is when a group makes faulty decisions because of group pressures. Groups affected by groupthink ignore alternatives and tend to take irrational actions that dehumanize other groups. A group is especially vulnerable to groupthink when its members are similar in background, when the group is insulated from outside opinions, and when there are no clear rules for decision making.

146. B

Community organization aims to develop leadership so that communities can better address their problems. Using the problem-solving process, the social worker should FIRST help the members to figure out which problem they would like to address. The social worker may help the group with other actions, but they are later in the process. The social worker must also not "take charge" because community organizing is about empowering individuals within the community to decide on the problems and take actions to make changes.

147. A

Social workers should not disclose identifying information when discussing clients for teaching or training purposes unless the client has consented to disclosure of confidential information. In addition, social workers should not disclose identifying information when discussing clients with consultants unless the client has consented to disclosure of confidential information or there is a compelling need for such disclosure.

148. B

Humans are sexual throughout the life course. Children are sexual even before birth, with males sometimes having erections in the uterus. Same-gender sexual behavior during childhood can occur as boys and girls tend to play with friends of the same gender. It is not related to sexual orientation or to whom individuals are attracted. It usually results out of exploration and access. Although there may be physiological changes that occur in older adults, they do not lose their desire to be sexual.

149. A

Hope is not a separate stage, but is possible during any of the five stages—denial and isolation, anger, bargaining, depression, and acceptance.

150. B

The client is clearly exhibiting a lot of emotion. In this state, providing direction or instruction will not be effective and can escalate the situation. Listening or being silent is a good technique to diffuse the hostility, but limit setting may also be needed. The client should be provided with alternate strategies for accessing the social worker if a need arises in the future.

151. A

In communication, there are two types of content, manifest and latent. Manifest content is the concrete words or terms contained in the journal. Explicit and overt communication also refers to the actual statements made by the client in the journal. Latent content is that which is not visible, such as the underlying meaning or themes of the words or terms used.

152. B

Social workers in fee-for-service settings may terminate services to clients who are not paying overdue balances if the financial contractual arrangements have been made clear to the clients, if clients do not pose an imminent danger to themselves or others, and if the clinical and other consequences of the current nonpayment have been addressed and discussed.

153. D

The endocrine system produces hormones, which are chemicals that control body functions such as metabolism, growth, and sexual development.

The digestive system is made up of organs that break down food into protein, vitamins, minerals, carbohydrates, and fats. The nervous system is one of the most important systems in the body because it is the body's control system. The lymphatic system is the defense system for the body.

154. A

Social workers can have many roles including, but not limited to, consultant, advocate, case manager, catalyst, enabler, broker, mediator, facilitator, and instructor. A social worker can be supportive in these roles, but is not supposed to be the client's support system. Instead, a social worker should assist the client to mobilize or build his or her own natural supports.

155. A

Tardive dyskinesia may result from taking high doses of antipsychotic medications over a long period of time. Symptoms may persist indefinitely after discontinuation of these medications. Thus, antipsychotic use should be closely monitored and prescribed at low doses, if possible.

156. A

Conversion is when mental conflict or disturbance is transferred into a physical symptom to relieve anxiety. The loss of eyesight after witnessing the incident may have resulted from this trauma.

157. D

When working with groups, a social worker should use the group as the major helping agent and not make decisions for the group. A social worker should only intervene when interactions or the communication pattern within a group is becoming fragmented or dysfunctional in some way. Social workers' interventions may involve assisting in opening up new possibilities or avenues of exploration; interpreting the assumptions, attitudes, or behavior of the group or its unconscious communication; and/or modeling ways of dealing with dilemmas or situations.

158. D

Reaction formation is when a client adopts attitudes or engages in behaviors that are the opposite of his or her unconscious belief. The behavior of the woman growing up and recently is in contrast to the way in which she feels about her sister.

159. B

Children with disabilities needing assistance should be provided with Individual Educational Plans (IEPs) that are revised at least annually. A team composed of social workers, teachers, administrators, and other relevant school personnel typically create these plans. The parents, and often the children, also participate. The IEPs include a statement of goals, means of attaining goals, and ways of evaluating goal attainment.

160. A

Social workers should represent themselves as competent only within the boundaries of their education, training, license, certification, consultation received, supervised experience, or other relevant professional experience. Listing herself as a "Dr." on a card for mental health treatment can be misleading to clients who would believe that the degree is related to the services advertised on the card.

161. B

In negative reinforcement, behavior increases because negative (aversive) stimulus (i.e., nagging) is removed. The word "negative" does not mean bad, but rather "removal." In positive reinforcement, a behavior increases because of the introduction (positive) of something desirable to reward it.

162. C

The core values include service, social justice, dignity and worth of the person, importance of human relationships, integrity, and competence.

163. C

Aversion therapy or treatment is aimed at reducing the attractiveness of a stimulus or a behavior by pairing it with an aversive stimulus. An example of this technique is treating alcoholism with Antabuse.

164. A

Language is a system of using words to communicate. It has two parts: using words and gestures to say what is meant (expressive communication) and understanding what others say (receptive communication). Receptive communication develops earlier than does expressive communication. Infants start learning in the womb, where they hear and respond to familiar voices.

165. B

A social worker's self-awareness about his or her own attitudes, values, and beliefs about cultural differences and a willingness to acknowledge racial and cultural differences are critical factors for effectively working with diverse populations.

166. D

A strengths perspective focuses on understanding clients based on strengths and mobilizing resources to improve their situations. It looks at making environment modifications when needed and the fit between the person and the environment. Focusing on interpersonal struggles is more indicative of a psychodynamic approach.

167. A

There is no indication that this behavior is typical. Nonverbal communication can be very powerful. Her behavior may be the result of something that she is reluctant to discuss. Asking her if something is bothering her will give the client an opening to disclose it to the social worker.

168. B

Racial definitions have changed over time—they were once based on ethnicity or nationality, religion, and so on, but are now primarily defined by skin color. Cultural, racial, and ethnic identities are passed on through customs, traditions, language, religious practice, and values. Individuals can be the same race, but different ethnicities (i.e., White and Irish or Polish).

169. B

Precontemplation is the first step in the change process. In precontemplation, a client is unaware, unable, and/or unwilling to change. This stage is characterized by a client arguing, interrupting, ignoring the problem, and/or avoiding talking or thinking about it. A social worker should establish a rapport, acknowledge resistance or ambivalence, try to engage a client, and recognize his or her thoughts, feelings, fears, and concerns.

170. D

The comment demonstrates some hesitancy or resistance by the client. During engagement, resistance can arise as the client is not clear about what will occur, including the client's role, the social worker's role, limits to confidentiality, and so on. Exploring this comment as a therapeutic issue is not appropriate as it is the initial session and it may just be a reflection of a lack of understanding—not a clinical issue.

Index